Lyn

A Story of Prostitution

Lyn Madden and June Levine

Attic

First published in 1987 by
Attic Press Ltd
Attic is an imprint of Cork University Press
Youngline Industrial Estate
Pouladuff Road
Togher
Cork
Ireland

Reprinted 2000, 2001, 2003, 2004, 2008

British Library Cataloguing in Publication Data

Levine, June
      Lyn: a story of prostitution
      1. Prostitution
      I. Title 2. Madden, Lyn
      306.7'42'0924HQ117

ISBN: 978-0-946211-45-6

Typesetting by Red Barn Publishing, Skeagh, Skibbereen, Co. Cork
Printed by ColourBooks Ltd., Dublin

All names and identities, excepting those of the main characters, have been changed, for obvious reasons, in this true story of the under belly of Irish society.

DEDICATION

Lyn Madden and June Levine dedicate this book to each other and, above all, to the courage of Dolores Lynch.

Acknowledgements

To all of those at my fortieth birthday party, especially the woman who hosted it. For obvious reasons, I will not name them, but you know who you are, and thank you.

Thanks to my 'escorts' who became my friends. Thanks to Inspector Mick Connolly for setting aside his duties and giving me time to talk out my fears.

Thanks to Ronnie Drew who rescued me when I was penniless after I missed the Liverpool boat home. When he asked me what I did and I said that I'd been a prostitute, he laughed and said 'So? You're a prostitute I'm a singer. They're just labels.' And thank you to Deirdre for being gracious when she might have been annoyed.

To the artist who kindly sent me £20 after the article in *Magill* magazine and to Colm Toibín who was editor then, thank you. Also to the RTE man who brought books to cheer me when I was in the Meath Hospital. Thank you, young Dr Riley of that hospital, for your kindness.

Surgeon Matt McHugh generously removed some of the scars of my teenage years and I want him to know how much I appreciated that. Also, thank you to Dr Moira Woods who saw me in her medical capacity, but by sparing the time to talk to me, gave me back a little respect for my body.

To Professor Ivor Browne who helped me grow towards freedom.

Lyn Madden

Preface

Nowhere is Woman treated according to the merit of her work, but rather as a sex. It is therefore almost inevitable that she should pay for her right to exist, to keep a position in whatever line, with sex favours. Thus, it is merely a question of degree whether she sells herself to one man, in or out of marriage, or to many men. Whether our reformers admit it or not, the economic and social inferiority of women is responsible for prostitution . . .

From Emma Goldman's *The Traffic in Women*

In the beginning I used to introduce Lyn to everybody. Then I started to recognise a sign from her which said: 'Did business with him,' and so I stopped. I did not want to know which husbands of the women in my life used women as prostitutes. Eventually, I dealt with that. However, without my having to ask, Lyn had clearly answered one of the most common questions about 'the game': 'What sort of man . . . ?' All sorts: politicians, business and professional men, priests, the guy who puts money by each week for the purpose, and the fellow who has a hand job because he cannot afford intercourse.

An insight into the nature of prostitution had come from an unexpected source. It was after the second wave Women's Movement erupted in the early seventies, when it was such a relief to share intimate conversations, feel free to ask any question that came to mind.

'How did you come to have fourteen children?' I asked the woman sitting next to me.

'I was trying to coax money out of him for a pair of shoes for one of the others,' she answered. 'You have to use what he wants to get what you need.'

Prostitution is the inevitable outcome of patriarchy. It has always existed because men have always been in a position to pay for what

1

they want, and women have always been in a position of need. In that context, with male sexual desires regarded as sacrosanct, female sexuality becomes a commodity.

There is a sustained effort throughout society, both within and outside of marriage, to keep women economically dependent upon men. Words like 'romance' and 'chivalry' are used to fudge a vital issue of freedom for women; they condition all of us to live in an atmosphere of prostitution. Everyone recognises a man's need to earn at least enough to support two people, himself and a woman. Because women are supposed to be kept by men, payment for their labour is considered of less consequence. And in a time of few jobs, it has been mentioned that those jobs should be given to men, the supporters, the bread-winners. The social norms are distilled out of a basic economic system which makes a woman dependent for the bite in her mouth as much as any luxury.

There is a vital need for all women, everywhere, to take a long, hard look at the reality of prostitution. The plight of women on the streets, women like Lyn, will not change much until all women recognise their need for economic independence. In its more subtle forms, prostitution is classless. Why, for instance, are women often expected to be economically helpless in public, always the guest of the man? And no, despite feminism, things have not changed much at all.

When I was very young, I thought I had to kiss a boy who paid for my ticket into the pictures. I did not admit that then; I buried it deep and quickly cloaked my subservience, in 'romance'. In later years, I have been rapped on the knuckles for embarrassing men when, in my work capacity, I insisted on paying for their lunches. I've been told it is unfeminine to ask for the bill, warned of becoming a castrating female. All I can say about this is that nature seems to have done too delicate a job on that organ in which the male ego is frequently centred. Why should a man always be expected to pay? Why should he wish to do so? What, at the very least, is expected of a woman who is 'paid for'? Why should one be economically paralysed by one's sex? What effect does such an atmosphere have on the growing girl?

I met Lyn Madden through a mutual friend who is a member of the Prisoners' Rights Organisation. This person told me that Lyn was state witness in a murder case in which three women were alleged to have been killed by a pimp and that Lyn was writing a book about it. Would I look at Lyn's work?

Now, Lyn says that she did not set out to write a book. She just felt compelled to write the nightmare out of her system, perhaps in an effort to make sense of it. In any case, Lyn wrote until her thumb was swollen and purple, but with that ability of hers to cut off pain, she continued to write. I was devastated and infuriated by what she wrote. And I was impressed by the book's potential value as a sociological statement. More than that, I liked Lyn.

I attended every day of the trial and undertook to help her by editing the work and pointing her in the direction of publishers. The book went the rounds of London publishing houses. All of them rejected it, mainly, as far as I can understand, because the central character was 'unsympathetic' and it was a bit raw. There was none of the acceptable 'whore with the heart of gold' element to dilute it, nor was there any glamour.

In 1987 Attic Press invited me to work on the book, and Lyn gave me a free hand. I have simply acted as an interpreter of a language, a way of life, which is foreign to the average reader. I have done my best to protect the original power of the story, the essence of Lyn. I regard myself as a translator of a culture which, through Lyn, I have come to understand slightly. I hope too much has not been lost in my translation.

My heart went out to Lyn when we first met. There, but for Lady Luck, went I. We clicked right off and struggled to understand each other. Now, it can be seen that, in sisterhood, Lyn and I have bridged the gap created by a patriarchal class structure.

Lyn never matched the stereotype of the whore, a word she hates and which, for this reason, is used only twice in this book. By day, Lyn always fulfilled those aspects of a woman's role which are most acceptable; shopping, cleaning, cooking, caring, looking nice. When we met, she struck me as so vital. Her hair was black, her eyes blue with long lashes and well-shaped brows. Her high cheek-bones were accentuated by the palest skin. Her mouth was full and she never wore lipstick, deciding years before that it made her look cheap. Close enough to kiss Lyn, I saw that she had scars, made by knives and punches.

I have never seen Lyn drink, swear or do anything more 'unladylike' than smoke. I cannot imagine her saying some of the things she quotes herself as saying in this book. I have never experienced, from her, that vulgarity she must have needed for her work.

'Vulgarity is like make-up. It is a defence mechanism, a sort of second skin. On the street, faced with men, cops, passersby, the disguise you need isn't innocence, or modesty, but vulgarity. That's what protects you.' (*Prostitutes, Our Life*, Failing Wall Press).

Once, Lyn and I were discussing prostitution and I snapped: 'Nonsense. Prostitutes are used like public lavatories.' She did not look me in the eye for days. Lyn could not bear the imagery; it made her feel frantic, but above all, she hated my vulgarity.

My experience with Lyn has taught me that an exploited woman often does not realise the reality of her life. It is not that a woman in Lyn's situation lies to herself. But by its very nature, the life of prostitution compels her to 'cut off' from feeling. The thing that makes it possible to keep going in prostitution is this 'cut off'. And the perfect cut off, as described by the psychiatrist and writer R D Laing, is so perfect that one does not know one is cut off.

In the past, Lyn was willing to speak to the media. Most of what she said (apart from its awesome pace of delivery) intellectualised her experience of prostitution, the world she felt she could not escape even when circumstances forced her to leave it. Today, her perceptions are different. She no longer regards prostitution as 'just a job', nor does she live with the fear of being 'sacked'.

'I'm 37 and it scares me. The day will come when I walk along the street and a car will stop. In the dark he won't see me and I'll open the door and he'll say: "Oh, you're too old." And I'll have to shut the door and walk home. That's going to kill me.' She told this to Rosita Sweetman in *On Our Backs*, a study of sexual attitudes in Ireland, published in 1979. Lyn was not to know then that she would escape the 'ultimate' rejection and live in fear of a terminal repetition – that of being tortured and murdered by her lover-pimp.

Lyn was addicted to men. Not to her clients, but to relationships with 'awful' men. I soon realised that Lyn's obsession with the men in her life was a reflection of her great need for the caring she had missed in her developing years. The care she gives, even now when she gets the chance, is the care she craves.

'If you have ever found yourself obsessed with a man, you may have suspected that the root of that obsession was not love but fear, fear of being unloveable and unworthy, fear of being ignored, or abandoned or destroyed,' says Robin Norwood, the American therapist who wrote the self-help book, *Women Who Love Too Much*, published by Pocket Books, New York, in 1984. It is a book that helped Lyn and me to understand a lot about our past lives.

Norwood explains Lyn's inability to leave John Cullen or to let

4

him leave her. To Lyn, being in love meant being in extreme pain. Each new relationship she tried with a man turned out to be more painful than the last. By the time her relationship with Cullen began to disintegrate, Lyn was terrified by the fact that she was 'failing', yet again, in a relationship with a man.

'I had shut off so much feeling as a child that I required all the drama that men provided, just to feel alive. Trouble with the police, involvement with drugs, financial schemes, crazy sex, these had all become the ordinary stuff of life to me. In fact, even with all of that, I still could not feel anything much.'

That is one of Robin Norwood's clients talking, but I could be listening to Lyn. When one realises what she endured as a child, it is no wonder, as Norwood's book explains, that Lyn formed the sort of relationships she did with violent, impossible men.

There are two common responses to prostitution. One states that it is morally wrong, based on the fear of sexuality in women, while the other claims that prostitution is essential to the preservation of the family and the virtue of 'good women'.

Even a successful campaigner for the rights of women in prostitution, Maureen Colquhoun, the British MP, used the 'necessary' argument. When she moved the Protection of Prostitutes Bill before the House of Commons in 1979, Ms Colquhoun stated 'I have spoken with eminent psychiatrists who say that it is accepted in their profession that prostitutes have a great therapeutic value in society. In this country the Reichian school of psychiatrists uses sex therapy. Indeed they help people deprived of sex to sort out their problems. Prostitutes deal primarily with all the sexual things that have gone wrong. The first people to whom men go when they have sexual inadequacies and problems are prostitutes.'

Psychiatrists are usually men, as was Reich. I asked the psychiatrist Ivor Browne about this service to society and its therapeutic effect. 'Surely that is beside the point,' he replied. 'To whom is prostitution therapeutic? Certainly to none of the prostitutes I've met.'

In any event, the sexual needs of men (or women, for that matter) are not sacrosanct. They are certainly not sacred to the point of deserving such human sacrifice and misery. Women are severely damaged by prostitution. They are punished physically, emotionally, sociologically, and legally. Women are driven into prostitution by the most negative forces, whether from the hurt sustained within their families or within society, or a mixture of both. How dare anyone expect us to accept that the prostitution of even a single female is necessary? Why is the man with money in his pocket of more importance than the woman who needs it? Wherever there is poverty, there is prostitution; and when poverty increases so does prostitution. Throughout the world, it is increasing at an even faster rate than other forms of violence against women.

The twin industries of prostitution and pornography have combined to create a worldwide plague, rotting the lives of women and children. In Bombay, one rupee (about six pence) buys the enforced sexual service of a kidnapped nine-year-old girl; sex tours organised for Western businessmen or Gulf oil sheiks fetch higher prices for young girls lured to the city by procurers who promise marriage or a better life than frugal village existence. And in America, that land of equal opportunity, the poor and the children of the poor are frequently used for prostitution, pornography and 'snuff' movies.

The effects of these twin industries are contagious, getting to all females in different ways. Men, too, are obviously affected. Anyone who doubts the possible effects of porn would do well to note how John Cullen reacted to it. It turned him on to sexual practices which he had never imagined until he read about them.

Perhaps *Ordeal*, the terrible story of America's former porn queen Linda Lovelace, ought to be prescribed reading for those legislators who turn a blind eye to video nasties, in their pseudo concern for freedom of expression.

Given women's position in society, what happened to Linda Lovelace could happen to any woman. 'Men queued up at parties,' writes Gloria Steinem, 'to be the beneficiaries of the sexual sword swallower trick Linda had been taught by her husband and keeper, Chuck Traynor. By relaxing her throat muscles, she learned to receive the full plunge of the penis without choking. A desperate survival technique for her, but a constant source of amusement and novelty to others.'

Steinem's piece on Linda Lovelace is included in *Outrageous Acts and Everyday Rebellions* and describes a woman's helpless enslavement. Lyn identifies greatly with Linda and says: 'You can be taken over, so terrified and lost that you believe there is no way out for you. I think that what happened to Linda could happen to any woman. She was beaten so badly, and tortured, that her rectum was damaged and she had to wear special stockings because of the injury to her veins. She tried to escape a few times, but he brought her back.'

6

The cheaply made *Deep Throat* starring Linda Lovelace, was the work of director-writer Gerry Damieno who told the story of a woman whose clitoris was in her throat and who was constantly eager for oral sex with men. The movie, made in a week at a cost of $40,000, made $600,000,000, a profit swollen by the sale of T-shirts, car stickers and sexual aids. Millions of women, says Steinem, were taken to *Deep Throat* by husbands, boyfriends and pimps, to learn what a woman could do if she really wanted to please a man.

There are, of course, all kinds of pimps. Strictly speaking, a pimp is a man who lives off the 'immoral' earnings of a woman or women. I am finding, however, that the word 'pimp' has developed a broader meaning in my mind's vocabulary. Pimping has come to mean living on all of a woman's energy, her ability to feel, her maternal instincts. Few Irish women in prostitution will admit to having pimps. The men in their lives are mostly husbands and boyfriends. However, all but a few women hand over their earnings to a man. And that brings me to John Cullen, convicted of, and serving a sentence for, the murder of Dolores Lynch in a fire which also cost the lives of her mother, Kathleen, and her aunt, Hannah.

In relation to Cullen, where did all that waste of human life begin? We could recognise the power of evil to dominate, but what forces combine for the development of that evil? To begin with, surely a society such as ours could do better by its orphaned poor. John Cullen was aged nine when his father died; why was there no one to help him cope with his grief? Could someone not have taken the inner child into account before institutionalising him for habitual truancy? Surely, he would have been better off unschooled than educated in the ways of brutality and revenge.

John Cullen is an epileptic, yet he drank while on medication. A more educative and caring contribution by some members of the medical profession might have helped in decreasing the disastrous effects of this combination. Cullen was in and out of prison all his life, a sitting duck for therapy, and yet it was never offered to him. Who knows but that he could have been helped to be a more reasonable man? Rehabilitation must have been possible at some point, long before he murdered three women.

So long as women are kept economically dependent in our society, no wonder men continue to believe in our masochism. After all, how many men would suffer such indignity without going to

7

war over it? It is a myth to presume that women enjoy economic dependency. Many a marriage has fallen apart when a woman became aware of her beggar status within it. It is an even greater myth which says that women enjoy being sex objects, subjected to sexual domination and even pain and debasement. It is truer to say that, through their economic power over women, men feel free to inflict pain upon us, than it is to say that women become willingly involved in it.

It is sad but true, as Gloria Steinem writes, that 'feminist groups are not strong enough to be a public presence in the world of pornography and genocide, or in the world of welfare and the working poor'. I believe that we have externalised the problem of the existence of women in prostitution in an unconscious effort to avoid the painful confrontation of prostitution in our own lives.

In their personal lives, women have neglected to investigate the atmosphere of prostitution in which the vast majority of women live. We must, as women, individually and collectively, claim economic independence, fight for it, believe in it. If we remember our childhood prayer 'Give us this day our daily bread . . .', let us be reminded of the cost of taking that bread from the middle-man.

June Levine

1

Lyn had soaked in the bath for about an hour. Suddenly she became aware that he was moving around the flat. John Cullen never moved from his horizontal position unless . . . Oh no! was he looking for something to tie her up with? she panicked. Hurriedly, she dried herself and got into her nightdress. She looked into the bedroom. He was lying down on the bed again and she took a quick look around. No sign of any torturing equipment. She went into the bedroom and sat on the edge of the bed. He told her to get dressed; they were going out. She looked at the clock. It was nearly 3.00 a.m.

'Where to, John?'

'Just do as you're told and get dressed.'

She obeyed.

As they were heading down Dorset Street she asked, 'John, where are we going?'

'Mind your own business,' he said matter-of-factly.

He didn't need to tell her then. If they were not going to the 24-hour shop, as was quite usual, there was only one other place to go to at 3.30 a.m. Liam Ryan's house. There were only seventeen days to go to the court case about the stabbing.

Messages were still coming about the charges being brought by Liam against John Cullen. One week, John heard that Liam was going to stand firm. The next week, he would hear that Liam might drop the charges. It was a war of nerves and Lyn knew that it was getting to John. At 3.00 a.m. on a couple of nights during the previous weeks, John had said: 'Get dressed.' and they had gone to Liam's house and just sat outside.

But now they were driving up Clanbrassil Street when John suddenly took a right turn. DOLORES! Lyn had noticed lately that Liam had replaced Dolores as the object of John's revenge. Before Liam had brought charges against him, John had sworn, daily, that he would get Dolores for having him nicked seven years ago.

John turned left, then right, and drove slowly up a street lined with semi-detached houses, counting out loud as they passed each house on the right-hand side. Lyn's heartbeat slowed to a regular beat. She felt her palms sweating and rubbed her hands together. What made her think of Dolores? Was it because he had turned off Clanbrassil Street? John told her that Dolores lived in a terraced house like the ones on Coronation Street. This estate was obviously not the one. Lyn did not know what he was doing; perhaps he had found another imaginary enemy, whatever or wherever. She guessed that it had to be related to the trial because something had been brewing for weeks.

Cullen parked the car on a hill and removed a pair of gloves from the dashboard. 'Get out,' he said.

Lyn got out and went round to the back of the car. She watched as he took a large blue holdall from the boot. He was wearing the gloves. Lyn looked at him questioningly, hesitating for a split second before he took her by the arm and said, 'Right, let's go.

They walked down the hill. A woman was walking towards them. John pulled Lyn close and buried his face in her hair, pretending to kiss her. The woman had a pleasant face. She smiled at Lyn.

They came to a road which Lyn later learned is named Clarence Mangan Road. As they walked, John was nodding his head at each house, counting. He stopped at a house, looked up and down the road, then stepped into the garden with Lyn close on his heels. He looked steadily at her and said, 'Right, now listen, I'm going over the wall here. Watch the lights in this house. If the lights come on, whistle. Watch the road for cars. If you see a police car and it comes on top, get a taxi home.'

He handed Lyn a £20 note. She watched as he climbed up on a high wall that had glass embedded on the top. Lyn looked nervously up and down the street. She heard the rasping sound of a bolt being pulled back. Then the gate was open and he picked up the holdall bag and pulled her into the garden and closed the gate. John laid the holdall on the ground just inside the gate, removing a Stanley knife, hammer and butcher's knife from it. Lyn gasped. Before she could speak, he looked sharply at her and put his index finger to his lips.

'Wait here,' he whispered and walked down the garden to a low wall. Lyn looked at the houses that backed into the garden. They *were* Coronation Street houses. Dolores. When John came back in a few minutes, he opened the bag again and took out two containers with firelighters and matches taped to them. They were exactly the same as the incendiary devices he had shown her once. Before Lyn could say anything he silenced her with a look.

'Come down to the bottom of the garden with me.'

John got up on top of the chicken wire which was on the low wall separating the two gardens. He flattened the wire with his feet, then got back down, picked up the two containers and put them on the flattened wire. Climbing on the wire very slowly and carefully, he jumped down into the small back garden. Reaching up, he took the two containers and placed them on his side of the wall.

Lyn looked nervously back at the house of the garden she was standing in. He grabbed her by the hair and turned her around to face him. His face was clear in the moonlight. He was smiling. This was his moment!

'Remember, Lyn, if you see any lights come on, whistle.'

'I can't whistle.'

She could feel hysteria rising; her legs were trembling.

'Well then shout, but don't shout my fuckin' name,' he snapped. He went down and tried the back door.

Suddenly something struck her. How had she failed to notice it? It must have been the shock. All the lights were on! Cullen was sliding up the downstairs window. She saw him pulling the curtains back to have a good look into the room. He came back over the wall and said happily: 'I didn't even have to force the window. The fuckin' thing was already open.' He could not believe his luck. Lyn's mouth was dry and she could not have answered him even if she had wanted to. He went back and started to climb up a small roof that reached an upstairs room. Lyn could not look. She wanted to sit down. Her legs were shaking so badly that she had to grip the chicken wire for support. She looked over her shoulder. If only someone would get out of bed and notice what was going on!

Lyn heard a loud, clattering noise like a slate being dislodged. She whirled to face the other garden and looked up at the roof. John Cullen was lying flat on his back, his arms stretched out on either side and his knees pulled up to his waist. He was staring down at her enquiringly. She shook her head and he eased himself back down off the roof. He went into an open shed in the garden and straightaway she saw a flare. The flare went out. It was very breezy. It went out another few times. Cullen then walked back over to the open window and placed the two containers inside – the windows were so low that he could lean over the sill. Lyn saw flames and ran. Down the garden, out the gate and up the road. Then she heard them. Simultaneously. Screams. A woman's loud piercing screams. Glass shattering. Then more screams. She ran faster, heard someone running behind her. John Cullen passed her. He stopped and turned and waited for her to catch up. She ran faster still. He was standing stock still, the street lighting illuminating him.

'Did you see the smoke?' he asked. She had never seen such a smile on a person's face except in pictures of saints. This was his moment of glory.

'No, I heard the screams.' He grabbed her before she could fall.

'Come on, Lyn, you'll have to make it to the car.'

They got into the car and he threw the holdall onto the back seat. He drove like a madman, through red traffic lights, until she screamed. He was smiling. He slowed the car and began to talk excitedly.

'Did you see the way it went up in flames, Lyn? When I was waiting for you to catch up with me, I looked down the road and you should have seen the blaze! It lit up the whole sky! The first lot blazed up easily enough. I had a hell of a job lighting up the second one. Lucky the fuckin' window was open.'

'That was Dolores, wasn't it,' Lyn whispered. It was a statement, not a question.

'Shut fuckin' up. Just watch the news tomorrow. If I have the right house, you'll know all about it.'

He threw the gloves out on the road one at a time and when they got back onto the Ballymun Road he suddenly laughed out loud. She looked at him. He was ecstatic. They finished the journey in silence.

John brought the holdall into the flat. As soon as he got into the hall, he told her to get some newspapers. He stood in the hall with the holdall until she'd brought the papers. He told her to spread them out on the floor. Then he placed the holdall onto the paper and stripped completely, dropping his clothes onto the paper, too. He told her to take off her shoes and deposit them onto the paper.

He was singing softly to himself. Stopping suddenly, he said, 'What are you looking at me like fuckin' that for? Do something, make a cup of tea, run the bath, look out of the window and see if the coast is clear.'

She did it all. As she was waiting for the kettle to boil he came back in and got into the bath, humming softly. 'I hope I got the right house,' he said, and continued humming.

When Cullen got out of the bath, he wrapped the towel around him and lay down on the bed. He let out a deep, satisfied sigh. 'Ah, that feels great. Pass me my tea.'

Lyn was scared to look at him in case John misinterpreted her look. She had not uttered a word since they had come back to the flat. Anything she said could upset him. He pretended not to notice her silence. He told her to wash everything he had dropped onto the newspaper and leave them, wet, in a plastic bag. He would dispose of them tomorrow night. He dried himself, wrapped the towel around himself again and went into the hall. Lifting the holdall, he passed it to Lyn and told her to wash it all over. He stood beside her at the kitchen sink to see she did it properly.

He got dressed then, kissed her on the cheek, smiled and said, 'Have to go now, Lyn. Get a good night's sleep. I'll be up around four o'clock tomorrow.' Then he was gone.

She locked and bolted the door, took a few Valium and lay

down on the bed, not bothering to get between the sheets. She knew she would not be sleeping. It was 6.00 a.m. Only two-and-a-half hours since he first told her to get dressed. So that's why he had been so cool the last few days. He must have planned this very carefully. He knew, for example, that her son Joey would be in Liverpool for the football match. Where had he made the petrol bombs? His mother's house? His wife's house? Here? At the back of it all, she could still hear the screaming.

That was her holdall bag he had taken, her hammer, her Stanley knife, her butcher's knife. When had he taken them? When she was in the bath? No, how could he have foreseen that she would take a bath when he was in the flat? But that would not have stopped him, because he would have made the bombs right under her nose. He knew she would not dare to interfere.

Not once on that night had Lyn considered stopping him or running from Cullen. She had seen too much of his violence. She certainly could not have prevented what happened. As for running away, even if she had made it out of the garden without getting her skull caved in or the butcher's knife between her shoulder blades, where could she run to? He had the keys to the flat. No matter when she had gone home, he would be there on the bed, smiling, waiting. She wished that she hadn't heard the screams. She couldn't stop them in her head. Who was the woman screaming? Dolores, or a complete stranger? He said he hoped he had the right house.

'Oh my God,' Lyn realised, Dolores' niece could have been in the house. She had forgotten about her. John Cullen knew there was a child there. Why had he dragged her along with him? He wanted her with him. He always said that if he ever got locked up again he would kill her before he went in. If anyone died in that house he would go to prison for life. So would she. Cullen had taken her life without raising his hand to her. Lyn told herself that no one had died – if she had heard the screaming before she left the area, so had others. The fire brigade would get Dolores out. 'Didn't I have two fires myself when the kids were small?' she asked herself.

'Yes.' She answered her own question.

'Did the neighbours call the fire brigade?'

'Yes.'

'Were you or the children burnt?' 'No, not a scratch. We all got out.'

'Well, stop worrying. But just pray that no one suffers.'

It was nearly 6.00 p.m. on Sunday night when Lyn stopped arguing with herself. Perhaps because the police had not arrived, she convinced herself that whoever was in the house had escaped. She had not switched on the radio all day, too terrified to listen to the news on her own. John said he would be up at 4.00 p.m. If there was any bad news, Lyn thought, she could not stand to hear it on her own. She switched on the TV at 5.55 p.m. because she had to know. Her nerves were frayed. He, obviously, was not going to show up. Typical.

The newsreader's face flashed onto the screen. A judge had been shot in Belfast etc. etc. She let her breath out slowly. He continued: 'Two women died in a fire in a house in Hammond Street early this morning. The daughter of one of them, Miss Dolores Lynch, aged 34, died later in hospital.' He continued. Something about X units of Dublin Fire Brigade. When a picture of the burned out house flashed up on the screen, Lyn jumped up and switched the set off.

She lay back on the bed, reached for her Valium, took several, swallowed them. She then ran into the kitchen and drank some water, her hands shaking as she held the cup. Then Lyn did something she had never done in her life. She stood in the middle of the kitchen floor and screamed as hard as she could, for an eternity. She did not cry. She could not.

'You bastard, John,' she screamed over again and again, and eventually she lay down on the bed again. Shock set in.

At 8.30 p.m. there was a loud knock on the door; she got up and looked out the kitchen window. John's car was parked outside the flats. She slid the bolt back and opened the door, noticing that her hands were still shaking. He barely glanced at her. Lyn locked the door and watched his back as he walked down the hall with his usual arrogant sway. He lay down on the bed, folded his hands under his head and said, 'Why haven't you got the telly on?'

'I had it on. Did you hear the news?' She did not look at him as she asked.

15

'Yes,' he said. 'I'm glad she's dead.'

He was smiling, yet at the same time he was completely composed. Lyn went into the bathroom and locked the door. She sat down on the floor with her back to the door. So he had watched the news at 6.00 p.m., heard that Dolores, her mother and her aunt had burned to death. Had he just sat around his house, playing with his children, small talking with his wife? How could he? How could he bear to touch his children with the same hands that had destroyed three women?

What had she expected, Lyn asked herself. Had she expected him to say how sorry he was for the deaths, how sorry he was that she had witnessed it? John Cullen had no feelings, she told herself. He was totally, utterly inhuman. She splashed cold water on her face and went back into the room. He was glued to the television, relaxed, serene.

'What are you standing there for? Come and sit down beside me,' he said. She lay on the very edge of the bed. He leaned over, pulled her towards him and was about to kiss her when she turned her head away from him.

'John, I can't. Please don't kiss me.'

He took his arm from around her. She felt him studying her and then he jumped up off the bed and said: 'Right. Get all the gear together and we'll get rid of it. I want to make an early start. The pubs shut at 10.00 p.m. and the police will be doing the road checks for tax and I want to avoid that.'

Lyn got dressed and put the clothes in a plastic bag. She was on her way out the front door when he said, 'Where's the holdall? Go and fetch it, eejit.'

She got the holdall and put the plastic bag with the clothes into it. They drove out to Portrane, stopping to get petrol on the way.

When they got to Portrane they parked on the cliff top. Nearby was a parked car with a courting couple. When the couple had gone, John Cullen told her to bring the plastic bag of wet clothes and follow him. She got out of the car but could not see him in the dark. He touched her arm and she jumped. He took his jumper and vest out of the bag and ripped them to shreds and told her to follow him. He set off down the edge of the cliff. Lyn tried to follow him but she tripped and fell and cried out. His voice floated back up to her, telling her to stay at the top. She walked back to the cliff top, going as near to the edge as she dared, and peered over. It was so dark she could just make out the outline of the rocks. She could hear the sea lashing against them. Haunted, she strained her ears to try and separate the sounds of the waves lashing and the sounds of a man. All she could hear was the waves. She could not see him. She took a step back and put her hand up to her mouth to stifle a scream. He was behind her.

'Jeez, John. I was looking over the cliff for you. I never heard you coming up behind me.'

He took his trousers out of the plastic bag and tried to rip them, but could not. He walked back to the car, got the butcher's knife and slashed the trousers to shreds. As she saw the blade flashing she longed to push him backwards over the edge of the cliff. She shivered.

Cullen went back down the cliff to dispose of the last of the stuff and was gone for ages. Fear set in again, the fear of standing on a cliff top in utter darkness and a three-time killer somewhere near. Had he contemplated pushing her over? Christ, why had she not thought of that sooner? Of course he would have to kill her and she would have to keep licking his boots. Keep licking them, all day, every day. He was back.

'Right. Let's go,' he said.

They drove back to Ballymun. As they neared Coolock Lane he said, 'I think we'll dump the holdall out near the knackers' camp.'

He drove down Coolock Lane and did a U-turn at the itinerant camp. Then he told her to throw the holdall out her window on the side of the road. When they got back to the flat he switched on the television, lay on the bed and told her to make tea and sandwiches. She brought them in to him. He didn't speak until the television finished, Then he leaned over her, put his leg across her stomach and kissed her.

'John,' Lyn said, 'I am not looking for trouble, but please don't. I'm too upset. It was bad enough last night, but when I heard the six o'clock news I was shattered. I still am. I can't make love, I just can't.' Her skin crawled with goosebumps.

'John, can't you understand how I feel? I love you very much,

17

but . . . You'll have to try and have a bit o' patience with me. I'll get over it in time, but right now I just can't. Anyway, I'm half-dead.'

He studied her intently, looking for signs of weakness. She controlled the muscles of her face and hoped it gave the impression that she loved him, while being in too bad a state to make love. At long last he spoke, 'Alright, love, I understand.'

He kissed her very gently and then lay back on the pillow. 'I suppose it's only natural you would feel upset. I suppose I shouldn't have taken you with me, but it's too late now. I won't try to make love to you until you feel ready. I promise you that, Lyn. I won't even try. You just let me know when you feel that it's all out of your system. Lyn, I love you very much, you know. If I didn't, I wouldn't have taken you with me.'

He lay very still then, brooding. So did she. He took her with him *because* he loved her? This was not the time to question that.

One thing she had to know. 'John, how do you feel now?' Her voice came as barely above a whisper.

'I just feel glad she's dead,' he replied.

There had been no reference to the fire, to Dolores, her mother or her aunt since he had walked in the door four-and-a-half-hours ago. Lyn waited. She sneaked a glance at his face. It had that saintly look again.

'John.'

He turned to look at her. 'What?'

'What about her mother and her aunt?'

He jumped off the bed.

'A fuckin' rat shouldn't *have* a mother and an aunt! I'm going home. I want to go early so as I can come up to you early in the morning. I want to get all the newspapers, see if the police are in on it. See you early in the morning.'

As she bolted the door after him, Lyn knew the fire was to be one of his taboo subjects. It would be dangerous to mention it, and if she did, she knew to expect: 'Shut fuckin' up.'

She went to bed and lay thinking. Dolores had been a friend. She had babysat with her children, but she and Dolores had drifted apart long before Lyn had met John Cullen. Lyn had not seen her for years, but now she thought about how Dolores had always been there when she needed someone. Dolores was always there, willing to help anyone. She had stood by Lyn more than once and never flinched from dangerous situations. As the Valium started to take affect, Lyn wished she could phone Dolores now and tell her what had happened. Tell her that she had stood motionless while John Cullen set fire to a house. Dolores would rush to be with her, to help, to give advice.

John Cullen was back early next morning and they drove down to Sean's 24-hour shop and bought all the Irish morning papers. On the way back he wanted Lyn to read aloud the articles relating to the fire. As she picked up the papers in the shop, photos of the burned out house had leapt up at her. She folded the newspapers so she would not be able to see them. Her money went all over the shop floor. She felt everyone looking at her. She told John she could not read, that she had started to shake again when she saw the house.

'So it made the front page,' he said. He chuckled and pushed his foot down hard on the accelerator. When they got back to the flat he flopped down on the bed, surrounded by newspapers, and told Lyn to make his breakfast. He had left his own house so early his wife was still in bed.

As she was cooking, he kept reading out bits about the deaths. She brought him his breakfast in bed. He ordered her to read the papers while he was eating it. It was all there, the house, Dolores, her mother and her aunt. Her mother and her aunt had been overcome by smoke. Dolores had lived for twenty-four hours with 80 degree burns.

2

As the firemen struggled to get Dolores' charred body out of the flaming house, she kept repeating: 'Help Mammy. Save my mother.'

For years, Mrs Lynch had tried to rescue Dolores from 'the Canal'. Mrs Lynch could never grasp the extent of her daughter's fear of John Cullen. She believed that if Dolores gave up her 'bad company' and came home, she would be safe. She did everything to coax her daughter back, sought help from anyone she thought might influence Dolores.

Eventually, encouraged by her involvement with the Women's Movement and other political activists, and with media interest in prostitution in the late 'seventies, Dolores managed to break away from that life. She got a job on the domestic staff of St James's Hospital and returned to live with her family. Up to then, when people found out about her, she had lost other jobs, but she told the supervisor all about herself at the beginning, and the woman said that she would stand by her. Dolores loved her work in a geriatric ward, and was furious about the deductions from her pay slip.

Dolores was still haunted by fear, so she took taxis everywhere, or had her sister Kathleen pick her up in her car. Sisters and friends (Dolores had made friends with an amazing cross-section of women), were inclined to think that Dolores exaggerated her fears, for it had been seven years since she had sent John Cullen to prison. They thought it was water under the bridge. When they heard the news of the fire, though, everyone suspected who had started it.

Dolores' trouble with Cullen began when she sent Teresa, a new girl, home from the Canal. Teresa had only been a week down among the women when Dolores spied her and, although Teresa swore that she was over eighteen, Dolores guessed that she was about fourteen and sent her off home in a taxi. Teresa looked so vulnerable. She was skinny with dull, naturally blonde hair and shabby clothes, a long skirt worn over stout brown boots, obviously not the 'full shilling', although possibly just childlike. Teresa stood there, expressionless, while Dolores, a threatening figure when she was angry, ordered her home. Teresa was back the next night.

On more than one occasion, Dolores had sent young girls off the beat in a taxi. She greatly admired Detective Sergeant Lugs Brannigan because he had often treated her in the same way: 'Get off home, Dolores, or I'll give you a kick in the arse,' he'd say. She did not know her mother had asked him to do it. When Brannigan retired she took up a collection from the women to buy him a present.

In the beginning, Teresa's earnings were far below the expectations of her pimp, John Cullen, and she may have told him that it was Dolores' fault. Not that anyone would have blamed her for lying – the women knew that Cullen had arranged for all his pals to rape Teresa up against a tree before sending her down to work for him. Teresa was terrified of her 'lover', yet she idolised him.

One night, Dolores was in a café when Cullen came in and attacked her with a sauce bottle. She ordered her current 'best pal' Gloria to go and phone the police but Cullen went after her. Gloria, a beautiful, timid young woman, was pregnant at the time, and one of three women who worked in Dublin for a foreign pimp. Cullen dragged her out of the phone box and into the car, and he and the other men drove to a park where they raped and beat her. She lost the baby she was carrying. Dolores implored her pal to charge Cullen, but Gloria went back to England, saying business was too rough in Dublin.

Cullen was incensed when Dolores had him charged. He

beat her up again and again and each time he did, she went to the police. While he was in Mountjoy Jail awaiting trial, he sent some of his friends to Dolores' flat to beat her as a warning not to go to court. It did not stop Dolores Lynch, even though she was so terrified that she kept pans and kettles of boiling water simmering on the stove so that she could pour it from her second-floor window down on anyone who came to hurt her. John Cullen was sentenced to three years' imprisonment.

It was in the early days of Dolores' battle with Cullen that Nora Lynch and her husband were driving past the Pepper Cannister Church off the Grand Canal at Dublin's Mount Street bridge, and they saw Dolores standing there. Nora was not aware her husband knew about Dolores, but he said: 'There's your sister. Are you not going to talk to her?'

Confronted by Nora, Dolores started to cry and gave the excuse that she was hungry. 'I told her that she needn't be hungry. All she had to do was come home. Mammy would give anything to have her back. But she didn't want our mother to see her bandages. I asked her what happened to her hand. She told me a pimp did it to her.'

'Why don't you go to the police?' Nora asked her. 'I'll get worse if I do that,' Dolores said. Nora gave her sister the three pounds she had in her bag. When she got back to her car, her husband said, 'Nora, three pounds isn't much.' So they brought her to a shop and bought her groceries, gave her more money and drove her home to her flat. 'It was the night before Mother's Day and she made me promise to give Mammy a card for her,' Nora said.

It was far from pimps that Dolores Lynch was reared. Hers was a close-knit working-class Dublin family with a mother devoted to her children. Mrs Lynch was one of those working mothers unaware of the Women's Movement; a woman who had always worked, in low paid jobs, who had no choice. She never questioned the justice of her lot or thought about whether she enjoyed her work. Her husband had left, there was no Deserted Wives' Allowance, and she was glad of any bit of work that came her way. Nor did any of Kathleen Lynch's children feel neglected because she worked long hours. A neighbour helped her with them when they were small and she shared everything she could with them. She went to Irish dancing lessons with her four daughters and did the mothers' reel. At Hallowe'en she dressed up and went the rounds of local streets with them. Even on the night of the disaster, there was an event organised by Mrs Lynch to get the family together. It was a regular card game in the house which she felt encouraged everybody to be at home.

Dolores was born in 1950. In 1967, she was on the canal when Lyn Madden arrived from England. The two women did not become friends right away because Lyn's common-law husband and pimp, Craig Nelson, forbade her to make friends with other women on the game. Lyn was a steady 'grafter' who kept to herself and it was almost ten years before she and Dolores became close. Theirs was not a lasting friendship, but then, such relationships do not exist among women in prostitution because of the nature of their lives and their reliance on pimps and clients. However, they were close for a few years, when Dolores baby-sat for Lyn and even lived with her for a while. It was while Lyn was back in England for a year during 1973-74 that she and Dolores lost contact. It was also during that time that Dolores got into trouble with John Cullen.

Dolores was larger than life in every way. She lived for excitement, involvement, gossip, company. Short and grossly overweight, her personality was as out of control as her appearance. She was enormously generous. She lacked personal boundaries, spilling over into other people's lives, wanting to be part of whatever was happening to them. She was 'there', wherever 'there' happened to be, mostly because she had to be in on things. She was easily led, but she would not be driven, as her mother well knew. Usually, Dolores made one-way friendships with other women. She would move from one woman to another as she exhausted their stores of interesting information.

'You suddenly became aware that she always happened to be where you were (and sometimes ahead of you), ringing you up etc., and if you were "it" you hadn't a hope of getting out of her clutches,' recalls Lyn. 'She cost me a fortune in lost business and she would root me to the path under the pressure of her chubby little hand on my sleeve. She'd giggle and look up at me and say "Ah, sure, wait 'til I tell you".' And down to the last woman in those days, they waited until she told them. She was a gifted storyteller, kept her audience rapt, and her laugh was infectious. She was a giggler. She giggled in court. Her giggles on the Canal would set the other women off too and she was sometimes overtaken by an attack of the giggles during the Rosary at the Legion of Mary House. There was no woman on the game who was less interested in doing business than Dolores. The women used to laugh about her lack of interest.

Dolores would stand out in the cold, moving from one woman to another, exchanging titbits of scandal, all the while brushing off clients who fancied her. She would tell a man, 'Drive 'round once more, love, I just want to tell this girl something.' And the man would eventually give up and go for another woman. It was at the end of the evening when there was hardly anyone else to talk to that she would do a bit of work, just enough to pay for her evening meal with the other women and her taxi home. It seemed that being on the game merely financed her desire to be in the midst of it all.

Dolores always wore an all-in-one corset. Lyn remembers one night a client was beckoning to her, and she told her, 'There you are, Dolores, he's looking for you.' Dolores shrugged and said, 'Sure I couldn't be bothered takin' me fuckin' corset off.'

The women remember her as always having a cigarette in her hand, a cup of tea in front of her, her chest wheezing as her eyes shone with laughter. And she could be exasperating. One night, she put on 'whore's' make-up and her peals of laughter could be heard floating through the trees as each woman met her and asked what she had done to herself. None of them made up like that, and Dolores did not normally wear any make-up at all. Some of the other women dreaded going out socially with Dolores because they knew she would be scruffy and wear something outrageous. Then, there was the time when she was going to a family wedding and everybody was ready and they were aware of 'the great unwashed' Dolores, still in bed. They were all in the car, ready to drive off without her, when Dolores waltzed out, immaculately dressed, her hair done. In response to the surprise on their faces, she collapsed in a fit of giggles in the back of the car. She had hidden the new clothes so that the family would think she was going to be 'a holy disgrace'.

Dolores rarely spoke about her family, never said where they lived. There had been 'something' in Dolores' early life and she sometimes hinted at this 'something' with sadness, spoke of a deep hurt in her childhood which she could not forget. Some believed she had a daughter. Others poohpoohed this story as 'just Dolores'. She rarely discussed her personal problems at all on the Canal. She was too interested in everyone else's business. She was a great listener, gave her undivided attention. She would have made a Samaritan, but she could not keep a secret.

'Now promise me, you won't tell anyone if I tell you something,' Dolores would say and eventually forget to whom she had told what. This caused rows among the women and often someone would not be talking to Dolores for months on end. Dolores waited for the right moment and would then sidle up to the woman and ask, 'Are you not talking to me?' with a chuckle.

John Cullen broke Dolores' heart long before he took her life. She had a boyfriend called Tony, a Donegal man who worked at odd jobs. The way Dolores worked, nobody would call her boyfriend a pimp. He was a likeable fellow, although he had given Dolores the odd thump. They loved each other. When all else failed and Dolores still persisted in giving evidence against John Cullen, he turned his attention to Tony, warning him that he had better find a way to stop Dolores going to court. Tony pleaded with Dolores not to give evidence, but she was adamant. Then he issued an ultimatum: if she gave evidence against Cullen, he would leave her. She refused. Tony had no doubt that his head was for the chop. He left the country. Dolores went ahead with the evidence.

Mrs Lynch was born Kathleen King in the house in which she perished, her mother's house. She returned to 15 Hammond Street when her widowed mother was old. She worked as a tailor in Dorene's fashion clothing factory for 35 years. It was her mother's trade before her and Kathleen and Dolores Lynch were both apprenticed to Dorene's when they left school. With Dolores, it was in the front door of the factory of a morning and out the back. She could not stick it and found less tedious things to do with her day. Nora, the eldest, and Rita, both married, worked in hotels.

With everyone grown-up and working and with Dolores in a respectable job, the Lynch family thought that they had left hard times behind them. At Christmas, a month before the fire, the daughters took their mother out to buy her a fur coat. The women were delighted with the outing. Mrs Lynch had suffered a heart attack, but the Friday before she died, a specialist gave her a clean bill of health.

Mrs Lynch worked until the day she died, and was the centre of her daughters' lives. They always told her where they were going and when they would be back. Except Dolores.

As a child, Dolores was 'angelic', quiet and solemn, content with a comic until she was about thirteen years old. She suffered from ear-ache and was petted by her mother because of it and she played on it a bit, the way a child will. She did not do well at school and was always naive in ways, believing anything she was told. She started off in the Junior Legion of Mary, and Nora always believed that it was through the Legion that Dolores got into bad company. Visiting the Legion House on the Canal where the women congregated of an evening she would certainly have met plenty of 'bad company'. There was also rumour of some woman in York Street who led youngsters astray. Anyway, shortly after leaving school, Dolores changed. She became self-willed and yet was easily led.

Her teen years were a constant anxiety for her mother and Nora, who was the eldest. However, Dolores was always religious in a 'sort of way', and in later years she was the only woman who cheerfully knelt down with the Legionaries of Mary and said the Rosary. Most of the women would make their get-away when the Rosary beads were produced. Dublin's women in prostitution have always had a love–hate relationship with the Legion of Mary, the group dedicated to save the souls of 'fallen women'. The women used the Legion House in Herbert Place, near the Canal, as a coffee centre, glad of somewhere to go in out of the cold, but they rejected incessant bids to save their souls.

Dolores had finally made it off the streets, but according to her sister was 'as mad as ever'. Twice she took a group of old people to Lourdes, getting financial assistance from her family. And they could not understand her involvement with activists.

The Lynches were watching the television one night when Dolores appeared on the screen, carrying a banner with Bernadette Devlin in Derry. They switched off the set for fear of what else they might see. She did not listen to what they told her at home, and outside, the sisters believed, people played on her vulnerability.

Dolores never had a bean; she had no sense of property. She borrowed and never thought to pay back, and anything she had she gave away. She did not believe in having two of anything. She was the first to bring clothes for a new baby or take up a collection. When she worked in James's Hospital, she brought home a man's dirty clothes for her mother to send out to the laundry.

Dolores had all the Lynches working for CASA, the Caring and Sharing Association. The Lynches had to care and share whether they liked it or not. She would have Kathleen driving and Rita and Nora baking. Kathleen would get boxes of sweets at Christmas and Dolores would give them away. She went through money like water, and it did not have to be her own. The Christmas before the fire she got coal and other things for less fortunate people.

Dolores loved the uproar of getting arrested, followed by the battle in the court-room. She loved the arena, briefing her brief and listening to the judge and her brief negotiating over her. She hated the idea of prison, though, and managed to avoid it. Once, a judge said he would let her off if she got a job. Dolores went to work as a chambermaid in a hotel. After work she went down to the Canal, and she would often offer one of the women her wages if they would pack up for the night and go for a meal and chat with her. She was lonely.

Even after she got her job in the hospital, Dolores used to drop down for a chat with some of the women who were her friends. She felt a sympathy for them. She knew about standing in the cold, waiting for business. She knew what happened to women who faced pimps, without enough money, at the end of a night.

Dolores met with feminists in the late 'seventies at a time when there were attempts from within the Women's Movement to relieve the hardship of women on the streets. One faction wanted to stamp out prostitution, an attitude which Josephine Butler, the nineteenth century feminist, said was '. . . like trying to stamp out slavery by making it criminal to be a slave'. Other feminists believed that prostitutes must be offered the solidarity of sisterhood.

The Federation of Irish Feminists, who were a follow-on from Irishwomen United, met with several prostitutes on a regular basis in a rented room at the Resources Centre of the Student Christian Movement on Rathgar Road. They discussed the possibilities of law reform and the establishment of a crisis centre – perhaps like a battered wives' centre, where women would help women who worked on the streets. At the time, the women were being picked up by the police night after night and often two women found it hard to get a flat because it was assumed they would be running a brothel.

The Wages for Housework Group in England and other international groups were also vociferous on behalf of prostitutes. The Dublin meetings broke up, however, because there was an objection to prostitutes being in the building. Many of these women had known Dolores, but did not know where she lived. And in those days, before she got the job at the hospital, Dolores talked about taking up the sewing again. She was a born actress and played on middle-class sensibilities by telling the women stories about the Canal.

The increasing atmosphere of violence against women internationally and in Ireland instigated the Women Against Violence Against Women March through the streets of Dublin in 1978. Thousands of women marched to reclaim the night, and as they walked past the Rotunda Lying-In Hospital, women hung out of the windows to wave their support. As they crowded around the speakers' platform in Parnell Square, doctors in a Dublin hospital fought for the life of a 16-year-old girl who had been found abandoned, after being gang raped in a house in Sean McDermot Street. Eight youths had so brutally raped the girl that it was necessary to remove one of her breasts and take out her womb. Thus salvaged, she was eventually moved on to a Dublin mental hospital.

Some men insisted on marching alongside the women, claiming that not every man was a potential rapist. But the march was intended as a symbol of women being able to walk freely in the streets of their own country. Their numbers expressed Irishwomen's awareness of rape as a reality in their lives. The Rape Crisis Centre had just opened in a grubby little room, and buckets passed around that night were filled with donations for the centre. When the crowd broke up in Parnell Square, Lyn Madden went home, but a small group marched to the Canal to show the women their solidarity. When Lyn went to work the following night, she was met by a group of irate prostitutes complaining about 'a bunch of fuckin' feminists coming down here and queering up business.' Lyn asked what had happened and Annie replied: 'They came down here with their bloody banners and put up a road block so the cars couldn't get down . . . So we asked 'em "what the fuck are you doin' that for?" and they said: "women are reclaiming the night.'

Annie told them 'We already have the fuckin' night, we had it long before you lot came down.'

'So what happened?' asked Lyn.

'We ran 'em, didn't we?' said Annie.

It was the awful death in 1978 of ex-prostitute, Teresa Maguire, off the streets for two years, that brought about the letter of proposals to the Minister. Teresa, who refused sex with her attacker, was found with an iron bar stuck up her rectum.

Dolores had accused the then Minister for Justice, Mr Collins, of evading the whole issue of prostitution. In a letter to the Minister, Dolores wrote: 'The girls who make their living on the streets of Dublin are very annoyed and disappointed that you have refused to meet us in the company of the Council for the Status of Women to hear our point of view about the injustice we suffer in the courts.'

The same letter proposed that the Government open a rehabilitation centre to help young girls to abandon their trade on the streets. Dolores was annoyed that letters from the women had been ignored and the Council for the Status of Women had failed in their attempts to get an audience with the Minister about the matter.

In spite of public reaction, the Minister told the Labour Party spokesman for Education, John Horgan, that it would not be possible for him to discuss a particular court case because the Teresa Maguire case was sub-judice. Her attacker eventually received a two year sentence.

Dolores continued to speak to groups of women in Dublin, in the universities and around the country. She spoke wherever she was asked. Ironically, it was Lyn Madden who had introduced Dolores to activism on behalf of prostitutes. Then, Lyn was working in Gaj's restaurant and was helping Jim Finucane, leader of Young Fine Gael and Michael Keating's secretary, with research into the problem of prostitution. Michael Keating was then Fine Gael's spokesman for Justice. Dolores was one of the women interviewed by Jim in a Government paper published under the title *Girls On The Street*. At the time, he said that Lyn Madden was the woman most likely to escape prostitution.

Finucane was appalled to discover the full implications of prostitution in Dublin: 'the slavery, the brutality and the way the system works against girls on the street.'

The findings of *Girls On The Street* recommended the establishment of Welcome Centres, and law reform. The centres would be run by ex-prostitutes to provide a homely atmosphere for women who needed help. They would also try to develop any talents that would encourage an alternative way of life, offer professional help when required, and provide protection and relaxation. One of the signatories of the report was Lyn Madden.

Dolores claimed that the law and 'the system' did not solve the problem of prostitution, but that they enabled all prostitute women to be treated unjustly. She wanted the law changed; but more than that, she wanted to get women off the streets. She understood that the class system generated prostitution and pimping. She felt the degradation of a woman who was driven to prostitution. She talked a blue streak about this and everything else, but never about her family or where they lived.

On 28 November 1979, Dolores was to speak on the topic of 'Prostitution', billed as a 'spokesperson' for Dublin prostitutes at a huge Feminist Federation meeting. (For a couple of years, Dolores had spoken up for prostitutes, but many of the women on the Canal denied that she represented them. She probably got her mandate from the few who had met in Rathgar.) Meanwhile, the Pope was coming to Ireland that year.

Dolores disliked herself for the way she had used her life and hurt her mother. She sought a 'cure' in her typically flamboyant way – she wrote to Pope John Paul II and told him all about herself.

When the Pope came to Ireland, Dolores went to the Phoenix Park with friends and a packed lunch. When he visited England she took the day off from the hospital to watch him on television. She thought him a 'common sense, lovely man', and she accepted the invitation that came in answer to her letter to visit him at his summer home in Castel Gandolfo. Her mother and Aunt Hannah gave Dolores £500 to go and see Pope John Paul. Dolores, always primitively religious, had become extremely devout and was sure that the 'cure' for her past life was meeting with the Pope.

The letter Dolores got from the Pope was black from being handled. It got to be a family joke. Her uncle would come in and say, 'Is there any chance you'd show us the letter from the Pope, Dolores?'

She never said what she talked to the Pope about, but she carried around the picture of herself and His Holiness, showing it to everybody. She made a special trip to the Canal to show the women. The photograph was her proof that it was possible to escape prostitution and be accepted in the best of company. Lyn told Cullen about the photograph. He sniggered dismissively.

During the last few months of her life, Dolores Lynch changed. Her sisters saw that she was under more pressure, even though she still laughed and joked. Her high spirits were all a front, for she was being threatened. Pope John Paul had absolved Dolores of her 'sins'. Then John Cullen sneaked hell through the open window of her home at 15 Hammond Street.

3

Lyn paid her rent every Monday morning at the office on Shangan Road and then went to visit her friend Róisín who lived nearby. The Monday after the fire, John waited while Lyn paid the rent. As they were driving to Róisín's flat, he said, 'Don't mention Dolores. Pretend you didn't see the news or read the papers. Wait and see what Róisín has to say.'

Róisín had just got out of bed when they got to her flat, and her boyfriend Willy O'Donnell was not there. Róisín made tea, and John went into the living room, put a film on the video and lay down on the settee.

The two women sat in the kitchen drinking their tea. Róisín was talking about work, clients, the police, the women. That was all Róisín ever talked about. Lyn got edgy, got up and stood looking out of the window. Róisín was still going on about some taxi driver and what he had said to her when she suddenly stopped and said excitedly, 'Lyn, Dolores Lynch is dead. I forgot about it. Another taxi driver was telling us in Gig's last night.'

Lyn turned slowly from the window, but did not speak. Róisín read the look on her face. She knew. She mimed: 'Was it John?'

Lyn nodded and Róisín looked shaken. She mimed: 'Were you with him?' Lyn nodded again and sat down. Róisín and Lyn were so close that they did not need words. Róisín put her hand over Lyn's and squeezed, pointing to the open door. They both walked into the living room. Lyn said, 'John, did you hear that Dolores is dead?'

'I'm fuckin' delighted,' he said, not shifting his eyes from the television screen. The women went back into the kitchen, Lyn shaking again. They smoked and chatted loudly about nothing. Mostly it was Róisín's voice to the fore, and they tried to convey what they wanted to say to each other with their eyes.

Willy arrived, opening the hall-door with his key, said hello to the women first, and then went into the living room to John. Now that the men were occupied with each other, Róisín said, 'Come into the bedroom, Lyn.'

Lyn and Róisín lay side by side on the bed as they often did, to talk. 'Oh Lyn, you must be in bits. I knew when you first walked in something was wrong, but I thought you had a row with John. I completely forgot about Dolores 'til I thought of Gaj's. The minute I said it I knew by your face. What happened?'

Lyn poured out everything. She could not stop. When she got to the part about dumping the gear over the cliff at Portrane, Róisín said, 'Oh my God, Lyn, were you not terrified going out there with him?'

'I didn't know where he was and he came up behind me while I was peering over the edge,' said Lyn. 'He didn't make a sound.'

Since the first night she appeared for work on the Canal, Róisín had never got on too well with Dolores. Now, as she stared at Lyn, she could see the state she was in. 'Lyn, what are you going to do? He might kill you!'

Someone was coming up the hall, so Róisín changed the subject. John looked at the two of them and said, 'What are you two dummies talking about?' He was smiling. Róisín, quick as ever, quipped, 'We're talking about your lovely wife. How is she? Still as slim and beautiful as ever?'

Róisín was forever teasing John, and surprisingly, she got away with it. She teased him about his accent, his walk, his wife, his mother, his car, his hair, his ex-girlfriends, everything. But then Róisín did that to everyone, in such a way that nobody could take offence. 'She's as slim as you, Róisín,' John said. 'Come on, Lyn, get moving, I have things to do.'

'Good-bye, Róisín,' Lyn said. 'See you Wednesday.' She felt as if she was being physically dragged from Róisín's flat.

John dropped Lyn home and went to pick up his takings from Teresa. She felt a bit better for telling Róisín and she knew that it would not be repeated because, for all her light-hearted teasing, Róisín was also terrified of John Cullen. John drove Lyn to collect her son, Joey, from the boat that evening and the two of them spent the whole night discussing football. Lyn was amazed to see that John was enjoying himself with the boy. He and Joey started to kick the football up and down the hall. This was something they did to tease Lyn. It was guaranteed to exasperate her, start her giving out. Tonight, Lyn just lay on the bed, pretending to read. She read the same page over and over and still did not know what it said. Eventually John said, 'That's enough, Joey. I don't think your Ma is amused.'

He walked into the room smiling and said, 'Jesus, Lyn, you're very quiet tonight. What's the matter with you?' He kissed Lyn and she snapped at him.

'Do you have to ask that?' She got up, went into the bathroom and locked the door behind her. She could hear them laughing. Young Joey said, 'She's in a right mood, John. Has she been nagging again? I don't know why you don't give her a few digs to shut her up.' Only fifteen, Joey was already sure how women should be treated.

John Cullen just laughed and said, 'That's what I keep telling you, Joey. Never get married. This is what you will put up with. A woman is like a garden, a few digs now and then is what they need.'

They laughed. Joey admired John Cullen because John had always been nice to him. When Joey had gone to bed, John told Lyn to run his bath. When he got into the bath, he shouted at her to come in and talk to him. Lyn sat on the seat of the lava-tory. He was washing his leg when he paused and said, 'What's wrong, Lyn?'

She felt on firm ground now that Joey was in the flat, safe enough to say, 'What the bloody hell do you mean – "What's wrong"? You know what's wrong. I don't have to tell you. I can't live with this. This is too much for me to cope with.'

He carried on soaping his legs as he considered her reply. He answered slowly, selecting each word.

'You only feel like that now, Lyn. You'll get over it. I've listened to you talking about your past life for the last two-and-a-half years. You've been through an awful fuckin' lot, d'you know what I mean like, but you have come through it. That's because you're strong, mentally, I mean. When you are telling me about something that's happened to you, I know it hurt you, but you've come to terms with it. I'm not fuckin' stupid. I know the reason you won't let me touch you. It's every time you look at my hands, you think of that. Right?'

He was lying on the settee later while Lyn ran her fingers through his toes and he said, 'Did I tell you that the women on the Canal are making a collection for Dolores?'

This was the usual thing. If one of the women was sick or if relatives had died or something, there was always a collection for flowers or a wreath.

'No, you didn't. How do you know?'

'Teresa said it when I went up this morning. She said Annie was asking all the women for a fiver for Dolores' family – I told Teresa that if I found out that she had given a penny to it I would break her neck. By the way, Lyn, Liam has to be got rid of this weekend. I think I will burn his house.'

'The Holocaust,' Lyn thought. She knew Liam's wife and his children and she vowed that John would have to kill her this time as well. 'I will not hear any more screams,' Lyn's voice shook. 'I will not just stand there again. I can't. Don't force me to go with you.'

He leaned over and kissed her cheek. 'It's OK, Lyn, I'll do this one on my own. I don't know why I took you to Dolores'. I didn't need you, d'you know what I mean? I think I did it to make sure you wouldn't talk. You'd have known it was me. You could have gone screaming for the cops. I had a feeling you were getting tired of me and wanted out. At least now I know you can't grass on me. You would only be setting yourself up. The perfect crime!'

Cullen left soon after and went home. Lyn lay wondering how his wife dealt with all this. He had told Lyn that he and his wife were sitting together on the settee when they listened to the news on Sunday and that she knew that it was the same Dolores who had got John three years in prison. She also knew what time her husband had arrived home, 6.00 a.m. According to John, she had looked at him, but not said anything. 'Probably,' thought Lyn, 'she did not dare. But how did she feel? Did she hope someone else had murdered the Lynches, pray it was someone else? Or did she know?'

Lyn did not remark on the hour when John arrived at 7.00 a.m. the following morning. From past experience she knew that he had got out of his house early because he was expecting a dawn raid from the Murder Squad. He told her to get dressed; they were going for the morning papers. They bought the papers and when they got back to Ballymun, he told her to cook him some breakfast. When he had eaten, he suggested they go and see the social worker in Belfast who had written to ask Lyn to come and talk about her youngest child, taken away from her father in Belfast and put in care. She was in no mood for this ordeal but when she had got the letter from Belfast, she had told John she wanted to go. He did not speak much on the way there. When they hit Belfast, it started snowing heavily. They had to keep asking directions to find the place. John was furious because the people could not understand what he was saying.

Lyn spent two hours with the social worker, talking about her daughter Leila, and the background to the child's being in care. The social worker had never met Lyn before. Lyn was in such a weird state that, later, she never could remember what the conversation was about. It all seemed irrelevant now, anyway.

When Lyn came back to the car, one glance at John's face told her it was going to be a lousy drive back. It was still snowing heavily. Visibility was bad and they took a wrong turn coming off the Antrim Road. Then he let loose.

'Fuckin' stupid northern bastards. You'd think I was from fuckin' Mars. Did you see the fuckin' dumb look on their faces when I asked the way? Who wants the poxy north, anyway?' Lyn laughed nervously. 'What are you fuckin' laughin' about? Stop. I'll fuckin' take your life if you take the piss out of me. You could set me up for life.'

'I'm sorry, John. Honest. It's not funny, just I'm a bit tired after all that with the social worker.' Gradually his facial muscles

36

relaxed. He put his hand over and squeezed her knee and said, 'Sorry for shouting at you, Lyn. It just drove me mad when they pretended not to understand what I was saying.' When they reached Dundalk he unwound, pulled into the side of the road and said, 'I think we'll stop here and go for something to eat. If that's Belfast they can keep it.' She followed him into the café.

John Cullen hated to be anywhere he was not known. He hated having to leave Dublin, above all; being in a strange city made him feel a loss of identity. The year before, his wife and children had gone to her sister in Manchester for three weeks. He had stayed with Lyn for two of those weeks. He was to go over to Judy for the last week and the night before he left he was very tense. He said he hated England. On his return Lyn asked had he enjoyed himself. He replied: 'Yes, Manchester is OK. We went to Blackpool for the day and I enjoyed that, too. Now don't laugh at this, Lyn. I felt kind of queer that no one knew me, d'you know what I mean, like?'

Over the meal on the way home from Belfast, he said, 'You know Lyn, I've won. I've been reading all the papers and there has been no mention of forensic being called in on the fire. Ha! It's fuckin' great, isn't it! I've waited all these years. If I had known it was so simple, I could have done it years ago.'

She put down her knife and fork and said, 'John, don't you think that every woman on the streets knows it was you that did it? How many people have you told you were going to get Dolores? Even if you hadn't, ordering Teresa not to give to the collection would start them thinking. You have enough rope to hang yourself, and if you do anything to Liam's house they will know for definite. In fact, Liam is no fool. He knows it was you killed Dolores. He has probably seen his solicitor to warn him that if he gets any mysterious fires, to go looking for you.'

'Oh, shut up, Lyn. You're just trying to spoil it for me.' She stared at him; he was beaming. When they got back to Dublin he did not stay very long in the flat. He left around 11.30 p.m., saying he would be up early the next day.

It was the day of the Lynches' funerals when Lyn woke next morning. She had never been to a funeral in her life, but she imagined it, hour by hour. The relatives, the getting ready to go, the cars, the three coffins in three hearses, the weeping, the church, the sound of the dirt being thrown on top of them. And the screams. The screams were bursting out of her head.

When John arrived, one glance told her that he was edgy, more than that. She cooked his dinner. He talked to Joey for a long time, and Lyn knew something was on his mind. A bath always relaxed him. Lyn asked if she should run the bath for him. He nodded. When he got into the bath she went in after him, closing the door so Joey could not hear.

'John, what's wrong?'

He did not answer for quite a long time. He kept soaping his body. Silently he washed and then soaped and soaped again.

'Dolores,' he finally answered, then fell silent again.

'Christ,' she thought, 'don't tell me it's finally hit him?'

'What about her?' Lyn asked.

'I was down the Canal last night. That's why I didn't call you. They are still collecting for her. I will kill every whore down there. I fuckin' hate prostitutes. How dare they make a collection for her? They know she's my enemy. They know she grassed on me. They know she's a rat,' he said. His face was white with temper.

'John, for Christ's sake, the woman is dead. She was buried today. Her mother and her aunt were buried with her. The funeral was today, for God's sake. Can you not let her rest?'

He looked up at her. The look on his face reminded her of one of the men in *One Flew Over the Cuckoo's Nest,* a sly, crazy leer. 'Yes, I forgot. I hope the maggots are eating her,' he said.

It hit her, suddenly. She had always known he had psychopathic tendencies, but now he had flown over. Nuts. She had to get away from him, fast. He was talking about Dolores as if she were still alive. 'That's it, then,' Lyn thought. 'I have to get away from him, but how? Where?'

On Wednesday morning, Lyn went to visit Róisín. She knew something was wrong the minute she walked in. Three vigilantes had marched into Róisín's flat the night before and confiscated two kilos of hash which had, only that day, arrived from Amsterdam. It was on the kitchen table. The men told Willy that if he dealt in any more drugs he would be knee-capped. Then they left. Neither Willy nor his mates made any attempt to stop them. 'It has a market value of £10,000,' said Róisín. 'And this means I'll have to go back to work again.'

'But Róisín, you've been going out again for the past month,' said Lyn.

'Not seriously,' Róisín replied. 'It's just been to get spending money for myself.'

Willy was always telling Róisín that she could not afford to have a baby. Lyn knew this was what was on Róisín's mind. Now she would have to earn enough to keep herself and her flat, and also provide for Willy O'Donnell, his wife and their five children.

4

The first time Lyn met Róisín, she was accompanied by her friend Tish, and they were surrounded by a band of shouting women. Róisín had tears on her eye lashes. Lyn had never seen anyone cry so prettily before. The tears did not fall from the blue eyes; they just nestled on her eye lashes and her nose was not red. Lyn saw at once that Róisín and Tish were new women, and the others would not allow them to work. Most of the hostility was against Róisín who was eighteen years old, tall, blonde and beautiful. Tish, built like a twig, was not that pretty.

Róisín was being pushed around when Lyn cut her way through the circle, took her by the arm and in a quiet voice told the women to back off and leave Róisín alone. Never at a loss for something to say, Lyn asked in her English Midlands accent, 'Scared of the competition, eh?' The women moved off and Lyn gave Róisín a tissue and took her for a cup of coffee.

Róisín was a chatterbox with an endearing, sweet personality. She told Lyn all about 'my Willy', who had only three children at that point, and how much she loved him. By the end of the night, Lyn was totally charmed by Róisín. And Róisín had found a heroine in Lyn, seventeen years her senior. The two women became close friends. Years later, Róisín told Lyn that she had nearly been put off the game by the first two women she and Tish saw that first night as they approached the Canal. They were Mona and Roz, two scruffy alcoholics. Róisín grabbed

40

Tish's sleeve and said, 'I don't think I can go through with it if that's how we'll end up.' And then she saw Lyn.

'I thought you must be a poshie,' Róisín said. 'You looked lovely in your blue dress, Lyn.'

Lyn never saw Róisín in a bad mood, and saw her cry only once, when Róisín's father killed himself. Over the years, Lyn wondered if Róisín would ever become bitter or cynical. It did not happen. Róisín never grew out of her girlish stage, and Lyn found that enchanting. Even when the weather was brutal and business was slow on the Canal, Róisín was lighthearted. No matter what anyone did or said to her, she did not bear a grudge or even get angry at the time. She was rarely serious, nor did she ever have a firm opinion about anything.

For all her vivacity and her facility for landing in trouble, Lyn was a serious woman, an avid reader. If ever she got into a deep subject, Róisín would distract her. 'Let's do something mad. C'mon, what'll we do? I haven't a clue what you're talking about.'

Many of the women were jealous of Róisín O'Connor's good looks and earning capacity, but she was well-liked because she was so nice. She was utterly undomesticated. Willy did everything around the flat for her and the one time she managed to cook a chicken she took a polaroid snapshot of it to prove that she had!

Róisín grew up in what outsiders saw as a happy family. Her father adored his wife, but their's was a tragic story. The trauma of this tragedy might account for Róisín's gaiety which probably covered *her* perfect cut off from reality. Her father had sexually abused Róisín and her two older sisters. They did not tell each other.

Róisín was seventeen years old when John Christy raped her in a flat in Ballymun. When she got home, she did not tell anyone. After four days of her silence, crying and not eating, her father demanded to know what was wrong, and she told him. Mr O'Connor borrowed a shot gun and blew Christy's head away. He was sentenced to two years in prison.

While Róisín's father was in prison, Róisín grew closer to her mother, and once, when they were having one of their long chats, Róisín and her sisters told her what their father had done. Mrs O'Connor was devastated. When she visited her husband in prison she told him what she had found out and that she would not let him back in the house. She still had a fourth daughter, the youngest, to consider.

Released from prison, Róisín's father moved into a flat on his own. One of his daughters used to visit him and one night she couldn't get an answer at the door. A neighbour helped her break in and she found her father slumped in a chair. He had gassed himself.

It was while Mr O'Connor was locked up that Róisín went on the game. Lyn remembers a policeman shouting at her one night, 'Go home Róisín, you cow. Your poor father is doing time for killing a man over you, and you out on the game.'

As for Róisín's friend Tish, she was a virgin when she arrived on the Canal and still was, years later, until she met her boyfriend. She remained a 'virgin' on the Canal, even after that. 'You'd only get the likes of it in Ireland,' Lyn said, but Irishmen understood perfectly well. Tish made a good living and never by sexual intercourse.

Now, Róisín told Lyn that all the women on the Canal had the raving horrors over John Cullen. They were not saying it to Róisín's face because they knew that John and Lyn visited her. But Róisín said they would huddle in little groups whispering, and when she came near they would start talking in normal voices about nothing.

They all knew the fire was no accident. And they all had it in for Teresa. Poor Teresa, twenty-two years old with a child's mind. When Teresa was asked to give money to Dolores' collection, she said, 'I wouldn't give a penny for her. She got my John three years in prison. I'm glad she is dead.'

On the day after the funeral, John kept on raving about the women collecting for Dolores, saying he wanted to kill every prostitute in Dublin. Teresa was the only one in his good books. 'John, please, please, stop it. You're freaking me out,' said Lyn. 'Dolores is dead. Let her rest,' she pleaded.

'But love, I don't mean I would kill you. I don't think of you as a prostitute. You are not nosey and interfering like them,' he said.

'I'm not talking about that. I mean the way you keep going on about Dolores. She's dead.'

'Do you reckon the maggots are eating her yet? She's been down there a day now.' His voice was questioning. This was new, the way he was looking at Lyn was like a child asking: 'Mammy, why did God make the dark?' She could not cope with this. She had never seen anything like it before. Cold crawled over her back and she tried to humour him. She had to get him out of the flat.

'Why don't you go up to your brother for a drink?' she asked, her voice sympathetic. 'It'll do you good. Why don't you?'

So many times, when things were good between them, she had objected to him going off for a drink without her. Now he said, 'Do you think so, Lyn? You wouldn't mind? Should I go for a drink?' It was a bit like getting a child from under your feet and out to play while he still thought it was his own idea – except that she was in bits when she bolted the door after him.

Shaking, relieved, Lyn's jaws ached and she bent over with stomach cramps as she walked up the hall. 'Do you reckon the maggots have eaten her yet?' And that smile. She would not let him in again that night if he banged for an hour. She would worry about the consequences when she was able to face him again. She would say she had taken sleeping pills and had not heard him. He would probably come back again when the pubs closed, but she could not face him again tonight. She doubled her dose of sleeping pills.

Lyn struggled awake. Saturday, a week since the fire. It was 10 o'clock. 'Jesus,' she thought, 'he's early for a Saturday.'

She opened the door to Kevin Mackey, Jenny Murray's pimp. 'Is John here?'

'No.' Her jaws cracked with a yawn.

'Willy is downstairs in the car. Will I tell him to come up?' asked Kevin. Half awake, she nodded and went into the kitchen to make a cup of tea. Willy O'Donnell, Fibbs and Kevin walked in. Willy asked, 'Where's Róisín?'

'I don't know what you mean, Willy,' Lyn said.

'John Cullen kidnapped her on the Canal last night and she has not been seen since,' Willy said.

Lyn sat down. John must have twigged that she had told Róisín about the fire.

'Willy, tell me from the start,' she said, her ears pounding.

'I was just getting out of my car outside the flat when Jenny Murray and Ted Summers jumped out of a taxi. They were waiting for me. They said John Cullen was down the Canal last night, very drunk, and he drove up beside Róisín and told her to get into the car. He wanted to talk to her. As soon as she got in, he drove off with her. The women did not know what to do. They went up to Gaj's and waited until 5.00 a.m. in case she showed up. Then they got a taxi out to the flat. They saw John Cullen's car parked two blocks away. They were too scared to go up to the flat, so they got the taxi to sound the horn. John Cullen looked out of the kitchen window. I thought Róisín might have come over to you for help.'

'Oh Willy, I told Róisín something,' Lyn said. 'If she tells John, he'll kill her.'

'I know. Róisín told me. I'm not worried about that. She'd be too terrified to say she knew. It's something else I'm thinking about.'

'John would not touch her,' Lyn said, 'definitely not if he was drunk. He can't do it on drink. He always falls asleep.'

The men exchanged glances. 'Is she not in the flat? Is John's car still there?' Lyn asked.

Willy said, 'I have not been in the flat, Lyn. Do you think I would walk into the flat and John Cullen waiting for me with a knife? I came here just to see if you knew anything. How will I find out if she's there?'

Lyn despised Willy at that moment. 'The gutless wonder,' she thought. 'His own woman could be trapped in that flat, even dying, and he didn't have the bottle to go in.' She thought for a moment. 'Why don't you get Stella to go into the flat and find out the score? He won't touch her because he knows she's straight and she will get him nicked. Stella has the bottle for it.'

Willy missed the sarcasm and said:

'Yes, right Lyn. I'll ask her.' As the three of them were leaving, Lyn said, 'Willy, will you call back and let me know if she told John she knew? I'll have to clear out fast if she did.'

'OK,' he said.

Joey got out of bed and asked why Willy had come and his mother told him. He smiled. Lyn was just finished dressing when she heard a car horn. She looked out of the window. A fellow was driving Willy's car and he beckoned her down. She threw on a coat and flew down the stairs, but he had gone by the time she got down. No one hung around when John Cullen was on the rampage. Lyn ran over to Róisín's flat. Willy opened the door. 'Did he?' she asked. He just stepped back to let her pass and she rushed to Róisín's bedroom while Willy went into the kitchen to the men.

Róisín was sitting up in bed, talking to Stella and drinking a cup of tea. Lyn saw with relief that there was not a mark on Róisín.

'Hello, Lyn,' Stella said in a funny voice and left the room. Lyn sat on the bed, and then it all came tumbling out. Róisín was totally distracted. Her speech was so fast that her sentences were all jumbled up.

'Oh Lyn, he pissed in my mouth. He kept me here until six o'clock. He kept on and on about Dolores. He said the fire was started with petrol. Lyn, he . . .'

Lyn shrank into herself as she recognised the details of the worst of Cullen's sexual fantasies, things in which she had refused to participate.

'He kept saying the maggots were eating Dolores. And he squatted over my face . . . Oh Lyn!'

Lyn heard Róisín's voice as if from a distance, recognising perverted details of her lover's attack on her friend. 'I thought he was going to bite off my clitoris. He said if the police found a hair of his head in Dolores' house, he would say that it must have blown there weeks ago.' Lyn's stomach churned as Róisín continued the vivid recounting of Cullen's attack.

'Lyn, he screwed me all night. Well, he tried. I tried to butter him up. You said you had to lick his boots and I was dead scared he'd tie me up and whip me. And he kept asking me did I like him and I said yes. I even said it was nice that we were alone for the first time, and he'd be alright for a few minutes, and lie still. And then he'd kneel over me again and make me . . . Oh Jesus, Lyn. Lyn, he came all over my face. He was alright for a while and then he started all over again. I've only stopped vomiting. He's mad, Lyn . . .'

Róisín was hysterical and Lyn, shocked and ashamed, held her. There was nothing to say. 'How could I have known such a thing would happen,' Lyn asked herself and wished that Róisín would stop, stop telling details that seemed to echo in Lyn's ears, but she did not try to shush her. Lyn accepted Róisín's outpouring like punishment. She had seen craziness in John Cullen last night – that was why she had got rid of him – and in pushing him out, she had destroyed Róisín.

The women sat rocking each other for ages, not saying anything. Willy walked in. 'Well, Lyn, now what?'

Lyn shook her head helplessly. The three of them sat on the bed for a while in silence.

'Willy, what are you going to do? You cannot let him get away with this,' Lyn said. She was finished with John Cullen. He had killed Dolores. Now he had raped Róisín and worse. He had to be stopped.

Willy looked for a long time at Róisín, then he turned to Lyn. 'I'll have to kill him. I bought a gun yesterday after the three fellows set us up over the hash. I will do it Sunday night when the pubs close.' And then Willy left. He went to place his weekly bet with the bookie's. No matter what else happened, it was Saturday.

Róisín calmed down a little and when Jenny Murray came to the flat to see how she was, they all went into the kitchen. Róisín went over the whole story again for Jenny's benefit. While she added things she had forgotten the first time, Lyn tried not to hear it all again. Jenny said that when they had called up to Róisín's flat the night before and honked the horn, they had seen John looking out the window and that he was naked.

Now, Maeve O'Reilly arrived at the flat to expand the story. John had pulled up on the Canal the night before to talk to Maeve. She got in the car and he asked her to go with him to Liam Ryan's house, to 'sort out' Liam. Maeve refused. He drove off at top speed. 'We're going to Sandymount. I'm going to screw the fuckin' arse off you.' Maeve was a lesbian.

'Y'are in your bib,' Maeve replied and fought like a demon while he tried to keep her in the car. The door could not be opened from the inside, but Maeve got the window down. While being dragged by the hair and back-handed across the face, she escaped out the window, even though Cullen tried to pull her back by the legs. She finally got away from him at Irishtown, and luck still with her, there was a taxi. John Cullen chased them, driving up on the pavement and through the traffic lights, but the taxi driver lost him when they reached the Canal. That was how John happened to be near the Canal when he spotted Róisín.

Lyn listened, stunned. She knew then that no woman on the Canal was safe while John Cullen was free. Maybe, like Peter Sutcliffe, the Yorkshire Ripper, he was starting off with prostitutes, but in the end any woman might be fair game.

'Was John sober when he left at 6 o'clock?' Lyn asked. He was.

'Lyn, when he was leaving, he said: "Well, Róisín, seeing as we both enjoyed it, we may as well get together again. I will come up and see you two or three nights a week." I asked him what about you and he said: "Lyn will understand. Anyway, perhaps you better not tell her."

Maeve did not know that John had killed the Lynches and she said, 'Lyn, he kept demanding to know which of the girls had given money to the collection for Dolores, and said when he found out who they were, he was going to kill them. Does he hate her that much?'

'And Lyn,' Róisín remembered, 'that's another thing. He asked me had I given anything to the collection and I said "No". I was rattling. Of course I had, just before he came along.'

Róisín begged Lyn not to tell John that she had told her about the attack. 'Don't worry, Róisín, I'll keep licking his boots. He'll stay with me. I won't let him loose again . . . I'd better get back to the flat in case he comes when I'm not there. If I'm not there, he'll know where I've been.'

When Lyn got home Joey wanted to know why Willy had sent for her. 'If you must know, John raped Róisín,' his mother said. Joey grinned and walked away.

Lyn followed him into his bedroom. 'I don't know why you think it's something to laugh about. Do you realise just how low rape is? At the very least, it's not pickin' on someone your own strength, is it? Do you think that anything John Cullen does is right? Well, it's vicious and cowardly, that's what rape is, but you think it's OK, is that it?'

Joey was flushed, wriggling his shoulders to shake her off. 'Stop nagging. I don't think rape is OK. It was only Róisín he raped. She was lookin' for it. John already told me about her. She was always playing up to him when you weren't around. Anyway, I'm not listening to you, you're always nagging him. Wait and see what he says.'

Lyn slammed the door and walked back into the living room. So he and John were 'boys' together? Joey. All he cared about was football. 'Just a kid,' Lyn thought. John Cullen had to get at him, discuss Róisín with him. What else had they discussed?

Lyn stared right through John Cullen as he stood grinning at her in the doorway. It was 7.30 p.m. He crossed over to her and kissed her on the cheek.

'Don't look so solemn, Lyn. I know I promised to take you for books for your birthday, but I got held up. I promise I'll take you into town on Monday. It will only be a day late.'

Lyn hated him. 'Don't you dare kiss me,' she hissed at him. 'I know you got held up. I didn't expect you to come up early. You needed to recuperate, you disgusting, perverted bastard.'

The smile never left his face. 'Jesus, Lyn, love, what's wrong?'

'What's wrong? Don't you dare ask me what's wrong. You bloody know what's wrong,' she yelled at him.

Joey came and stood in the doorway. He laughed at John and said, 'Willy O'Donnell came over here this morning looking for Róisín. He said you kidnapped her. Then me Mam went over to Róisín and Róisín told her you raped her. She's been nagging all day. You should tell her to shut up, John.'

Lyn jumped up and pushed Joey out of the room, shouting at him, 'Get out! How dare you tell him to tell me anything! Get out!'

Joey laughed and went into his own room.

John Cullen was smiling when he said, 'Lyn, if you are going to start, I'm going for a drink. I did not rape Róisín. I never touched her. She's lying.'

There was a time when she would have believed anything he said. In spite of all she knew about him, she had once been besotted. 'I know you raped Róisín,' she told him. 'She told me about you urinating in her mouth and squatting over her face. Does that ring any bells? How do you suppose Róisín could have guessed that was your dirty hang-up? How common d'you think it is? Anyway, there are three witnesses. Three of the girls got a taxi up to the flat at 5.00 a.m. and you were seen lookin' out of the window, naked.'

'So Jenny is stickin' her fuckin' nose in again,' Cullen said. 'I'm going over to Balcurris Road right now and I'm going to beat the shit out of her. I'm goin' to clear the Canal. I won't leave one woman down there in one piece. Róisín and Jenny will get it first for interfering, then all the rest. I'm sick and tired of brassers and the trouble they cause. I wish I had never set eyes on the Canal.'

Lyn faced him. 'You are sick of brassers? You have caused a reign of terror down there. I heard about you gettin' Maeve in the car. You intended rapin' her, too. Every woman down that Canal hates your guts. It was a sorry day for Dublin's prostitutes, the day you went into the pimping game. You won't find an Irish girl on the Canal tonight. The word is out, what you did to Maeve and Róisín. They are all terrorised. None of these girls did you any harm, and you have made a bloody good living from the Canal. So now you are going down the Canal. If you walk out of here now, I swear I will be gone when you come back. I work with these women. I won't stand by and let you terrify them.'

He stared thoughtfully at her. Lyn felt the tension easing away. He walked back into the room and lay down on the bed.

'Take my socks and shoes off,' he said.

'Ask Róisín to take them off,' Lyn spat at him, and shocked herself.

He did not look at her. He took his own shoes and socks off and said, 'Look Lyn, I'm staying in with you tonight because I love you, and I know you feel hurt, but if you know what's good for you, you will shut your mouth.'

Lyn had never known what was good for her. 'John Cullen, you left my flat last night to go for a drink. "Do you really think I should go, Lyn?" she mimicked. 'What do you do? You go down to the Canal, you pick Maeve up, you try to drive out with her to Sandymount to "screw the arse off her", as you say. The only reason you didn't succeed was because she had the bottle to fight back. Then you go back down the Canal and pick up my best friend and drive her out to Sandymount. But it's not comfortable enough for you, so you drive her out to Ballymun,

49

where you stay until 6 o'clock in the morning, degrading her. You tell her you would like to make it a regular thing, three nights a week. What three nights, John? The three nights I will be back down on the Canal working for you? I told you before if you ever went with one of the girls on the Canal you would want to make sure she was worth it, because it would be the end of us. This is the end!'

She forgot. Overcome by hate and jealousy, she forgot.

He grabbed her roughly and said, 'Lyn, baby, you are in no position to make threats. You are only reminding me that you are a danger to me over Dolores. You would want to be very careful what you say to me, d'you know what I mean, like? Let's get one thing straight. I did not rape Róisín. I screwed her. Did you see any marks on her? When we got to Ballymun, I parked two blocks away from her flat. She could have made a run for it, but didn't. When we got into her flat I told her to strip off. She said she wanted to wash herself first, so she went into the bathroom and locked the door. Now Lyn, you know what I'm like on the drink. I lay down on the settee waiting for her and I fell asleep. When I woke up I looked at the clock. I had been asleep for an hour so she could have got away. She could have, but she fuckin' didn't. Do you know what she said? She said how this was the first chance we had ever had to be alone together, without you or Willy around. I kept asking her did she fancy me, and she said, "Yes, John, for a long time." I told you she always wanted me to screw her. I told her to suck me and she did, and when I started pissing I was looking down on her and Lyn, she didn't even flinch. Just carried on fuckin' sucking. I couldn't get you to do that. I told you Róisín was a kinky little bitch.'

Was Róisín lying? No, Róisín knew John had killed three people. She knew John Cullen. She didn't want to die.

John was convinced that Róisín was crazy about him. Lyn could not tell him that Róisín had only catered to his whims because he was a three-time killer. She wasn't supposed to know that. Róisín would not sleep in her flat anymore because she was scared he would go up again. Fibbs was moving out of his flat in Ballymun because he thought John was on the rampage and 'you wouldn't know where Cullen might strike next'.

Lyn was sick and she recognised the feeling: jealousy over Róisín. 'I can't be jealous of *that*,' she told herself, but she knew that she was jealous. Had he always fancied Róisín? A couple of hours passed and she would not speak to him. Images of Róisín and John together tormented Lyn. Was this how a woman felt when her man raped another woman? Maybe this was normal. Why had she never read about this anywhere?

Suddenly, Cullen said, 'Lyn, I don't know what you're sulkin' about. Since the fire you said you didn't want me to make love to you. It's your fault I screwed Róisín. If you had let me make love to you I wouldn't have had to go down to the Canal lookin' for it.'

'Don't pull that one,' Lyn spat. 'It's only a bloody week since the fire. Are you trying to tell me that you had to go and rape a woman? Nobody *has* to. John, I'm no dummy. I know all about you, about men. I ought to.'

Lyn felt that she had been relegated to the position of Wife Number Two. When they had first been in love, they had made love two or three times a day, every day. He could not get enough of her, and then gradually he had started asking for 'kinky' sex. Lyn refused, and he had eventually accepted that it was not her scene. 'He still had to get his fantasies and perversions out of his system,' she thought now, 'and if he went home to his Irish catholic wife she would be lighting candles and sprinkling holy water on the sheets.'

'You say you hate all other prostitutes,' Lyn said, 'but they won't get you nicked, will they? So the odds are in your favour. You tried Maeve because you know she's gay; that was a challenge. Ha! How dare she get away? Then who do you spy? Poor Róisín, the softest, most easily frightened woman on the Canal. How many other women have you raped? The way I see it, after what Róisín told me, I wouldn't trust you with your own mother!'

He moved his arm suddenly. Lyn jumped. He scratched his chin and she said, 'And what's more, you told Róisín that you set fire to Dolores' house with petrol, that it wasn't an accident. You have a big mouth on drink.' She was trying to defuse the time bomb she had just primed, and afraid at the same time that Róisín might have let slip that Lyn had told her about the fire.

If in the future it came out, Lyn would turn to him and say, 'I didn't tell her, John. You did.'

That forced him to speak. 'I didn't mention Dolores to Róisín,' he said emphatically.

'Ha, you didn't what? You told her you lit the fire with petrol. You said if forensic found a hair of yours in the house, you would say it must have blown in there weeks before. You said Dolores had to die for getting Paul three years as well as you. You told Róisín she was for it if she had given any money to Dolores' collection. Oh, you told her plenty,' Lyn said.

He considered this, then said, 'Did I? I don't remember. I was very drunk. Perhaps I better lay off the drink for a while.'

He fell silent for a few minutes before he said, 'Anyway, it's all the one. I don't give a fuck what I told Róisín. The silly bastards still think it was an accident, so there is fuck all they can do about it.' End of conversation.

The night passed with him refusing any more discussion about Róisín. He was brooding, though. He left early.

5

The next day was Lyn's birthday. She attaches a child's importance to birthdays. Thirty-nine years. And she was deeply
depressed. Last year's birthday had been just three weeks after
she and Liam Ryan had been stabbed. She had thought at the
time, 'Will I live to see thirty-nine?'

It was only eight days since the fire. Two days ago, another
friend had been raped and debased by the man who was her
lover. What a crazy word. Lover, love, lover. Lover of what?
'Someone would have to find a new word for a man who shared
your life, but who was not your husband,' Lyn thought.
Boyfriend? He was no boy. He was certainly no friend.

John Cullen called around six o'clock, grinning. 'Happy
birthday, Lyn. I'll take you into Eason's tomorrow and you can
pick out some books. We will go for a drink tonight.' He kissed
her on the cheek. Hm. She ignored him.

Shortly after seven, he nudged her and said, 'Come on,
John's baby, get ready.' She ignored him, but he was not ruffled.
He had been the same after the fire. Fulfilled. Lyn decided 'ful-
filled' was the word to describe John's mood. Obviously, raping
Róisín had been fulfilling.

'Come on, baby, it's your birthday. Let's bury the hatchet.
It's months since we went out together. I want to go for a drink,
but as you said last night, I talk too much and that's dangerous,
so come with me. Come on, Lyn, show me how much you love

me. If it will make you feel safer, you can bring Joey with us. He would pass for eighteen. He can drink orange juice.'

She considered it. She could not trust John to go for a drink on his own. He would head for the Canal, and the women would be in peril. She knew John wouldn't do anything to her while Joey was around. It was safe enough.

'OK,' she said and got dressed.

They went to the Swiss Cottage. Joey sat opposite. He had never been in a pub before. He was posing, trying to look grown-up, his eyes nearly popping out of his head looking at the young girls. He had left his little world of football for the night.

After four pints John was all lovey-dovey, clasping her hand affectionately. It left her cold.

'Lyn, do you love me?'

'Yes.'

'You don't sound very convincing, love. Tell me properly,' he said.

'I love you very much,' she said.

'You still don't sound convincing, Lyn.' He kissed her. 'I think I know what the trouble is. I should never have made you get that abortion. We will have a baby. You can work for another two years, then pack it in and we will have a baby then.'

They were still holding hands. The sadness of it all hit her. She had loved this man desperately. Eons ago she would have done anything for him. He thought she was sad because she had got rid of their baby. She had been at the time, but that was before he had killed three women and raped her friend.

'John, I don't want to go over all that again. I'm sad about the abortion, but I will never have a baby for you now. I'm too old to be considering a baby. Things are all messed up for us. I don't know how we will end up, but let's just mess up our own lives, not a baby's.'

She got another kiss.

'Lyn, you only feel like that now because you are upset over Róisín. You shouldn't be. She's only a tramp. She proved it by letting me screw her when she pretends to be your friend. She hates you really. She's jealous of you because she knows Willy is only using her, but she knows I'm crazy about you. She knows you have class. I guarantee that in ten years time we will have it

54

made. We will have two houses let out into flats. We can use the money from the rents to open a little book shop. That's what you'd love, isn't it? Our child would be about seven years old then. My own kids would be grown up and Róisín will only be a bad memory to you by then.'

'You know we won't last ten years,' Lyn said, her voice low.

He kissed her again and looked intense and sincere as he said, 'Lyn, love, I wish I could make you realise how much you mean to me, d'you know what I mean like? If anything happened to you I would kill myself. If I didn't believe in an afterlife, I would leave my wife tomorrow and move in with you. I would get a divorce and marry you.'

Surprised, she sat up. 'John, what has an afterlife got to do with all this?'

'Well, y'know Lyn, if I knew for sure that when you died you were just buried and that was it, well, it wouldn't cost me a thought. I don't love her. I do love you. But I respect her. She has been a good wife and a good mother. I suppose although I don't go to mass I still have enough of my catholic upbringing to be scared about meeting God if I left my wife.'

Incredulous, Lyn said, 'What about the Lynches? What do you think your God thinks about that? If you leave your wife, he won't forgive you? Do you think he's going to say, "Hi, John, don't worry about Dolores and her family", and open up the pearly gates for you?'

He withdrew his hand from hers in agitation and said, 'We're back to that again. Look, God knows I'm in the right. He knows Dolores got me nicked. He understands.'

'Oh my God,' Lyn laughed flatly. 'Where would you get it? Only in Ireland. You really believe that, John? You are nuts, you know that, don't you? If there is a God do you think he would consider Dolores in the wrong because she made a stand against your brutality? And what about her mother and her aunt? *They* didn't grass. You and your wife make me sick. I suppose I'm as guilty as her. I've no faith in God, but if I had it wouldn't be in a God who condones murder and rape, but would never forgive you if you got a divorce. For your information, there ain't no such thing as divorce in Ireland, so you needn't worry because you can't get one anyway. You must have committed adultery more than any one I know. You've been screwing Teresa for years and have three children by her. What about me? You've been screwing me for two-and-a-half years. Doesn't worry me, but what about your God?'

'Just shut fuckin' up. NOW. I don't want to hear any more. I can't please you no matter what I do, y'know? I made a big effort to control myself yesterday when you started nagging about Róisín, but I should have shut your mouth. Permanently. I brought you out for your birthday, and I try to be nice to you, y'know, but you sit there and sulk. I'm telling you, I can't put up with this much longer. If you want to carry on living, you'd be wise to can it.'

Her big mouth could cost her her life. The danger was palpable. Joey couldn't hear what John said, but he looked scared. In a panic, she reached for John's hand and held it for the rest of the night. He did not withdraw it. She wanted him to think that she was hurt over Róisín, and that she still loved him.

Lyn had not had a drink for months and got pretty sloshed. When they got home, she asked Joey to make the tea. She fell asleep. John pushed her awake, saying, 'Joey says O'Donnell keeps driving up and down outside the flat.' She had forgotten. The gutless wonder was going to kill John Cullen tonight. This was Sunday.

There was not a bother on John Cullen. 'Joey, is he on his own?'

Joey shouted back from the kitchen. 'No, he keeps pulling up outside and looking up at the window. There's three other fellows in the car.'

'How dare the rat come to my flat,' John fumed. 'I'm going to burn his car for that.'

'John, who says Willy is looking at this flat? Dublin is a free country. He's entitled to drive anywhere he likes.' Lyn watched his face. He was getting more incensed by the second.

He said, 'No, that's typical of O'Donnell. He knows I screwed his woman. That was two days ago. He was not man enough to come and face me. He has to wait till he gets tanked up, then collect a few heads before he dare come. If he comes up to this door, he will be the first to get it. Fetch me the knife, the sharp one.'

'John, a knife is not going to do much good. You know Willy bought a gun after the three heads commandeered the hash. He's not going to come unarmed.'

He laughed. 'Lyn, Willy would not have the bottle to come to this door if he had a machine gun. He's gutless, a wanker. He may pay someone else to come. It's all the same anyway. He has signed his death warrant. Him fronting me up!'

Lyn kept quiet. She knew that Willy was a coward, but he had said that he was going to shoot John for raping Róisín. It was like having a pet dog that you loved; the dog bit people, savaged a child, had to be put down. You loved and missed the dog, but the dog had to be stopped. John Cullen had become worse than a mad dog. He had lost the power of reason.

Willy O'Donnell drove off. A non-event. But it left John seething. He was going to burn Willy's house and car and he was going to go over to Róisín to screw the arse off her, then beat the hell out of her. He would then go up to Liam Ryan's house and give it to him. Lyn listened to this litany, strangely unimpressed.

'John, you are not a one-man army.'

'Oh, but I am, Lyn. I am.'

His tone was absolute. That was the first time she had ever heard him brag. Everything about him was understated. He never said he could beat any man, he just dismissed them all. 'He's only a wanker,' he would say, and some of those in question were tough men.

She managed to quiet him and he fell asleep. He awoke with a hangover at half past five and staggered out the door saying he would be up the next night. Lyn relaxed. The beast would go to his lair to recuperate.

It was rent day again and Lyn went on up to Róisín's flat. Róisín, Willy and Fibbs were there, all in deep dark states of depression.

'What happened about the shooting, Willy?' Lyn asked with a straight face, wanting to see him squirm.

'Don't talk about it, Lyn. I paid a fellow to do it. He made up all sorts of excuses the minute he heard it was John Cullen he was to shoot. Then he saw Joey looking out of the kitchen window and we knew Cullen knew we were outside the flat. No one had the guts to go up to the flat, so we had to knock it on the head.'

'Including you, Willy, and it's your woman that was raped,' Lyn said sarcastically.

'Including me, Lyn,' he admitted. He sounded weary. 'I'm not able for this pressure. Róisín and me have only just come into the flat for clean clothes. We are sleeping on the floor of Colm's flat. Róisín is too scared to be in here on her own at night. I don't mind admitting that I'm scared to go home to my own house, I think he will come looking for me. If I am not there I don't think he will do anything to my wife and kids.'

'Willy,' Lyn said, 'I know Róisín told you about Dolores. It's gone to his head. He has had a taste of the power of killing something that got in his way. You and Róisín are next. I could not keep silent about the rape. I'm sorry, but I lost my head and accused him of it. John is crazy about me, you all know that, but he knows the rape was the final straw for me. I just don't feel anything for him. He doesn't want to lose me, but he knows he will. In his crazy mind he can't see that it was the fire that finished me. As far as he is concerned, you and Róisín are the guilty ones. You told me about the rape. He was going to burn your car last night, but I stroked his head till he fell asleep. He will rape Róisín again, he told me, and he'll get you because you had the nerve to drive around outside my flat. He even asked me where your mother lived. He was talking about Róisín's mother's house. He wanted to burn that down, too. Look, he was a borderline case before. He's slipped over the edge, is all. Don't presume he won't touch your kids if you're not there. He is liable to do anything, Willy.'

Willy did not answer her. He went into the living room while Róisín and Lyn sat in the kitchen.

Róisín looked years older. They all did. All except John Cullen. Róisín had been too scared to sleep the last two nights. She and Willy had lain awake all night talking. They had lain on a mattress on the floor of Colm's flat with the Colt.45 beside them.

'I didn't think John Cullen knew where we were,' Róisín said, 'but still I kept expecting him to boot through the door at any minute. Lyn, it's Willy I feel sorry for. My heart goes out to him. He's so upset and he doesn't know what to do.'

That was Róisín, loyal to Willy to the last. She said that Willy's mate Patser had moved his wife and kids out of their flat for fear John Cullen would go for him when he could not get his hands on Willy.

Willy came back and said, 'I've decided, Lyn. We have only one option open to us. You have to go to the police and tell them about the murder.'

'Oh no, Willy, you're crazy. I only came to warn you what he's thinking about. I don't want to see any harm come to Róisín. It's only another seven days till he goes up for the stabbing. He's capable of doing a lot of damage in that time, but surely you can all lay low for a week? You're asking me to grass. You're a man, you're supposed to protect Róisín. You've been pimping off her for the last five years. I don't think it's fair of you to put it all down to me. I don't know what to do. Even if I went to the police it wouldn't end there. OK, so he's arrested, and me, too. What then? He would be bailed out and you would be back where you started. He would make sure I was bailed out, no way would he leave me in Mountjoy when I am a witness. And he'd know I had grassed him up. I'd be another Dolores. Only more so. This is a murder rap. He'd get me and torture me and then arrange a little hit-and-run accident or something mysterious. No, it's asking too much of me. It's up to you, Willy. You sort it out!'

'Lyn is right, Willy,' Róisín said, 'we would only be putting her life in danger. And he would guess that we were the ones who put her up to it, so we'd all be for it anyway.'

Róisín did not press the issue. They talked a while longer, tried to find a solution that would not boomerang, and then Lyn left. As she walked back to her own flat she thought it was only a matter of time before the police came pounding on the door. And that was likely to lead to more mayhem.

John did not show up all day. Had Willy already gone to the police about Dolores? Lyn heard John's key in the lock at 11.45 p.m. after the pub. He swayed in. 'Get me something to eat.' She did not answer him, just went into the kitchen to do as she was told. When she had cooked him a dinner and brought it in to him, he was fast asleep, snoring. Lyn stood in the doorway looking at him. He looked normal in his sleep, no sly smirk, no evil eyes narrowing in temper, no elated, weird smile. What would she have to do to rid herself of him? Would it take a silver bullet, or a stake through the heart?

'John, love, it's five o'clock. Time to go home.'

He opened his eyes wearily. 'I guess I fell asleep, huh? Jesus, I drank an awful lot. You look worn out, Lyn. I should stop coming up after the pub. I'll come up early tomorrow and make it all up to you. I know I should have called up today. I still didn't get you your birthday present.'

He kissed her and was gone. Birthday present. 'What a bloody farce,' Lyn thought, 'Who was your victim tonight, John? Who did you rape?'

He was back at around 3.00 p.m. the next day. He took Joey and Lyn to Crumlin Shopping Centre. She bought some groceries, some tiles for her bathroom. He wanted her to choose some books for her birthday. She refused. 'What I wanted for my birthday you're in no position to give,' she said and Joey flushed. John ignored the remark. He drove them back to Ballymun. He chatted to Joey and they watched television while Lyn made dinner.

'Run my bath, John's baby.' He got into it. Lyn slammed the bathroom door and went to lie down on the bed. An hour later he shouted, 'Lyn, come and run some more hot water in this.'

She went in and turned on the hot tap.

'That's enough.

She looked at him and made no move.

'I said that's fuckin' enough.'

His voice rose one decibel. Danger. She lost her nerve, turned the hot tap off.

'Sit down and talk to me,' he said.

She sat on the lavatory seat.

'Say something, Lyn.'

'I've got nothing to say to you,' she replied and watched as he stood and scrubbed his body all over, then sat down and rinsed all the soap off. He stood up and scrubbed himself again, sat down again. He must have done this half a dozen times. He did this every day. It had not occurred to her before, but now she noticed that his scrubbing of his body went beyond being thorough. It was obsessive. He couldn't stop it. He paused in the middle of scrubbing his legs to say, 'I love you, Lyn. You know that, don't you? No matter what I have done over the last few weeks, you know what I mean, like, I want you to know that I love you. Róisín was nothing, that was just to get at Willy. Can you understand that? Don't let it come between us, Lyn. When a man screws a woman it doesn't mean a thing. I just wanted Róisín to know that she's dirt. I wanted Willy to know his woman is dirt.'

'No, John,' she said wearily, uninterested, 'I don't believe anymore that you love me. It's an obsession. I had it all with Dave Black and Craig Nelson. That's not love. I don't know why that's the way men love me. You hurt my best friend just to get at her boyfriend. Can't you understand how that hurt me? You could have got Willy some other way. You could just scare him witless, for Christ's sake.'

He would not answer, kept on scrubbing his legs. He lay down on the bed after his bath and told her to dry his body all over. She did that. Then he asked her to run her fingers through his toes. After a while, he started into what Lyn called his pre-love-making verbal, barely above a whisper. 'Lyn, in a minute I am going to kiss you from head to toe. I am going to start with your toes, I am going to lick and suck them and work all the way up. Now, love, kiss me.'

Lyn jumped off the bed and threw the towel at him. 'That's what you bloody think! If you want to lick or kiss anything, go home to your lovely wife and do it. Or better still, why don't you go and visit Róisín? It must be about time now for one of your three weekly visits!' She stopped, out of breath.

He got up and dressed himself, slowly. When he had finished, the colour had drained from his face. He reached for his car keys, gave a look that made her blood run cold and said, 'I'm leaving now, Lyn. I will not be coming back. It's over. I have to get out now before I do something we'll both be sorry for.'

He marched down the hall, out, and left the door swinging open. She bolted it after him, ran down to the kitchen and, with her heart pounding, watched him getting into his car. He took off with a screech of brakes, skidding up on the path and away.

Lyn took a few Valium and tried to calm herself. She had gone too far. She could still have got out of letting him make love to her if she'd played her cards right. She could not control the reference to Róisín and knew even as she spoke that it would set him off. Lyn felt guilty about Róisín and her own relentless jealousy. She loved Róisín; she just could not keep her jealousy to herself.

Now that he was gone, she was terrified. She should have carried on crawling, grovelling, humouring him. He would be back. He would not leave it at that, not when he started brooding on what she knew. At dawn, Lyn fell into a restless sleep, and kept dreaming that John was standing over her, knife glinting, smiling.

There was a banging on the door. 7.00 a.m. 'Oh Christ,' Lyn said. Why hadn't she run last night? He would take the door off the hinges. Joey walked into her room, fully dressed.

'Mam, it's the cops. You'll have to open the door.'

Relief. Lyn looked out the back window. There was a huge garda* standing out the back watching the balcony. That is standard practice in Ballymun when they do a raid. Men have been known to descend eight storeys down over the balconies to escape. She threw on a dressing gown and went to the front door and shouted: 'Who is it?'

The banging stopped.

'Police. Open up.'

There were five or six men. One of them said, 'Who's in the flat with you?'

'Just my son, Joey,' Lyn answered. They were searching the rooms. The same guy said, 'Get dressed. I am arresting you under Section 30**. Joey, make your mother a cup of tea.'

She got some clothes from the bedroom and went into the bathroom, threw water on her face, dressed herself and combed her hair. She went back into the living room. Joey had made her

---

* Policeman
** Section 30 is the Act under which people can he held for interrogation for offences against the state

a cup of tea. She sat down and drank it. She was very groggy. She had only slept three hours and could still feel the Valium.

The officer said, 'You know what it is about, don't you?'

She nodded.

'Right. Let's go, Lyn. Your mother will be alright, Joey. We will call you later.'

6

They drove, in silence, to Kevin Street Garda Station. Lyn planned to tell them everything; relieved that she would not have to face interrogation on top of everything else.

Once inside the forbidding old building, a ban garda* searched her, took her handbag and handed her back her cigarettes and lighter. Tea next, and then they began the questioning. Lyn clammed up. Years of habit silenced her. Being in a police station had brought her defences up. As a child she had experienced this feeling of being in a hostile place, and through the years she had learned how to resist, defend herself in a police station. Had they questioned her at home, it would have been easier for them, but now her deep conditioning took over. She was not aware of what happened to her until later – but now she locked her jaws.

Two gardaí questioned her in relays. No Mutt and Jeff routine, both doing the nice guy bit, she thought. One sat facing her, the other pulled his chair up at her right-hand side until he was about two inches from her. She would not, could not, co-operate. They would have to go through the process of getting it out of her if they could. They were the enemy. She settled into battle, even though it was not what she had planned to do.

They asked her about Dolores, and Cullen, and the fire.

---

* Policewoman

They wanted to know where she had been, and they told her how Dolores had died. Dolores. Her friend.

Lyn said she could not tell them anything. If she did, she said she was as good as dead herself. She begged them not to tell her any more about Dolores. Lyn felt tormented as the questions continued. She was hung-over from the Valium, sweating and unwashed, and she had started menstruating a week ahead of time.

Hours later, and Lyn hadn't told them a thing. She was saturated with sweat and menstrual blood. She could smell herself, could feel her blood oozing heavily. If she had been arrested for anything else she would have demanded a ban garda and asked for sanitary towels and a wash.

They asked her to help them to stop Cullen before he killed or maimed more women. Then they told her that Teresa and Róisín had been picked up and that Róisín had made a statement. And all the time, they said, Cullen had been there, smirking, sure that Lyn would never grass.

The police read Róisín's statement to Lyn and showed her the signature. Lyn was still not sure. She asked to see Róisín.

The three gardaí looked at each other and the one who read the statement out said, 'Right.' He turned to the other two and said, 'We might as well. We've tried everything else.'

Róisín walked in and stood with her hand on her hip. She was fighting!

'Róisín, did you make that statement?'

She straightened her shoulders and said, 'Yes, Lyn, I did. I've decided that John Cullen is not going to push me around any more. I can't take any more. I can't even sleep in my own flat. Willy can't go home to his own house. I am putting a stop to John Cullen.'

Róisín was white. Lyn had mental flashes of her humiliations at John Cullen's hands. She was breaking, but she held on. 'Róisín, if I make a statement, will you stick by me?'

She put her arm around Lyn's shoulder and said, 'Lyn, you make your statement and I will stick with you all the way along the line. Willy said he will, too.'

'Oh Róisín, I'm so scared. John will kill me when he knows. I can't do it on my own. You are the only friend I have. I need you. He will never rape you again. But promise me you will stick by me, I need a friend.' They rocked each other, just like the time after the rape. 'Lyn, I told you, me and Willy were talking about it. We will stick by you.'

Lyn struggled to stop crying. 'Róisín, will you do something for me? Will you look after Joey? Get him out of Dublin. Pack his bags and get him over to England. Close the flat up, you can leave all the stuff there. Just take the video and telly and my briefcase. And Róisín,' she whispered, 'I got my period. Bring me some clean clothes down?'.

Róisín left and they asked Lyn if she would make a statement. 'Yes, I will. You should have let me see Róisín sooner.'

Lyn made a half statement. She told them only so much. She was conscious that every word she uttered was another nail in her coffin.

Lyn knew that, whatever she said, she would pay for it, that somehow, John Cullen would get her. She wondered if she could get through it all, even if Róisín stood by her. Taken to a cell, she fell asleep instantly.

In the morning, Lyn awoke to the voice of a man reciting the renewal of Section 30. A policewoman brought her some tea, and at around 9.00 a.m., the questioning began again. Where had she been? What had she seen? Heard? Details, please.

More and more questions. She had admitted she was at Dolores' house with Cullen. Why didn't they charge her and take her up to Mountjoy? At least she could have a bath and get into a cell by herself. At 7.00 p.m., Joey was allowed in to see her. She tried hard not to cry but she did and told him she would be locked up a long time. 'Go back to England. I know it will be hard for you with no one to look after you but you'll have to fend for yourself now. You're a big boy. I've let you down again. Maybe, someday, you'll understand.'

They questioned her again until around 8.30 p.m. When they all went out of the room for a while, Lyn lay her head down on the table.

When they came back, one of them had her statement in his hand. He said, 'I want you to come with us now, Lyn, and face John Cullen with your statement.'

She started to shake. 'Oh, no. I can't.'

'Lyn, he won't touch you. I promise you. Now come on. You had the guts to make the statement. Now face him. It will be over in a minute,' one of them said soothingly.

Lyn got to her feet stiffly and they walked her down a corridor, her legs trembling on high heels. One of them put his hand on a door handle, and she stepped back, the panic rising in her throat. She made to turn back. 'I can't,' she said.

He took her gently by the arm. 'Lyn, you can,' he said.

'Stand in front of me, please. Don't let him get me.'

They opened the door. John was sitting on a chair with his back to the window. He glanced up at her. She dropped her eyes and looked at the floor. Four gardaí had gone in with her and there were already two in the room. One said, 'Are you Elizabeth Ann Madden?'

'I am.'

'Is this your statement?'

'It is.'

'Is this your signature?'

'It is.'

She kept her eyes glued to the floor. If they didn't hurry this up she was going to fall, her legs were going. The garda said to John, 'Do you want us to read the statement out to you now?'

'No,' he said.

'Do you want to have a chat with Lyn?'

'No.'

It was over. They ushered her out. 'Oh my God,' she said and leaned against the wall for support. They put her back in the room.

One of them said, 'Róisín is going in now with her statement.'

Lyn felt sorry for him, felt pity for him. He had looked defenceless for the first time since she had known him. They brought Róisín in, ashen.

'Lyn, they want me to go and face John and tell him I made the statement. I can't do it,' she said.

'I thought I couldn't either,' Lyn said, 'but I did it. Don't ask me how.'

Lyn and the gardaí tried to convince Róisín that John Cullen would not be able to harm her. 'Róisín, come on. I'll go in with you,' Lyn said, 'I can face him again.'

Lyn stood behind Róisín after they entered the room with the gardaí. She was shaking. 'Are you Róisín O'Connor?'

'Yes.'

'Is that your statement?'

'Yes.'

'Is that your signature?'

'Yes.'

John Cullen lifted his head, narrowed his eyes at the women. He stared at the floor while the women bumped into each other in their rush to get out of the room.

'That was probably the bravest thing either of us have ever done,' Lyn said. No matter that six men were there to prevent him from attacking them. Lyn and Róisín knew that they were now public enemies number one for John Cullen.

'Keep your fingers crossed for us, Lyn,' one garda said. 'We are going to the DPP* with what we have.'

Wearily, she raised her head to look at him. He had his two fingers crossed. Lyn nodded. Two of them stayed in the room with her talking, questioning her.

'I don't want to talk. I'm too tired. I just want to go up to the 'Joy.'

They let her be.

There was a rush of feet to the door. Four of the Murder Squad walked in, obviously having been home, spruced up and beaming. One of them leaned across the table, shook her hand and said, 'Congratulations, Lyn. We have him charged with murder.'

She watched bemused as they shook hands with each other and exchanged congratulations. It was like something from an American television soap opera. Two of them lit up cigars.

'What am I charged with?' Lyn asked, amidst the rejoicings. 'Please God,' she prayed, 'don't let it be murder. Let it be an accessory.'

They remembered she was there and were all smiling now.

---

* Director of Public Prosecution

'Lyn, you are free to go. The night is young yet. Róisín is waiting downstairs for you. Some of our lads will take you home.'

Lyn could not believe her ears. She was free. Lyn and Róisín rushed to hug each other. They both cried openly and stood rocking each other. One of the murder squad shouted to Lyn that they would be in touch. Two Special Task Force men drove them home. Lyn wept quietly. One of them said, 'Well girls, the ordeal is over. He is locked up for good now.' 'I don't know,' Lyn said. 'This could be just the start.'

The STF checked Róisín's flat before leaving. Lyn was utterly exhausted, beyond talk, and when Róisín ran a bath for her she got into it and closed her eyes in relief. She soaked for about half an hour, washed her hair, wrapped a towel around herself and lay down on the settee. They switched on the late news.

'A man has been charged at a special sitting of the Dublin District Court with the murder of Miss Dolores Lynch. He is John Cullen, a married man, of 58 Mount Olive Road, Kilbarrack.'

Róisín cheered. 'Switch it off, Róisín.' Lyn said.

Róisín kept talking. 'Lyn, I'm so happy you are home. The Murder Squad were down the Canal all night on Wednesday questioning all the women. They all started talking then. He raped Annie Doyle while you were away at Christmas, and beat her up. She was too scared to tell anyone 'til she knew he was locked up. The police said that the word spread like wildfire that it was John Cullen who was being held for Dolores' murder and they got about fifty phone calls, all from women saying they were glad he was caught. There was a terrible atmosphere down the Canal over it. The girls knew they were all in danger.

The police had arranged that they would arrest Willy on Wednesday morning when he went to sign on the labour. That way, his fellow criminals would not know he had grassed.

'I don't see the logic of that,' Lyn said. 'John Cullen is a murder suspect. Who would connect him with Willy O'Donnell?' Willy had refused to make a statement when they brought him to the station. It was up to Róisín, they said. She was the one who had been raped. No one would condemn Róisín, but Willy would be finished.

Lyn was immediately wide awake with anxiety. The relief was

gone, as was the feeling of being purged of guilt. She was simply afraid. John Cullen could be out on bail today, and he would head straight for herself and Róisín. They decided to stay in Róisín's flat, because there was no way that Lyn could face her home, where there was so much of John's presence. Besides, she was still exhausted after the past weeks, and the long interrogation. She would rather stay with Róisín. Lyn was lying on the couch when Joey walked in. 'What did you have to go and grass on John for?'

'Joey, he killed three women. You liked Dolores when you were a little boy. Don't you remember she minded you? And he raped Róisín and Annie. What was I to do? Just leave him on his rampage?' Joey had never had a man treat him with the kindness which John had shown. He was scarlet, on the verge of tears.

'It doesn't matter what John did. You didn't have to grass him, Mrs Black,' he said. Lyn winced at the name. He was referring to the Christopher Black supergrass trial.

'Joey, please, I know it's hard for you to accept, but John had gone nuts at the end. There is so much you don't know about John. Lots of things I haven't told you. He couldn't be allowed to walk free, just go on as he was doing.'

'I don't care what he did to anyone. He never did me any harm. You shouldn't have grassed on him.'

'Joey, for Christ's sake, Hitler never did you any harm either, but . . .'

Joey was storming out of the flat. Lyn was shattered. Grassing had not come easy; she had had to fight herself, all her beliefs. And now this. Mrs Black. Supergrass. Her feelings had been confused these last two days. She was glad that Dolores had not died in vain. The world had to know that she had been murdered for her courage, her sense of justice, and why Mrs Lynch and Aunt Hannah had died with her. Yet, on and off, she ached with pity for John Cullen. She told herself that he was a monster, but she had known another side of him. She had shared love with him. He had been good to Joey. She had no illusions about herself and that, above all, facilitated her pity for John Cullen.

7

Lyn was born in Cork in 1944. She remembers being sent to a convent school in England when she was seven, being in a large room with her mother, Bridie Madden, and a nun. Her mother left with the nun, saying, 'see you later.' The nun came back into the room, alone.

She slapped her hands together and said, 'Come on, Elizabeth. Take your coat off and I will take you to your dormitory.' Lyn vividly remembers staring at her and not answering. Had she not been alone in the room, she would have thought the nun was talking to another girl.

The nun got annoyed. She undid the top button of Lyn's red coat, saying, 'Come now, none of your cheek. Let's have this coat off.'

Lyn jumped up off the chair, did her button up and stood against the wall trying to press her body into the woodwork to escape. The nun crossed over to her, tried to undo her buttons again. Lyn held her buttons tightly in her clenched fists and started to cry.

'No,' she said, 'I'm waiting for my mammy.'

The nun slapped her across the face and said, 'Stop that at once! You are staying here. Your mother is not coming back. She doesn't want you. Now, take that coat off. Now.'

Through her tears Lyn looked in the nun's eyes and was afraid. She took the coat off. The nun took it from her and put it on the chair on which Lyn had been sitting. She told her to follow her. Lyn attempted to take her 'Elizabeth' brooch off her coat but the nun would not let her. Lyn had been so proud of that brooch. She followed the nun.

They seemed to walk forever in the largest building Lyn had ever seen. Finally they entered a room where the nun pointed to a bed which she told Lyn would be hers. She then took Lyn to a large room with tables, which she called the refectory, and told an old nun there to give her a glass of milk and bread. Lyn drank the milk. She tried to eat the huge chunk of bread because the nun who had slapped her was watching. But she could not. She was crying so much she was choking. Then she was taken to a large room with wooden benches all around the walls, and lots of girls. Most of them seemed older than Lyn. The nun left.

There was silence as the other girls looked Lyn over and quickly turned their attention back to each other again. No one spoke to her and she stood for ages in the middle of the room. A nun was seated at a table, embroidering. Suddenly, she shouted, 'You there, standing in the middle. What is your name?'

The other girls stopped their talking. All eyes were fixed on Lyn.

'Elizabeth,' Lyn said, self-consciously.

'Elizabeth what?' the nun thundered.

'Madden, Missus,' Lyn whispered.

'Sit down, Elizabeth Madden,' she ordered. Lyn sat down. Still no one spoke to her. When a bell rang she followed the other girls. Benediction. Refectory. Bed. She cried and cried when the lights were put out. Her mother had said, 'See you later.' She had not said she was not coming back. Lyn wanted to go home. The night carved out her future relationship with her mother. She never forgave Bridie.

Bridie Gleeson had married 'that no good Madden fellow', against her father's wishes when she was seventeen years old. She got an old family friend to forge her father's signature on the consent form. Bridie's husband Denny Madden was twenty-four years old, a soldier, from farming stock and considered a good catch in the rural Ireland of the 'forties. Bridie was more concerned with the fact that he was a great dancer, and all the other girls were after him.

The priest refused to let them marry at the main altar because it was not a white wedding, even though Bridie was a virgin, and she walked up the aisle in her pink suit, auburn curls gleaming. Denny's only suit hung in the pawn shop, but he looked dashing in his uniform. The wedding celebration was in the local pub with a few friends, and Denny had to report back to barracks while Bridie moved into a rented room in Cork's McCurtain Street. She played house while she waited for Denny's leave. A few months later she hurried from the doctor's surgery to tell Denny that she was pregnant. She was perplexed to discover that her young husband was not delighted.

Denny changed. Soon, he neither called her 'my love' nor went dancing with her. He came home later and later and sometimes did not show up at all. And when she asked where he had been, he hit her. 'Don't you ever dare to ask me to account for my movements,' he shouted at her, and punched her in the face. It was the first of many beatings for Bridie, and she knew that he resented the loss of her figure. She was also aware that he was courting other girls.

Bridie sat home alone without even a radio to relieve the tedium, and then one night she followed Denny to the local dance hall. As she entered, she spotted him across the dance floor, his arms encircling a girl. He was furious at his wife who stood in her maternity smock, tears streaming down her face. He rushed over, grabbed her by the hair, pushed her outside the door and beat her to the ground. She cried that she wanted nothing more than for him to go home with her, and he yelled, 'Well, I don't want to go with you. You're too old.' She had just turned eighteen.

Upon Lyn's arrival, the couple were evicted from their room because the baby cried too much, made too much noise. They rented a cottage down a boreen* for four shillings a week which left five shillings from Bridie's Army Wives' allowance. Denny rarely came home at that time, preferring to stay at his sister's

---

* a narrow country laneway

house where he could be sure of a square meal. Then Denny got hold of a bike and cycled to the outlying village in search of girls.

When Lyn was four months old, Bridie took a job as a house-keeper a few miles away. She could not afford to pay someone to mind her child, so she left her in a drawer for the morning. The children from the farm at the top of the boreen would listen for Lyn and when she cried, they talked to her through the letter box. Bridie spent the nights dozing in a chair, armed with a sweeping brush to frighten the rats. As her health suffered, her looks faded and her husband grew even more distant, although she did become pregnant again. This time, Denny disappeared for four months before his son was born. He was not enamoured of Donald, or Donny, as he was called, and whom Lyn adored. They were all beaten by Denny, especially Donny.

One day, Bridie was seated at the kitchen table when the door burst open and a woman ran in screaming, 'Where is that animal Denny Madden?' She was dragging a young girl after her. Bridie jumped up, startled, as the woman lunged at her and chaos ensued. The woman's thirteen-year-old girl was pregnant by Denny Madden. Denny's reaction when he came home was to beat Bridie senseless. And then, because he feared repercussions, he deserted the army and the entire family journeyed to Dublin. They ended up in the workhouse in Capel Street.

Lyn remembers sleeping on the floor in the corridor while her father slept over in the men's building. Bridie spat on her hankie in the mornings to wipe Lyn's eyes, glued together with yellow matter. Into adulthood, Lyn had panic attacks when she thought she was blind.

The family queued for 'penny dinners' which cost tuppence, but Bridie could not afford tuppence for Lyn, too, and she used to put some of her food into a clean handkerchief and feed the children while Denny went in for his dinner.

Little Donny contracted croup in the workhouse and died in the hospital, holding a piece of an Easter egg that the nurses had given him. He was saving it for Lyn.

A short time later, Bridie had a baby girl who died when she was four months old. Bridie had a nervous breakdown then, and Lyn was sent to live with an aunt in Dublin. At some point, Lyn remembers, Bridie came to fetch her and brought her across the sea to live with her father in London. They had a nice flat, but it was not long before they were evicted and ended up in the London workhouse.

Lyn was about six then and shortly after, her mother and father parted. Bridie is a workaholic to this day, but for several years she never had a job that paid enough to enable her to have Lyn at home. She paid Lyn's keep in the convent. Bridie was romantic about having a baby before Lyn was born, but by the time she was nineteen years old, Bridie had lost any maternal feelings she might have developed under normal circumstances.

After that first night in the convent, crying for her mother, Lyn learned not to cry in institutions. She considered crying to be the supreme weakness, and never, ever, let them know they had got to her. Over the following weeks, the other girls became less hostile and began explaining things to Lyn. Her later life taught her that there was no immediate acceptance for a new-comer in institutions. A person was appraised, then designated to a particular bunch. Lyn made it to the top bunch in the convent because she never cried.

The convent was Nazareth House on Hammersmith Bridge. Sisters of Mercy. Lyn never saw any mercy in all the time she was with them. Not in four years.

Lyn's mother came to see her once. It was on the day she made her First Holy Communion when she was eight and her mother gave her a lovely cross and chain. Lyn had the cross and chain for a week before the head girl on her table took it from her. She warned Lyn not to tell the nuns that she had punched her in the face and pulled her hair.

There was a glass case in one of the rooms in the convent in which all the girls' valuables were put for safe keeping. Lyn's 'Elizabeth' brooch was there and she never missed a day standing with her forehead against the glass, looking at it, her link with home.

The girls used to get sixpence a month which they were allowed to spend in Woolworth's. On a Saturday morning, about twenty of them would go into Woolworth's where they would rush excitedly from one counter to another, looking at all the possibilities for their sixpences. Except for Lyn and her best

75

friend Eileen Flynn. The two liked to shop on their own. Eileen always bought pretty lace hankies which she kept hidden at the convent, and Lyn bought safety pins. To this day, Lyn does not understand why. There would be one large gold-coloured pin with lots of little ones of varying sizes suspended from it. She never counted them and she never took the little ones off the big pin, just loved the way they glittered, all shiny and she loved holding the big one in her left hand and running the index finger of her right hand along them. Eileen and Lyn never talked about their purchases. Lyn hid her pins in secret places in the convent and around the grounds. She was happy just knowing they were there, but if she was upset about something, she would unearth a bunch of pins and sit fiddling with them until she cheered up. She kept her best set hidden in an outhouse which the girls were forbidden to enter, and when she felt miserable, she would slink in there to play with the pins.

It was outside this outhouse that Eileen was teaching Lyn the words of Alma Cogan's new song *Give me five minutes more, only five minutes more in your arms*. That was as far as they got. A nun pounced on them and slapped them both sharply on the face.

'Common little sluts,' she said, her face red, 'follow me.' She took them to the Mother Superior's office, dragging them in by the hair of their heads. She pulled Lyn's knickers down while Mother proceeded to hit her again and again, first with her cane, then with her hand. Lyn screamed inside her head, but she did not cry. She did not know what the word 'obscene' meant, when the nun told Mother Superior the girls were singing 'obscene' songs. All the girls were caned for minor infringements of convent discipline, and it made them wary of the nuns.

Lyn discovered reading while she was in the convent. She read anything she could get her hands on, even though it was all religious material. As an adult, she could still quote parts of the mass in Latin, but she always disdained religion.

One day, when Lyn was eleven, her beautiful mother appeared to take her home. Lyn was so proud to say, 'This is my mother.' She hugged and kissed Eileen Flynn, said goodbye and felt so sorry for Eileen who was an orphan.

Home was one room in Sumatra Road. A blanket hung from a string on the ceiling as a divider between the two beds. There was a man there. His name was George. Lyn was to call him 'father'. He slept with her mother.

Their drinking water was kept in a bucket on the table, and one morning Lyn woke feeling thirsty. She got out of bed, pulled back the curtain to get a cup of water and saw George lying on top of her mother in bed. Bridie's eyes were closed and the bed was bouncing up and down. Lyn dropped the blanket and slid silently back into bed, forgetting her thirst. She did not know what they were doing, but she did not like it. She was upset and wanted to get sick, but it would mean going to the bathroom. She might see them again. She swallowed the bile in her throat, hating George for what he was doing to her mother.

Bridie was cleaning for a Jewish woman up the road. The woman had four daughters, so she gave Bridie loads of girls' clothes. They were prettier dresses than anything Lyn had ever seen. Also, at that time, there always seemed to be unusual food in the flat. And then one day, Lyn's mother came home with a lovely little clock. On another day, she arrived with the most exquisite solid silver dressing-table set. Lyn played with the lovely pieces for hours. The next thing she knew, her mother no longer worked for the woman. No more lovely dresses.

Lyn loved her mother with a single-minded intensity, but Bridie found her a difficult child, 'quiet, but a pain in the neck'.

There was the time Lyn nagged to join the Girl Guides because of the uniform, and when her mother finally got it for her, Lyn did not want to go back to the Guides after a couple of meetings. Then there was the time Lyn was in the dance chorus of a concert. After the show, her mother would not let her take off her stage make-up before they went shopping in Petticoat Lane. People stared and Lyn snivelled. Her mother hated her to do that and back-handed her across the face.

'But everyone's staring at me,' Lyn whimpered.

'Fuck 'em,' Bridie said. 'While they're staring at you, they're leavin' someone else alone.'

Lyn remembers her mother seemed to talk in 'sayings' a lot. 'Children should be seen and not heard.' 'A shut mouth catches no flies.' 'What's good for the goose is good for the gander.' 'Your mother's the best friend you will ever have.' 'I don't care what so and so thinks, they don't put bread on my table.' And 'Fuck the begrudgers.'

Whenever Lyn did anything that really annoyed Bridie, her mother would say, 'I hate you, you bastard, you. I've always hated you. I've hated you since the day you were born. You're just like your father, rotten all the way through.' Lyn knew that speech so well that whenever her mother started it, Lyn would say it fast in her head, before her mother finished. One day the landlady knocked on the door in the middle of one of Bridie's tirades, and when she had gone, Lyn's mother said, 'Now . . .' but could not remember what she had been saying.

Straight-faced, Lyn prompted, 'You're just like your father, rotten all the way through.'

Bridie was a pretty woman, tall and broad-shouldered. She was animated and, even today, her energy and vitality put her daughter to shame. Bridie chain-smoked until she was forty and had a heart attack. She had a husky voice. She walked tall, and Lyn recognised the click of her heels as she came up the street. Bridie was noticed everywhere she went. She loved dirty jokes and Lyn lived in dread of what she might say. Bridie failed to notice when someone did not want to listen and Lyn would cringe as people went glassy-eyed.

Bridie worked hard. Always. As far back as Lyn can remember, her mother always had two jobs, day and night. Once, she worked in a factory that made dolls' eyes and brought home loads of them. At the same time, she washed dishes in a café.

Lyn thought her mother could read her mind. She played truant from school a bit because she was teased for being scruffy, and used to go down to the railway track to watch the trains. One day when she came home, her mother asked her what she had done at school. Lyn replied, 'rithmatic,' because she knew her mother was bad at sums and would not question her about the subject. Bridie battered her.

'You haven't been to school, you liar, your coat's drenched,' she said. Lyn failed her 11-plus exams, not because of truancy, but because the nuns had taught her more religion than the subjects she needed for the exam.

Lyn never got pocket money, and one night when her mother was asleep she crept out of bed and stole sixpence from her purse. She put it in the pocket of her gym slip and closed the top up with a safety pin so that it would not drop out. When she got to the shop the next day, she removed the safety pin and put her hand in for the sixpence. Empty. Lyn could not believe it.

Years later, Bridie told Lyn that she had not been asleep when she took the money and had retrieved the sixpence. 'All those years I wondered what had happened to the sixpence,' Lyn says. Lyn's hair was infested with lice. She had to attend a clinic every couple of weeks, on her own. The nurses examined her hair and when they found lice, they combed Suleo through it. Still, she used to enjoy sitting down each night and watching the lice fall with the sound of light rain onto the paper on her lap as she fine combed her hair.

'Lizzie's got fleas, Lizzie's got fleas,' the kids used to shout in the playground, and Lyn hated it. She got the idea that if she bought them presents they would like her. So one morning when she was down with the landlady, Mrs Sewell, Lyn saw a £1 note on the mantelpiece and took it. She went to the shop on the corner and asked for its value in sweets.

The old lady asked Lyn where she got so much money and Lyn said, 'Me Mam won the pools.'

When she got to the playground, she doled out the sweets to the large circle of children who surrounded her. When she got home, Mrs Sewell knew she had taken the money. Lyn waited all day for her mother to come home from work. She met her in the street, walked along beside her and asked, 'Can I carry your bag, Mam?' Just as they reached the house, Lyn blurted, 'I've done something awful, Mam,' and slowed down. Bridie did not lessen her pace. 'I've stole a pound from Mrs Sewell,' she said. Her mother never said a word. When they went into the house, George looked at Lyn funny, but nothing was said. Lyn went out to play after tea and an hour later, she saw her mother leave to go to her night job.

George always got Lyn ready for bed and that night when she had stripped off to wash, he beat her hard on the bottom and legs again and again, with his hand and then with the wet flannel, muttering, 'I'll teach you to steal! I'll teach you!' Lyn never forgot that her mother knew George was going to beat her and kept silent, and that George waited until she was stripped before he did it.

'My mother's worst fault was that she was unpredictable,' says Lyn. 'This was the same woman who met me from school one afternoon (much to Lyn's surprise) and bursting into tears said, "Happy birthday, Lynda. I'm sorry I couldn't get you anything better." Lyn had not known that it was her birthday.

Her present was a book, *Grimms' Fairy Tales*. It was not a new book. It had 'Anne Green' inscribed inside, but to Lyn it could have been the original *Book of Kells* in solid gold. It was the first book she had ever owned and she loved it.

Later that year, Lyn was rooting around in the wardrobe when she found an *Eagle Annual*. She used to get the comic every week, so she took the book out and read it before she put it back. It was to be her Christmas present. On the last day before the Christmas holidays the school had a party. The pupils were told to wear their best clothes and if they had any presents for other children they were to bring them along. That put Lyn in a pickle. She had nothing to give, and no money. And she liked a boy called Christopher, because he, too, was so shabby.

She got the *Eagle Annual* from the wardrobe and wrapped it up in a bit of wallpaper as a present for Christopher. She did not have anything nice to put on and went to school worried sick that she only had her ordinary clothes to wear. She sat next to Christopher who wore a dirty jumper with a run in the elbow, but who had on a clean pair of trousers. Christopher kept his hand near his pocket, over the place where the grey trousers were patched with navy blue. Lyn handed him her annual. Christopher looked highly embarrassed and muttered, 'Thanks,' then hung his head and said, 'Ain't got nuttin' for you,' and blushed furiously. 'Don't matter,' Lyn said, happily. Nothing mattered to Lyn except that she was not the only one in the class who looked scruffy. Through the afternoon, as Lyn watched Christopher's grubby little hand trying to cover the patch on his short trousers, she fell in love with him.

On Christmas Eve, Bridie was raging, 'You little bastard. I suppose you gave it to that little snotty-nosed brat, didn't you?' Lyn was not disappointed about not getting a Christmas present. She had been able to give something to Christopher.

It was shortly after this that Lyn was playing hopscotch on the road when a man in a soldier's uniform asked her where a certain street was. She wanted to go on playing hopscotch, but went with the soldier instead. She was wearing a pale green sun dress with a tiny square bit on the front and shoulder straps. They reached the street and he took her gently by her hand and guided her into an alleyway. She was confused, and he pushed her back against the wall, pulled down the straps of her sun dress and fondled her flat chest. She thought that she should have breasts and was ashamed that she did not. The soldier was about twenty years old, but he seemed ancient to Lyn. Then he pulled up the skirt of her sun dress. Lyn was mortified because she was wearing her navy blue school knickers. He stroked her 'there' and with his other hand, undid the buttons of his trousers and brought out a mass of flabby flesh, grotesque and covered in curly hair. Lyn stared in horror at this, and at that precise moment, cold water showered from above and a woman shouted, 'Leave that little girl alone, you dirty bastard.'

The soldier ran from the alleyway. 'Wait there, ducky,' the woman with the bucket said. 'I'll come down and take you home to your mother.' Lyn ran. If that woman talked to her mother, she would be in terrible trouble because her mother had told her not to leave their street. It was hours before her mother came home from work. Something told Lyn not to tell Bridie what had happened, but she worried about the soldier for weeks. She guessed she would have to wait until she found another friend like Eileen Flynn to ask her what was wrong with the soldier.

8

A few weeks after the episode with the soldier, Lyn's mother said they were going to Australia. Lyn raced around to the few friends she had made since leaving the convent and told them, 'I'm going to live on the other side of the world, in Australia.'

They were not impressed. 'It will be awful hot there,' someone said. And another girl said, 'You'll eat fruit all day, like in the zoo.' Angela, who was younger than Lyn, said, 'You might get eaten by sharks.'

Moving day came. All their tatty belongings were piled into the back of a removal van and Bridie and Lyn sat in the midst of it all. It was freezing cold. Lyn wondered where George was, but she did not ask her mother. She was one of those rare children who never asked questions. All day long, they sat in the back of the van, too cold to sleep, though Bridie did doze off for a bit.

At last they had arrived at a small terraced house in Leicester. Bridie's sister, Kitty, lived there with Uncle Bert and this was to be their home for the next six months. Lyn got on well with Auntie Kitty and asked her when her mother and herself were going to Australia. 'You should not have told the child you were going to Australia,' Lyn heard Kitty tell Bridie. 'Why couldn't you just say you were moving to Leicester?' 'I don't believe in tellin' kids me business,' said Bridie.

Six months later, they moved to a flat over a shop in a little village outside Leicester and George appeared again. Lyn had missed George. He did not ignore her like her mother did. He used to keep her enthralled with his stories about the merchant navy in which he had spent most of his adult life. He showed her the scars of a bullet wound he had got in his leg during the war. And then, a girl named June came on the scene. She was Lyn's sister! June was about eight years younger than Lyn and she got on well with this new sister of hers. June told Lyn about the years she had spent in different children's homes.

Bridie was working in a factory and she had a friend there named Gladys. Gladys and Bridie started going out together a few times a week. One night when Bridie returned from a night out with Gladys, a row started between her and George. She kicked him out. June and Lyn felt sorry for him, but knew better than to ask questions.

Lyn had two friends who were about her own age, Ann and Margaret. They would set off early in the morning to nearby fields. One day they were making a rope swing; Margaret had pinched an old rope from somewhere and they scoured the fields until they found just the right tree. They were clambering over the wall when a man seemed to appear from nowhere.

'Hey, you, with the curls,' Lyn heard, She was the only one with long, black, curly hair. She sat on the wall and turned to look at him. He pulled his jacket open. He was pulling at a mass of flabby skin with his hand. He had the same illness as the soldier. He was walking towards her, pulling furiously at his hairy growth. Lyn sat absolutely still, staring at him, and suddenly Ann and Margaret were pulling her down off the wall, into the field. Margaret shouted, 'Go away, you dirty old man. Her father is a policeman. We will make him arrest you.' The three girls stood and watched him as he backed away, still pulling at himself.

'Stop lookin' at the filthy thing,' Margaret said, annoyed. 'Why did you keep lookin'?'

'I felt sorry for him,' Lyn explained. 'There was something wrong with him. Did you see all that saggy thing, growing out of his belly? I saw a soldier in London and he had that, too.' Margaret softened. She was two years older.

'Lyn, all men have that,' she said. 'It's called a dick. Your father has one. That's how they got you. So if you ever see a man showing you his dick, run. He might do something wrong to you. Didn't your mother tell you?' Lyn did not want to admit that she had lived in convents until some months ago and did not know about 'dicks'. Did George have one of those things growing out of him, and if he did, how could her mother bear to be close to him? Lyn was not sure that Margaret was telling the truth.

'Well, if all men have one, why did that man show it to me, and the soldier, too?'

'Because you're pretty, stupid. There's a girl you'll meet when you go back to school, Betty Foster. She's very pretty and men are always showing it to her,' Margaret explained patiently. Then she climbed the tree and tied the rope tightly to it. They took turns standing on the tree, grabbing the rope, sitting on the knot with knees crossed, then hurtling down. But the day was spoiled for Lyn. When she got home she stared in the mirror. Pretty? She had unruly black curls and long black eye-lashes. Maybe she was pretty, but she wished she was ugly. She did not want to be shown those awful 'dicks'.

One day June and Lyn were told they were going into town shopping with their mother. They got spruced up, but mother did not take them shopping. Bridie took them to the Children's Department and said she wanted to place the girls in care. The Department refused because they were not homeless. Not to be thwarted, Bridie took her daughters to Hillcrest, a place for homeless people, and they stayed overnight.

'God, it was an awful place,' recalls Lyn. 'The lights were out in the dormitory when we arrived. June and she shared one bed and Bridie was in the next bed. Lyn did not sleep. There were people snoring and old men coughing and spitting, and there were no sheets on the beds, only an itchy army blanket with red stitching on the end. Lyn could see her mother's eyes shining, so Bridie could not have got much sleep either. In the morning, they were given a bowl of porridge, very salty, no sugar. And then they went back to the Children's Department and Bridie left. June cried with fright and confusion and the girls were sent to separate homes. Lyn went to The Beeches and a while later June joined her there. The Bennet's, who had one daughter, ran The Beeches. The couple were OK, but the daughter was always reminding the kids that they were orphans. One day, Lyn offered to peel the potatoes. After that she became 'official' potato peeler. It was done in an outhouse and it offered privacy, so she loved shutting herself away in there every day to peel spuds by the sinkful in freezing water.

Lyn started to sleep-walk regularly. She was moved out of the dormitory which was at the back of the house and taken to the main house where the staff slept. Her mother called to see her one day, and she was slim and sun-tanned. Lyn told her she looked beautiful and Bridie said she had also been to keep-fit classes. 'Feel the bones here,' Bridie said, offering her hip bone.

Lyn watched from an upstairs window as her mother left. She bit her lip to stop herself from crying. Inside her head she begged her mother to take her with her. Bridie did not look back.

One day, Lyn was told she was wanted in the office of The Beeches. When she entered, the man, Mr Bennet, smiled kindly and said, 'Your father is here to see you, Elizabeth.' Lyn expected George, but a man walked in and they looked at each other. The man burst into tears, rushed over to Lyn and hugged her tightly, sobbing, 'My little baby, my little baby.' Lyn was deeply embarrassed and struggled to free herself. What mad scheme had Mammy thought up now, she wondered. The man held her at arm's length, studying her, still crying. Lyn turned to the man in charge of the home.

'He's not my father,' Lyn said. But yes, the man was indeed her father. When Bridie sued for divorce and maintenance, Denis Madden had found out that his daughter was in care. Mr Bennet told her to show Denny around the home. Lyn walked in silence with her father alongside her. He asked her to show him where she slept. Lyn went into the dormitory to which she returned when her sleep-walking stopped and pointed silently to her bed. Denis picked up a photograph in a frame which she kept on her locker. It was her mother. She was going to snatch it from his hands until she saw that he was crying. She dropped her eyes and studied the polished floor boards. She heard him blowing his nose.

Denis Madden put his arm around his daughter's shoulders and said, 'Poor little Lynda, your mother never was any good. I never knew she had you put away all these years. I am taking you home to live with me. This is your new Mammy. Isn't she pretty?' He had taken a photograph out of his wallet. Lyn looked at it without speaking. Denis was standing beside an extremely pretty woman, and in front of them sat four children. 'These are your little brothers and sisters,' Denis went on, 'We will all be happy together. Your new Mammy and me will be down to collect you next week. She's Italian, she loves children.' Lyn made no reply.

Lyn ran away from the home that night. She wanted to find her mother, but she did not know where to look. The police picked her up at daybreak and took her back to the home. Her mother arrived later on in the day, annoyed with Lyn for speaking to her father.

'Anyway, you're coming home with me. Denis Madden is not getting his hands on you.'

Her mother lived in a real house! It had an upstairs and a downstairs. And a bathroom! It came complete with a new father. His name was Lol, short for Lawrence. She was to call him Dad, but the word would not come out. George was her Dad.

Lol was a lovely, gentle man. His first wife had died of cancer. He had a grown daughter living in France. She had been to University and when Lyn expressed an interest in her books, Lol gave them to her. They were books that Lyn would otherwise never have read.

When her mother was at work one day, Lyn came across her diary. Reading it, she realised that all the times Bridie said she was out with Gladys after work she had been with Lol. So that was why June and she had been put into care. Poor George, how hurt he must have felt. Lyn's mother told her she had married Lol. Lol did not know Lyn existed until the day her mother brought her home.

June was in a home about a mile away from Lol's house, and Lyn used to go and visit her on a Saturday. She was under strict instructions from her mother not to mention June to Lol. One Saturday morning her mother appeared in the living room, dressed to kill, a carnation pinned to her dress, and she and Lol went out. They came back a few hours later covered in confetti.

Lol announced they had just got married. Lyn's mother moaned at him, saying she had told Lyn they were married ages ago. Lyn said nothing. She knew they had not been married before because she had read her mother's diary. June was brought home. The first time Lol saw her, he said, 'You're very welcome, June,' and then turned to her mother and said, 'Look Bridie, if there are any more, I'm entitled to know.'

Just before Lyn left school at Easter her mother went on a holiday to Ireland for two weeks, alone. While she was away, Lol stayed at home to look after the girls. It was his annual holiday. One evening, he sent Lyn to the chipper for chips and she met some friends on the way back and lost all track of time. When she got home the door was bolted. She knocked and Lol let her in and battered her.

'You're just like your bloody mother,' he kept shouting. Lyn did not cry. The next morning he acted as if nothing had happened. Lyn forgave him, anyway. She liked him.

Lol drove to the airport that night to collect Lyn's mother and the minute they got back they started shouting at each other. Suddenly the door to Lyn's bedroom opened, her mother hurried in, lifted up the edge of the lino and put something underneath. 'Don't let Lol get at that!' she said. When she had gone back downstairs Lyn lifted the lino and took out the packet she had put there. It contained photographs of her mother and a grey-haired man. Most of the photographs were taken on a beach. There was one of Bridie kissing the Blarney Stone with the grey-haired man holding her waist. He was Sean Flynn, from where Bridie worked. When Lyn asked why she had gone with him, her mother said, 'He had plenty of money. It's better to be an old man's darling than a young man's slave.'

Lyn felt utter revulsion. The atmosphere in the house changed. Lol was hurt. Bridie despised Lol for his failure to stand up to her and she taunted him constantly with jibes about different men she was meeting. The short spell of happy family life was over.

Lyn had her first date. She was fourteen, he was fifteen years old. Susan and her friend had made the date for her, and six of them were going to the pictures. Lyn had no interest in boys then, but since it was so important to the others, and Lyn wanted to be in with the group, she went along. Susan and Mandy and their boyfriends started necking the minute the lights went out. Lyn stared uneasily at the screen. Her date slid his arm around her and planted a sloppy kiss on her lips. Ugh. He tried to grope inside her blouse, reminding her of the soldier and her green sundress. When the intermission came, she acted sick and told them she had to go home.

A few weeks later, a week before her fifteenth birthday, Lyn got her first period. Lol and her mother were still fighting. Lyn's illusions were dimmed and she vowed that she would never get married, but more importantly, any man in her life would have to be strong. Lyn had been shattered to see her mother walk all over George and Lol. It was then that she had her first crush. He was a guy who lived nearby, a ringer for the film star James Dean. Lyn used to time his going and coming from work, worshipping him from behind the net curtains of her bedroom.

She had bought five Woodbines at the newsagent's one day and bumped right into her idol. As she apologised she felt herself going crimson. He was so 'manly'. He put an arm round her shoulder and said, 'No need to apologise, Sexy. How about a date? Meet you on the corner at seven-thirty tonight.'

Lyn floated home. She could not believe her luck. She spent hours plastering her face with cake make-up, bright red lipstick, the lot. She rummaged through her mother's wardrobe, tried on several dresses, chose one and stuck safety pins everywhere to keep it from falling off her skinny frame. She was ready. 'James Dean' took her to the local youth centre where they danced, talked. He walked her home. He led her into an alleyway and he kissed her.

'His lips were very soft. It was so romantic, just like I had read in the teenage magazines,' said Lyn. He took her hand and gently pushed it down his body until she felt soft, hairy balls of flesh. She dragged her hand up sharply. She thought of the soldier and started to cry.

'Hush, don't cry, Lyn,' 'James Dean' said. 'I'm sorry. Are you a virgin?' She nodded. He buttoned up his trousers. He stroked her hair very gently, kissed her and said, 'I didn't know, Lyn. You look real sexy. I could kick myself. Do you forgive me?' She nodded. He took her home, kissed her, and said that he would see her again, and then he was gone. She lay awake that night, thinking. She felt attracted to boys, but she hated their genital organs. She had now discovered that she loathed the feel of their testicles, their penises. 'James Dean' was a nice boy, but he had made Lyn touch what the soldier had showed her.

9

Lyn left school at fifteen. She had nineteen jobs, one after the other, but could not settle in any of them. She liked the job she had as an assistant in a bookshop, but she had to leave that when she dyed her hair blacker without using gloves and her hands got so stained that she could not go to work.

She did not get along with her mother at all. Bridie would leave instructions for her, like 'light the fire, and put on the potatoes'. Lyn would start the chores, then take a break to read and forget about the rest. Or she would let the fire go out and leave the potatoes to burn in the pot. Arriving home from work to face all this drove her mother crazy. Lyn was sixteen, and felt ill done by. Her mother came home to one more fiasco and there was war. 'Just get out,' she said. 'Just leave this house and leave me in peace.'

Lyn and a girlfriend, Kay, hitch-hiked to Great Yarmouth by the sea. Just for kicks, they stole a cigarette lighter from a shop, were caught and charged. Kay's mother took the train down and bailed her out. Lyn's mother refused to help her and Lyn was sent to a remand centre for three weeks, at the end of which she appeared in the juvenile court. As she walked up the stairs, her heart lifted when she saw her mother standing at the top. She smiled, but her mother turned away. Kay's mother spoke up for her and she was given probation. Bridie was boiling. 'I want nothing to do with this one,' she said. 'I've done my best for her and now look how she behaves!'

Kay's mother said that she would accept responsibility if the court would put Lyn into her care. The court refused, and Lyn was sent to the Good Shepherd nuns in Manchester for twelve months. These nuns were the opposite of the Sisters of Mercy. They were caring nuns. Their punishment was withdrawal of privileges. Lyn's class were due to stage *The Pirates of Penzance* for the public and Lyn was excited to have the role of Mabel. Then she was caught smoking and the part was taken from her and given to a new girl. The night of the play, Lyn had to stay in bed and she could hear the audience applauding. It nearly killed her. All the weeks of singing her heart out, fantasising stardom, had gone up in a puff of smoke.

When she left the convent a year later, her mother did not bother coming to meet her. Lyn sat on the front door step for four hours waiting for Bridie to come home from work, and when she finally did appear, she made it plain that Lyn was a nuisance to her. Lyn was still delighted to see her.

Soon Lyn picked up with her shoplifting friends again. At the same time, she met Craig Nelson. He was nineteen years old, dashing and good-looking. They hung around together for a few weeks, then she threw him over. He was too serious and intense for her. She got arrested for shoplifting again and was sent to prison for three weeks for medical reports.

In theory, the court had decreed that she was a recidivist. They wanted a psychiatric report on her to find out why. In practice, she was sent to Strangeways prison in Manchester and put into what was called a 'hospital ward'. She saw a psychiatrist for five minutes. His main interest was the extent of her sexual experiences. Years later, looking back with the benefit of experience, she knew that he had not been searching for any Freudian links. He was simply kinky.

There were hundreds of women in that prison in those days, although it is 'men only' in Strangeways now. The woman in the bed next to Lyn was on remand, charged with murdering her husband. She had caved his skull in with a hatchet, and was convicted while Lyn was there. The woman on the other side of her had drowned her baby in a rain barrel. Lyn was the youngest prisoner there at the time. She never cried, but she was terrified all the time and hardly slept. When she went out on the daily half-hour exercise in the prison yard she met most of the female prisoners. A few of them were just a few years older than Lyn and she smiled at them in an attempt to make friends. After the first three days or so, they gradually dropped their defences and let her walk with them. Three of them were pushing prams with young babies. They exchanged the usual prison pleasantries. 'What are you in for?' or 'How long did you get?' Most of the women were doing three months for prostitution. One of them was extremely pretty, but what struck Lyn most at the time was how 'ordinary' the others were. When they heard that Lyn was on remand for shoplifting only three months after her release from the convent, they all agreed that she was foolish.

'Listen, kid,' a woman called Ryan said, 'there is no percentage in shoplifting. Next time you are in court you will get two years. For what? For a new skirt or something? Go on the "game". You can make £30 a night and the money is your own. You have the looks. You could make a fortune. You'd be the queen of the line, cars would be queuein' up for you. You can buy a car, a house, a holiday abroad.'

It seemed to make sense to Lyn, who never thought to ask them what they had to show for being on the game.

'But how can you put up with dirty old men?' she asked. They all laughed.

'Are you a virgin?' the Irish woman asked. Lyn refused to answer, too shy.

Toni, the pretty one, said, 'Listen, kid, when you start having sex you will find out that all men are dirty old men. If you can put up with a boyfriend screwing you, you can put up with the clients. After a while you won't even know you are doing it.' Lyn could not believe that. Not then.

They were coming in after exercise one day and as they crossed the 'chiefs circle' in front of the Governor's house, Lyn saw a girl, about twenty years old, crying loudly. 'That girl's gettin' out today, because they are hangin' her boyfriend day after tomorra,' one of the women told her. The boyfriend had got the death penalty, and the girl two years for a mugging in which an old woman died. The Home Secretary had agreed to release the girl so that she would not be in the prison when her boyfriend was hanged.

On the morning of the hanging the sirens woke the 'hospital ward' inmates. At 4.00 a.m. they were told to dress quickly and were then taken and put into separate cells. Nothing was explained to them. At 7.55 a.m. Lyn learned why. She heard a train rumbling in the distance and then: Bang, Bang, Bang, Bang, Bang, Bang.

'Christ,' she thought, 'we are at war! Manchester is being bombed.' The banging was swelling from the guts of the prison and it was getting nearer, nearer. It was here now, in the next cell, and it passed to the cell on Lyn's right and continued on. Tears came to her eyes, but she held them back. She knew what it was – the prisoners were banging their tin mugs on the cell doors. It had started on the men's side and was picked up by the women. 8.00 a.m. Bells tolled. The banging stopped. Justice was seen to be done. A young man was murdered in cold blood, for revenge. The prison was silent for the rest of the day.

The hanging had a deep effect on Lyn. Resentment and rebellion rose in her as she sat in that cell. She thought about the murdered woman, but could not see that her 'avengers' had done any better than her murderer. So that was justice. It was a justice she could not respect, did not want to be part of, and it made the society which condoned it an alien place. She formed a code of her own. 'I didn't know what I would do on my release. I did know that I would never work at a "normal" job,' Lyn says. 'Society could stuff its double standards.'

Lyn's three weeks were up and she went back to the court. A clerk handed her a report to read. It was a duplicate of the one that was, at that moment, being read aloud to the magistrates. Her mother had condemned her. Lyn was no good, and after she had devoted her whole life to her. The 'shrink' had found that Lyn was intelligent and introspective, but was 'normal' in spite of showing a decisive disrespect for authority. She lacked concentration. This made Lyn worthy of six months' detention in an experimental centre. It was such a new place she was only Number Five. It was supposed to impose 'a short, sharp lesson'. Lyn learned plenty, including: always use a contraceptive; get the money first; how to defraud a post office and forge cheques; smash a human skull with a bottle; how to fence stolen goods. She was put to work digging the garden. She woke one morning and looked out of the window and saw that the gardens were covered in heavy snow. Lyn had always suffered from the cold so she called a meeting and suggested that the prisoners refuse to work unless they were supplied with gloves. Everyone agreed. They lined up for work with Lyn heading the queue. They stood silent as the screw opened the door and motioned them out. The women refused to go. The screw got red in the face with anger.

'What is this?' she thundered.

'We're not working unless we get gloves,' Lyn said.

'You're not what? Get yourselves out there at once,' she ordered.

'No, either we get gloves or we strike,' Lyn countered.

'Right, we'll see about that. I'm fetching the Governor,' she said.

'So fetch the bloody Governor,' Lyn replied. The girls shuffled uneasily; they were terrified of the Governor, a disciplinarian. 'Don't worry about her,' Lyn said to them. 'She'll have to give in if we stick together.' A few minutes later the Governor stormed in, her eyes bulging.

'Well, Madden, causing trouble again. So you're refusing to work unless your pretty little hands are warm?'

Lyn stuck her chin out. 'That's right,' she said, 'we're all refusing.'

The Governor smirked. 'All who?' she inquired. Lyn grinned back at her, and turned her head to indicate her backup. The hall was deserted. Lyn lost two weeks remission for that and served the full six months, having lost all other remission for breaking petty rules.

Upon her release, Lyn met up with her old friend, Sandra, ex-shoplifter now turned prostitute. She also met Craig Nelson again and they began courting. Craig and Lyn moved into Sandra's flat. Lyn liked Craig and he was crazy about her. They slept together for weeks, but did not have sex. They had no privacy, with Sandra and her boyfriend sleeping in the same room. They could hear the other couple at night and Craig thought that Lyn was too good for that kind of thing. They stayed in bed a lot, reading, cuddling and talking.

One morning, Lyn announced in a grandiose tone that as it was Craig's birthday and since she had no money to buy him a present, she would let him make love to her. 'Big deal', Craig said. They broke open the gas meter and bought two bottles of wine and went back to bed for the day. It was no big deal.

'Craig kind of liked the idea I was cold,' Lyn recalls. 'It set me up on a pedestal. Sometimes I would feel turned on by Craig, but I daren't show it.'

Craig was getting £2 a week Unemployment Benefit and Social Security gave Lyn £3 a week. She could not live on that. Sandra bought her food, fags, stockings. Lyn's independent streak had developed fast. Sandra had decided that Lyn should not go on the game. For Lyn, however, prostitution was one thing; being a parasite quite another. When she told Sandra that she was going out on the game with her, she said, 'I don't mind, Lyn, it's your life. But what if Craig finds out?'

Lyn thought about that. 'Why should he mind? It's my body,' she said.

That evening they went out to work. A car stopped and the driver said, 'I'll have her,' nodding at Lyn.

'She's new,' said Sandra. 'She won't go on her own, first time. I'll sit in the back.' He let the two of them in the car and pulled into a car park. Lyn sat in the front seat with Sandra in the back. The man handed Lyn £2. Sandra pinched Lyn on the shoulder and whispered, 'Don't just bloody sit there! Get him undone.'

Lyn undid his zip, then turned to Sandra. 'Oh, for Christ's sake, I'll do it,' Sandra said. She leaned over in between the seats and massaged his penis. When he got an erection, she passed Lyn a contraceptive and told her to put it on him. Lyn ripped the tin foil from it and she stared. It was so tiny. How would it stay on? Sandra laughed, snatched the contraceptive from her saying, 'You bloody fool, it unrolls. Look. You roll it down over his dick. You hold the teat between your fingers, like this. That way you won't get any air in it and it won't burst. Right. Get on with it,' Lyn lay back and guided him. Then she looked at his face for the first time and felt sick. It was over. She threw up all over the door and window. Lyn's first client yelled at them to get out of the car. Sandra and Lyn walked away from the car with Lyn distraught.

'Oh, Sandra, it was awful. I'll never do it again.'

'You will, Lyn. The first is always the worst.' The next day

Lyn went into C&A and bought a skirt and a blouse. Then they went for a meal and she was broke. She told Sandra she wanted to go to work with her again. Sandra nodded.

Lyn did not bother telling Craig where she got her money from; he thought her mother gave it to her. When he found out he nearly killed her. Lyn lay on the floor covered in blood, tufts of hair stuck to her jumper, and Craig spat on her. 'I thought of you as something special.' He was weeping with frustration. 'I put you on a bloody pedestal and you've broken my fuckin' heart.'

Lyn was apathetic. He kept telling her to say that she was sorry. She said it because he was hitting her, but could not see what the fuss was about. Exhausted, he walked out. Lyn could not have cared less. Her fellow prisoners in Strangeways were right. After the first two nights on the game, she did not have to work at switching off. It just happened. What was going on with her body had nothing to do with her. Her mind was her own.

Craig walked back into her life four weeks later. He told her that as she had hurt him so much and his friends were laughing behind his back, she was going to stay on the game. 'But you are going to do it right,' he said. He came from hard-working parents, but could not stick to a job. Although he was violent, he had no bottle for robbing. They would do this in style, he vowed. He set Lyn up in a business flat. She was not allowed to mix with other prostitutes because he thought Lyn superior to them. She never did heed him about that. She was always well-dressed. He chose her clothes, told her what to wear, where to work, everything. Her whole future was mapped out for her and she honestly did not care at that time.

'How could I have foreseen what a lifetime on the streets did to a woman?' Lyn asks. 'I bore him three children and we lived well. No, *he* lived well. He had holidays abroad, wore expensive jewellery, drove a fast sports car, wore Chester Barrie suits, gambled. I stood on street corners, freezing. OK, so I screwed the night away, but I was usually so damn numb with cold by the time I picked up a client that my assets were frozen! Often when I was haggling over prices with a client I was saying inside my head, "For Christ's sake, please let me in out of the cold." I could feel the warmth from the open window.' Lyn was always freezing. When she got kidney trouble, Craig rubbed her with wintergreen ointment and fetched and carried. In a way, it was Lyn who made Craig a pimp. He was extremely puritanical about sex and would not have initiated her going on the streets. However, he learned fast. 'Craig was a mass of contradictions. He was a family man terrorising us with his bullying and violence. If he could have got some way to sort out his violence, he was an OK guy,' Lyn says. 'But he was extremely violent, and would fly into a rage at the smallest provocation. He taught our sons to be violent.' Both of their boys have done time for violence. 'He used to get them up out of their sleep to box with them when they were little. And, of course, violence was normal in the house. The table was often upended at meal times.'

Craig had a scrap book he called his 'indictment of society', in which he kept newspaper cuttings of injustices perpetrated by mankind: rape, brutality, plunder, slavery. He was obsessed by what the Nazis had done under Hitler and romanticised everything Jewish. He admired close-knit Jewish family life, the rituals that created order in everyday living and the fact that Jews helped each other. He would have liked to be part of such a community.

Craig used to keep Lyn awake, going on and on about the state of the world and would get furious when her eyelids began to droop. He expected her to sit up and take notice of man's inhumanity to man, after she arrived home from an eight hour stint on the streets.

Lyn never wanted to have children but Craig had a thing about being infertile. She did three months while she was pregnant for the first time. Each of her three children, two boys and a girl, were in prison before they were born.

She never wanted to marry either. Anyway, Craig had been married at seventeen and had two daughters, and living with him seemed to amount to the same thing. She viewed marriage as just another form of prostitution. Bridie, her mother, was always marrying and, in her seventies, married again in 1987. Glad she did not marry, Lyn feels she should not have had children either. She was not maternal and the fact of giving birth did not make her so.

She was expecting their first son, Chris, when Craig visited her in prison. He was on crutches, having hitch-hiked 150 miles on a broken leg. On her release, he had a nice flat waiting for her and made her retire from the game. He had a job as a nobber, a brick carrier, and Craig could carry sixteen bricks on his head, but he lost the job when winter came. His car needed taxing so he stole a disc off another car, was caught and sentenced to six months in prison. Lyn was left with an eviction order, an empty food cupboard, no coal for the fire, and her baby. She was back in prostitution. Craig heard this through the prison grapevine, appealed his conviction, got bailed out, caught her on the streets and battered her. He would have had to go back to prison if they had stayed in Leicester so they moved to Birmingham and as a further punishment, Lyn was sent out working the streets again.

One weekend, Craig drove over to Leicester to visit his mother, and on the way back stopped off at a village inn for a drink. He got into a terrible fight, was arrested and charged with causing an affray. Out on bail, he decided they would now have to get out of Birmingham before the court case, or he'd be in for a long prison sentence. Their babysitter at that time was a young Irish man called Michael. Michael told them that Dublin was a great city for prostitution, so Craig and Lyn decided to give it a try. They went over to Dublin for one week, leaving their two children in Michael's care. Lyn had not written down the name of the street where Michael said the women worked (Percy Place) but she remembered that it sounded something like 'purse'. She stopped a woman and asked for a street beginning with 'purse' and she said, 'Oh yes, Pearse Street'.

They had arrived. Six nights Lyn walked up and down Pearse Street without a car stopping, Craig walking a few yards behind her, carrying her coat and umbrella in case it rained. On the seventh night they were both exhausted and were on the point of giving up and returning to England. Lyn trudged wearily along Pearse Street and Craig hissed, 'Turn right at the next corner.' She did. A car stopped.

'Lookin' for business?' Lyn asked.

'Yes, how much?' he replied.

'Three pounds,' she said hastily. Craig had told her to ask for a pound more than Birmingham because she was a new face.

'OK, jump in, love,' the client answered.

On the boat to Ireland, Lyn had said, 'Jesus Christ, Craig, it's dawned on me it will be all Paddies I'll be doing business with.' In England she'd been led to believe that Irishmen were too often dirty and violent.

Craig said, 'There must be some middle-class Irish.' Her first client in Ireland took her back to his flat. He was OK.

When she was leaving, he said, 'Thank you, you're a nice girl,' and shook hands with her. 'Oh, and by the way, love, it's £5 in Ireland.' They both laughed. He also told her where she was more likely to pick up business in the city. Craig and Lyn flew back to England the next day, collected the children, then flew back to Dublin.

Lyn was twenty-one years old. The 'sixties passed her by. When other young people were discovering the word 'freedom' and smoking pot, she was convinced that because she was not clocking in and out of a low paid job, she was beating the system. It was years before Lyn began to notice that other women had the same material things that she had, but they did not have to sell their souls to acquire them. She still saw marriage as a form of prostitution, but she had to admit that many husbands, on the whole, worked and seemed to care.

Night became the colour of Lyn's life. Looking back, she cannot remember the days. She never had a holiday. There must have been days when Craig and Lyn took the children to the beach or out for the day somewhere, but when she tries to recapture the past, Lyn can only envisage streets, night, cold. Once she went to a hypnotist in an effort to stop smoking. There were a group of people in the room, and the hypnotist told them all to relax and imagine a happy scene in the past. She became aware that everyone else in the room had slipped into a sleeping hypnotic state, imagining happy memories. She had none. She could not summon a single pleasant scene to mind, a place to which she could return, under hypnosis.

Lyn earned £180,000 in fourteen years, but Craig gambled and drank it as fast as she brought it home. He wore mohair suits and had wealthy, respectable drinking friends. He blamed Ireland for making him an alcoholic. Their boys were growing up, and they noticed that their mother went out at night. So

Craig decided on a post office fraud scheme, which, if successful, would give them enough money for her to retire from the game, return to England and open a book shop. The stuff of dreams. They were arrested and released on £1,000 bail. Obviously, they could not risk both of them being sent to prison; it would mean the children being placed in care. So they skipped the country. Back in England with the children, they stayed with Craig's mother near Coventry for a while, but they argued incessantly. His mother could not understand how anyone could lie in bed after nine in the morning. People went to work, that was normal. 'Besides,' his mother said, 'work was good for the soul.' After one particularly ugly scene between Craig and his mother, they left his parents' home and moved to Birmingham.

It did not enter Craig's mind to get a job. The anti-vice laws had tightened up in England. If Lyn had gone out on the streets she would, inevitably, end up in jail, so Craig said she had to get a job. Lyn worked in Lewis' Department Store as a cashier, earning £18 a week for a year and it was worse than she had ever imagined it might be. She found it more demeaning than prostitution, saying 'Yes, Madam' and 'No, Madam'. She hated it. She has always been hopeless on the telephone and remembers answering it one day, 'Ladies coots, suits and rainwear,' and collapsed laughing. The customer was annoyed. Says Lyn, 'I was only tryin' to talk posh.' Craig would not let her go to lunch with anyone and every day brought her a bun with cheese and milk. And she was faced with a sinkful of dirty dishes and a horizontal common-law husband when she arrived home from work at nights.

Craig started drinking again. Three weeks running, Lyn handed him her wage packet on a Friday night and the money was gone by Saturday morning. They had an eviction order on the flat and Lyn got pregnant again because she had not had the money for her birth control pills. 'You'll have to go back on the game in Dublin. There's nothing here,' said Craig, and she went.

Craig stayed in Birmingham with the two boys and Lyn worked the Dublin streets for a week before she was arrested and sent to Mountjoy prison on the fraud charge. While she was awaiting trial, Craig was arrested and extradited to Ireland. Lyn got six months and Craig was sentenced to twelve months. Their children, Chris and Joey, were taken into care by the Church of Ireland Social Services.

10

When Lyn had served her six months, the Church of Ireland Social Welfare people sent her to live with a family as a live-in child-minder. The family treated her well, but she was not paid and did not even have money for a pair of tights. She went back on the streets twice weekly and told them that she was visiting friends. Being heavily pregnant, Lyn found it hard to attract clients, but managed to earn enough to buy cigarettes, a few baby clothes and some toys for her sons.

She went into labour just after she left the streets one night and gave birth to a baby girl. Craig visited her in the hospital, handcuffed to a prison officer. Lyn was bursting to tell him the name she had chosen for their daughter, but he informed her that he had decided on a name for her. Fiona. Lyn had to leave the baby at the hospital because of her child-minding duties. The day she left the hospital, the Children's Home rang to tell her that Joey was seriously ill. She had not seen him for a week. Lyn went to see him right away. A psychiatrist had examined him because he would not eat or talk, and diagnosed him as 'pining'.

Lyn had visited the boys every evening until the people who ran the home stopped her. She was upsetting the other children who did not have mothers, they said.

Now, she walked into the room where Joey sat, listlessly twiddling the knob of a radio. He barely glanced at her before he turned away again, but she had seen the state of him. His lips were sticky with black scum. He had lost weight. His eyes were lifeless. He was lost, heartbroken, crushed.

Lyn knelt beside him, 'Joey, Joey,' she said and hugged him, but he did not respond. She rocked him for a while and said, 'Talk to me, pet?' He did not answer.

'Joey, I love you.' Still, he hung his head as if it were too heavy for him to raise. She took a bag of sweets out of her bag and offered them to him. He just left them there. Joey's desolation was palpable. He could pine away, literally, she realised, simply die because he would not fight to live.

Shocked, Lyn said, 'Joey, in seven days you are coming home. Seven days makes a week – count each day until it's seven and then Mammy is coming to take you home. I promise, Joey. I'll be back tomorrow and after that it will only be six days, and five more and then you will be back living with Mammy. Please, Joey, get well. I love you. Mammy had no house. But in seven days you will have a house and your own bed. Promise, Joey.' The child lifted his head, like a senile old man. There was a glimmer of hope before he rested his head on her shoulder. Then he lifted it again and managed a smile.

Lyn went out on the streets that night. She told the men she picked up that she had just had a baby and they were 'considerate', though not one made her a present of the money she obviously needed so badly. One man was turned on by her request for him to take it easy and rammed himself into Lyn with such force that she screamed.

She was sore and exhausted three nights after she had given birth, but she gritted her teeth and got on with the job for six nights. On the seventh day she rented a house in a working class suburb of Dublin and collected Chris and Joey from the home and Fiona from the hospital.

Two months later, Craig was released from jail. They decided that having a daughter meant a fresh start. Fiona's future depended on Lyn getting off the game. It was agreed that Lyn would work for a year and they would save enough money to emigrate to Israel. Craig was convinced that all he had to do was live among Jews and he would be living 'right'. They changed their names by deed poll in preparation for Israel. Lyn went back to work with gusto. Lyn's buddies at that time were Jenny, Deirdre, Isabel and Dolores. Jenny was closest to Lyn then. She was not long back from Greenwich Village when Lyn met her. She had worked as a waitress there, loved the Village and talked a lot about it. But when Lyn, who had always wanted to travel, asked her why she came back to Dublin, Jenny smiled mysteriously and said, 'I can assure you it wasn't me mother I missed.'

For Jenny the game was an enormous ego trip. Most of the successful women get a buzz from making so much money, being chosen as queen of the line, but in Jenny's case it was more than that. Jenny came from a large family in Drimnagh. She said that her father was only there to bring home the money, her mother ran everything, and when Lyn visited, she saw that it was true. All the children had done exceedingly well, educationally, were well-qualified and had well-paid employment. Except for Jenny.

Jenny was intelligent and well-spoken, and forever in and out of mental institutions, mostly after suicide attempts. Her arms were ugly with scars and she often had electric shock treatment. The women had got her to the hospital a few times after she had overdosed. She could be extremely violent and had left a few clients badly scared. Lyn saw her break a bottle over a man's head once. Nobody knew what it was about, but there was blood everywhere and the women made a run for it before the police and ambulance arrived.

Jenny was into sadism with her clients. She enjoyed whipping them and she would rather do anything than have to have intercourse with them. She was tall with dark skin and a strong, handsome face. She had struggled against her feelings of being attracted to other women for years, but could not bear anyone to know about that. Her marriage was stormy and she was badly beaten, but she always returned to her husband-pimp.

Most women on the street need something to help them get down to work at night. With Irish women it is usually booze, although drugs were used as they became more readily available. Cutting off sex in relation to clients was the easier part of the life. Apart from that, the night might include muggers, weirdos who just wanted to beat them up, the police and, not uncommonly, the hassles with each other as well as curious sight-seers.

Jenny was hooked on Mandrax. She popped it the minute she hit the Canal and kept on taking it all night until it was time to go home. Her ego trip came when she was doing well at work, but she could never face a new night. Eventually, after about a year with Jenny, Lyn joined in and they spent every night stoned. Lyn would sneak home, hoping to God that Craig was asleep or that he would not notice the state of her. Under the influence of the drug, she took risks by getting into cars with men she would not normally have trusted.

One night when Craig was out of town, Lyn and Jenny got completely zonked. Lyn could not stand, let alone work. She took a taxi home and went straight to bed and fell asleep smoking. She woke up to find the bed on fire. There was thick smoke. She succeeded in getting the fire out, but the bed was destroyed. So she went into the children's room, shifted Chris into Joey's bed and fell into the empty bed.

She woke the next morning to find a dustbin man standing at her bed, 'Get up, Missus, get up. The house is on fire.' The dustbin men rescued the children and threw Lyn's mattress, which had smouldered through the night, out in the garden.

Lyn shook all day. That night, at work, Dolores produced an evening paper and there was Jenny's car wrapped around a lamp-post. The caption read, 'Housewife Has Lucky Escape'. When Jenny returned to work, Lyn refused to take Mandrax from her.

Lyn worked a double shift to erase any sign of the fire before Craig returned in a week's time. She bought a new bed, wardrobe, carpet, bedding, curtains, lampshade, wallpaper and paint. By day she set to work to repair the smoke damage that permeated everything. She washed half the clothes in the wardrobes, took the rest to the cleaners, and scrubbed, scrubbed and scrubbed – walls, ceiling, skirtings, windows. Then she redecorated, laid and cut the new carpet and by the day Craig was due home, Lyn was satisfied that he would never know there had been a fire. She went to work, telling the babysitter to keep replenishing the joss stick.

Craig was waiting for Lyn after she paid off the taxi driver in the small hours of the morning. He grabbed her by the hair and kicked her all the way up the laneway to the house. He punched her and spat in her face, so enraged that the only word Lyn could make out as he shouted, was 'fire'.

She lay on the ground with gravel imbedded in her knees, hands and chin. 'Please, Craig, I'm sorry, Craig. I'm sorry, I'm sorry, I'm sorry, please stop.' And he kicked her in the ribs.

'Sorry, you bastard? You're sorry? I'm not going to kill you for the fire, you stupid fuckin' cunt,' he hissed, spraying spittle on Lyn's upturned face. 'I'm going to kill you for not leaving a letter.'

'Craig,' she sobbed, on her knees, 'I don't know what you mean. What letter . . . ?'

'I know you don't, you stupid cunt. Well, I've just bloody got Chris out of bed and battered the poor little bastard, because I thought he had set fire to the fuckin' house.'

Craig had got into bed when he arrived back from Belfast and was lying reading. He kept looking up from the book trying to figure what was different about the room. And there was an odd smell. Suddenly, it hit him that the smell was stale smoke and the entire bedroom was new. He presumed it was Chris because Chris had set fire to their bedroom in a previous house. Craig went bananas. When he woke Chris up, yelling at him, the ten-year-old boy was bleary-eyed and could only mumble.

After this Jenny and Lyn drifted apart, but they still worked alongside each other.

Lyn's friend Deirdre was six years younger than Lyn and lived in what was once a disused barracks, turned into a warren of flats for the poorest of Dublin's poor. She was intelligent and a great conversationalist, married with two children. Her husband, Dan, was terrified of her. He was a dead loss as a petty crook and, more in exasperation than anything else, she went on the game. She refused to give him a shilling of her earnings and could be violent. She gave Lyn a beating one night for something Lyn was supposed to have said. Lyn got the worst of it, but she fought back and after that Deirdre had a grudging respect for her. Lyn liked to listen to Deirdre tell a story, but she could be treacherous, too.

Bernie arrived down among the women in the mid-seventies when she was eighteen years old. She looked like the movie star

Ursula Andress, same bone structure. She was from a farm in Cavan, and was a kind and generous person and absolutely crazy about a married man, twenty years her senior.

Bernie's friend lived with his wife and three children in Slane and travelled to Dublin in his BMW Monday through Friday to spend the days with Bernie and collect his takings. They were *both* in love with each other in the early days and started out staying in hotels all over the country and leaving without paying the bills. When they got to Dublin, skint, Bernie just sort of slid into the game. She had three kids for Ted: one was put up for adoption; her mother looks after Ted junior; and Bernie has kept the last one herself, in Dublin. Ted drives down to Dublin on Saturday mornings and drives Bernie up to Cavan where she spends the weekend with her family. Then he picks her up again on Monday.

Ted's wife is under the illusion that he has a business in Dublin, 'which,' Lyn says wryly, 'he does, doesn't he? A thriving one.'

When Lyn first arrived in Dublin in 1967, the women worked where the Vice Squad ordered. The police would drive up to tell them they could not work where they were and move them on. Eventually, they shifted them to Fitzwilliam Square, mostly offices and doctors' suites in fine Georgian houses surrounding a private park. This was where Lyn, Jenny, Deirdre, Bernie and Dolores worked when trouble came, via foreign pimps. There were other Irish women there, but Lyn's little group kept pretty well to themselves.

There were also some English women working the Square; they never mixed. As time passed, more and more English women moved in on the scene. They flew in from the Midlands, mainly Derby, and worked for the foreign pimps. Finally, the Irish women were outnumbered and feelings of resentment rose among them. It brewed. The English women beat up two timid young Irish women one night and told them to get off *their* beat. Then they started standing in a big group on the street corners, and if the Irish women wanted to pass, they would have to walk out into the road. There were other petty provocations which went on for a while before the English women dropped the biggest possible clanger: two of them approached Dolores

Lynch and told her to get off the Square. War was declared. Lyn, because of her English accent, was elected 'scout'. Her job was to approach any woman she thought was English and ask, ' 'ave you gotta light, Luv?' If she answered with an English accent, the Irish women would beat her up and tell her to get the hell out of the country. The English women could not believe this; the 'natives' were revolting. A few English prostitutes were beaten up before the Irish women noticed a decline in their numbers. They thought that they had won the war.

The foreign pimps did not like their women flying back to Derby sporting black eyes instead of money. A carload of them arrived on the square and spread about, threatening the Irish women. They drove down to where Lyn was working and one of them jumped out and said, 'Who you workin' for, woman?'

'I'm workin' for the white man, Honey,' Lyn flung back and received a black eye for her lip. She went right home and woke up Craig Nelson to tell him about it. Craig went nuts. He was always racist. 'We get out of England to escape the bastards and they dare to come over here?' he said.

Jenny arranged for Craig to meet her husband and draw up a plan of action. Over the next few nights the two men toured the beat in Craig's BMW, threatening all the English girls to leave the country or they would beat them up. Most of the women packed up and left. The Irish women were happy. The money started flowing again.

Only two English women remained. They were pretty quiet and gave no hassle, but the Irish women decided one out, all out. A few of the women warned them off the streets, but the two English women asked would Lyn and Jenny set up a meeting between them and the men. The women asked that they be allowed to stay in Dublin, and would Craig contact their pimp, Sonny.

Craig rang Sonny and the two made a deal. Sonny's two women, Gloria (who was to become a close friend of Dolores) and Teddy, were allowed to work for a fee of £50 per week, and the Irish women would befriend them. If any hassle came on the Dublin side, the Irish pimps would handle it. As it happened, the Irish women became very pally with Gloria and Teddy and they always ate together when the night's work was finished. With all the competition removed, everyone was earning more, not that the war had evolved for that reason. The English women just had not realised the implications of trying to drive the Irish women off their own pavements. Their gall had been like a red rag to a bull, to Dolores Lynch.

After a spate of adverse publicity, claiming that Craig had terrorised the English prostitutes, Craig and Lyn started to get phone calls from men with northern Irish accents claiming they were the Provisional IRA. They gave Craig twenty-four hours to leave the country. He left. Dolores moved in with Lyn, who was not sure they believed that Craig had left the country. Lyn moved house again and Dolores went with her to mind the children while Lyn worked at night. Dolores could not work the streets herself because she had been to court on a loitering charge. Her solicitor had prevented her from being sent to prison by promising the judge and the arresting officer that she would obey a curfew. She had to keep off the streets between the hours of 8.00 p.m. and 6.00 a.m. The taboo streets were named by the police. The courtroom scene was hilarious. Every time the judge raised his rubber stamp to stamp whatever judges stamp, he would be interrupted by the policeman naming another street which had come to mind. Afterwards, the women pooled their vast experience, but they could not come up with as much as a cul-de-sac he had overlooked. Dolores was well and thoroughly grounded.

Lyn's son Chris contracted meningitis, so Craig Nelson flew back to Dublin. They spent the night at the hospital until Chris was out of danger. Then Craig and Lyn went to bed, exhausted.

The following night Lyn left work early and took a taxi home to get a decent night's sleep. As she neared the house she saw two dark haired men scaling her garage roof.' Hey, what the hell are you doing?' she yelled. They jumped to the ground, turned: they had balaclavas, not black hair.

One lined a sawn-off shotgun up on her and shouted 'Make one move and I'll blow your fuckin' head off!'

Move? Lyn ran, yelling. She was jerked back with force, pushed face down onto the ground while someone sat on her back and pressed the cold muzzle of a gun into her neck. All she could see was her large floppy hat within eyes' reach on the ground. Footsteps, someone running.

'Take your fuckin' hands off her' Lyn heard Craig's voice, and then he hit the guy straddling her with such force he toppled over Lyn's head. She jumped up, knees grazed, in time to see the guy with the sawn-off gun push Craig.

Craig put his hand up, palm outstretched and said, 'Please don't, I've done nothing.' The man who had been sitting on Lyn's back retrieved the .45 which had fallen when Craig struck him. Now he, too, lined his gun up on Craig. Lyn suddenly saw that Craig was naked apart from a frilly pink dressing gown of hers. He had been taking a bath when he had heard Lyn's screams and grabbed the first thing that came to hand. At the time, no one laughed. The two guys told them to get inside the house. Once inside, one of them said he was the boyfriend of an English woman from whom Craig was taking protection money and it had to stop. He was an IRA man. Craig was always a smooth talker and this time it paid off. It ended up with the Provos helping to rid Dublin of the foreign pimps. When they went to bed after the incident, Craig fell asleep immediately, but sleep eluded Lyn.

She dared not tell Craig that it was her fault the two Provos had come. Craig had returned to Dublin secretly and Lyn had told English Gloria that he was in town. Gloria was Lyn's friend. She had been sent over to Dublin by her pimp, without as much as a change of underwear. He already had another woman working for him in Dublin who used to batter Gloria into earning more money.

Lyn had taken a liking to Gloria who was gentle and quiet, and had asked Craig if she could stay with them. Craig was soft in some ways, and had agreed, but he said that on principle she would have to pay him a nominal fee of £30 a week. Principle? Gloria and Lyn laughed behind his back, but she paid up. Then Gloria told Lyn that she had met a Dublin guy who did not want her on the game. Lyn did not tell Craig because he would have wanted to vet the guy. Gloria must have been scared when Lyn told her Craig was in town.

Craig left for England the day after the incident with the gun. Gloria's boyfriend was arrested for a post office hold-up and

110

sent to Mountjoy on a charge of membership of the Provisional IRA. While he was in prison, Gloria started getting hassle from a man named Fred. She rang Lyn one night, crying hysterically. Fred and some friends of his were in her flat, drinking heavily and terrorising her. She had run out, without her shoes, to phone Lyn who managed to calm her down. She told Gloria to get a taxi out to her house and Lyn would pay for it. Fifteen minutes after she arrived the phone rang. It was Fred.

'That you, you English bastard? I know where you live. I'm on my way.' Gloria and Lyn panicked and searched the house for something to defend themselves with. Finally, in desperation, Lyn took the pitchfork out of the garage and placed it beside the bed. They settled down to wait. They woke at ten next morning.

A couple of months passed uneventfully; the threatening phone calls decreased. Craig, missing the kids, flew back to Dublin. The children were delighted Daddy was home. Craig and Lyn thought that perhaps now things had settled down they could get on with their original plans for saving enough money to retire to England and open a book shop. In England they would save enough to go to Israel.

Sunday was Lyn's only night off. Two Sundays after Craig came home, she lay awake watching him sleep, wishing she could take the violent streak out of him. With Craig, his violence was more than physical. Many times he had forced Lyn to crawl across a room at his command. Sometimes when he hit Lyn and she refused to cry he would go berserk.

Right, you slut,' he would say. 'Get down on your knees.' Lyn would kneel, chin jutting out. Bang, he would punch her on the jaw, *then* she would cry. 'Now crawl over to me,' he would say and sit on the far side of the room facing her, watching her. She despised him, but it never occurred to her to leave him. She had had three children with him.

Now, as she watched him sleep, she thought of how much he adored the kids, how tender and loving he could be, until something clicked and he flew into a rage. 'Oh well, that's life,' she told herself.

She heard a noise. She got out of bed. Craig sat up, wide awake. 'Where are you going?' he asked.

'There's someone outside,' Lyn whispered. He was up in a flash, over to the window and stuck his head out.

'Get down here, you fuckin' English pig,' a voice said. Craig hurriedly pulled his head back in.

'It's Fred and another guy. They've got a gun. Phone 999,' said Craig. She heard glass shattering. She picked up the phone and dialed. Craig dressed himself and took the pitchfork out of the wardrobe.

'Hello, which service do you require?' 'Police,' Lyn said frantically. Craig walked out and closed the bedroom door after him. 'Hullo, this is Mrs Nelson, 34 Cabinteely Avenue. There's two men kicking my door in and they're armed.' She heard more glass breaking, then a man screaming. 'What?' she shouted into the phone. 'No, it's not my husband breaking in. My bloody husband's probably dead right now. Will you for chrissakes hurry!'

'Oh, I'm dying! Shoot the bastard,' a man groaned. Lyn was sitting in darkness. The door handle turned and she screamed. 'I think I've killed one of them,' Craig said from the doorway. He switched the light on. His face was white and splashed with blood. Lyn jumped up and threw her arms around him.

'Oh, Craig, I thought you were dead. Where are they?' she said.

'I got Fred in the neck with the pitchfork as he was coming up the stairs and he shouted to his mate to shoot me and his mate aimed the gun at me so I pulled the pitchfork out and threw it at him like a spear and it stuck in his chest. They were hitting each other to get out of the door. They ran up the street.' Lyn ran down to close the front door.

Craig and Lyn held each other as they stood looking out of the bedroom window. Dolores came trotting up the street. She had been talking to the Vice Squad when it had come over the radio that Lyn's house was under siege. She jumped into a taxi. Dolores would have made a great detective. She usually beat the police to a scene. As they waited for the police, the three of them assessed the damage. Glass lay everywhere; blood was splattered on the walls and ceiling. Blood trailed out of the house and down the street. The children still slept.

When the police did arrive, they took the usual details, checked the hospitals and located Fred and his friend. Fred had fifty-six stitches in his neck and shoulder, his friend was in a critical condition. The pitchfork had punctured his lung. The police asked Craig to press charges and he asked them to give him twenty-four hours to think about it. Craig and Lyn discussed it and decided that they would press charges.

'I'll have to go back to England and you'll be left on your own with the kids,' Craig said.

It was the second attack on the house in as many months. It was not an easy decision to make at that time, even though, like all pimps, Fred was nothing but a bully.

11

Lyn's health began to suffer because she was too worried to go to sleep in case there was an attack on the house. Her children were feeling the strain of living with a mother who was frightened to talk to them in case she missed a noise. And Lyn discovered that her sons had heard the two battles at the house, but had been too scared to get out of bed. Joey started refusing to go to bed at night although he would not admit the reason; his father had brought him up to be tough. Lyn asked Craig Nelson if they could call it a day and move back to England. He agreed.

It broke Lyn's heart to leave Dublin, where they had lived for ten years. She loved the city, but she could not cope with its violence. Once, years before, Lyn had flown to London's Heathrow with Craig and the kids. She started to cry the minute they landed. Craig shook her.

'There must be a reason. You don't fuckin' cry for nothing. What's up?' he asked.

Without thinking, Lyn said, 'I want to go back to Dublin,' not knowing the reason, and surprised herself.

Back in England they bought a lovely dormer bungalow in a peaceful country village. Lyn was ecstatic – it was the first house they had ever owned. They had lived in lovely houses, but they were other people's houses. It wasn't so much the fact that the house belonged to them; it was more that Lyn felt that she belonged to the house. She could never understand some of the things other women wanted. All she had ever wanted was a home. She wanted it so badly that she could not talk about it; she and Craig and the kids in their own home.

It was lovely, but it could not last. Nine months later, Craig announced that their savings were down to £6,000 and Lyn would have to go back to Dublin to work. They had no income, knew nothing of life in the real world. They were both scared and their savings were dwindling, so Lyn agreed.

The book shop thing had only been a mad dream, anyway.

Lyn became a commuter. She flew to Dublin for ten days at a time, leaving the kids with Craig. In Dublin, Lyn had a flat and after paying rent, taxis, food, clothes and air tickets, she flew back to England with £1,000 clear profit. She had come full circle.

'I suppose I felt the way a slave must have felt in America when she escaped and was brought back,' Lyn says. 'My dream of a house had come true, but so what?' Occasionally, she went to a pub to relax. She drank little at the time, but one night she met a fellow who invited her to a meeting of the Prisoners' Rights Organisation. She was not much interested in the idea, but Tom, the man who brought her, treated her 'so nice', and although their relationship faded, it was not before he had introduced her to other men and women who befriended her.

She met Margaret Gaj, well known for her work with prisoners, and Frank Crummy, another Dublin activist who was then a social worker. They took Lyn under their wing, and, in Margaret Gaj's restaurant, the meeting place of so many activists of the 'seventies, where the founder group of the Irish Women's Liberation Movement (IWLM) had gathered weekly, Lyn met Lady Longford and a cross-section of other people concerned, in one way or another, with social justice.

Lyn did not tell Craig Nelson about her new friends. She was careful to be respectful to him on the surface, but he sensed that something was going on. 'Perhaps I was guilty of dumb insolence,' Lyn recalls. He had always beaten her because of sexual jealousy, plus things like forgetting to put salt in the potatoes or arriving home from work ten minutes late. Now he beat her without giving a reason. Whenever she arrived back in Dublin without bruises, following her weekend off, she thought that she was lucky.

Lyn worked for ten days in Dublin, then went home to Craig and the children to be faced with ten days of washing, cleaning, ironing and Craig's needs, 'nothing kinky or difficult,' but more work, exhausting. Having fulfilled all those duties and being kicked and punched at intervals, it was back to Dublin to start all over again. Margaret Gaj, Marie McMahon (a founder member of IWLM), Frank Crummy and others talked to Lyn for a year in an effort to make her see what she was doing to herself. But Lyn felt bound to her children, and to their father who thought it was a big deal that he had protected her from other men all those years. He never saw himself as a pimp, or a criminal, and was unaware of how the life they led was destroying Lyn, destroying the whole family.

One Christmas Lyn arrived at Castle Donnington Airport and was met by Craig wielding a camping axe. She backed off and he flew into a fury.

'You stand still,' he said through clenched teeth. Lyn stood stiff with fear. 'I rang you three nights in a row at 5.00 a.m. in the morning and you were not there. Who the fuck were you with?'

'I was at work,' Lyn said.

They stood for an hour in the arrivals lounge while Lyn pleaded and grovelled. She had gone for a meal with the other women after work, but that was one of the things she was not allowed to do when she was away, so she could not say.

All through Christmas Craig nagged and beat her. She grovelled more. 'Craig, I'm so worried at the strain you're under, looking after the kids on your own. It's too much for you, too much to expect. That's why you feel so mad at me. Let me take the kids back to Dublin, at least for a while. It'll give you a break.'

She had no firm thoughts of leaving Craig for good, but she was desperate for a break, and she took the children, just in case. She was only back in Dublin a day when Craig started phoning her. He had always phoned her every day; that was another expense she had to cover. He used to wait in a call box while he got the operator to reverse the charges. Then he would moan and nag for hours. She could never listen to it all. She used to hold the receiver away from her, or on her chest, while she took a rest for ten minutes at a time, then say 'mmmmmm', or 'yes' or 'no'. He never caught on. Once when it was twenty degrees below freezing, one of her friends in the Prisoners' Rights Organisation slammed the phone down on Craig and dragged her out of the phone box. Then he took her home and spent an hour massaging her feet to help the circulation.

Craig always started a conversation to Lyn with, 'Is that you, slut?' And she would say, sweetly, 'Yes, love, how are you?'

One fateful night when the children were asleep and Lyn was reading, the phone rang. 'Hullo,' Lyn said.

'Is that you, slut?' Craig said.

'Yes, ponce,' she answered.

'How dare you, you bastard! You dare to talk to me like that?' he said.

'Yes, ponce, your 'phonin' days are over,' Lyn said.

'Get back here, this minute,' he ordered.

'Craig darlin', it is four-thirty. There are no boats or planes,' Lyn answered calmly.

'Well, fuckin' swim,' he screamed.

'Goodnight, love,' she said and put the receiver down. She lay back and laughed for a couple of minutes. Then she panicked. She jumped out of bed and packed all their clothes, woke the kids, dressed them, rang a taxi, bundled them into it and drove to her business flat. She had finally left Craig Nelson.

Lyn went into hiding for six months and members of the Prisoners' Rights Organisation and feminists helped her enormously with friendship and finances. Although her friends wanted nothing in return, Lyn felt she had to pay her own way. She went back to work.

Two weeks later she arrived home at 11.30 p.m. and sensed something different as soon as she walked into the house. She threw her handbag down and ran into the bathroom. Hearing a noise, she turned to face it and Craig Nelson pushed her backwards into the bath.

'Scream and you're dead,' he said.

Scream? She was dazed with shock and sitting in a bath filled with soaking washing, her legs dangling over the side. Craig had one hand around her neck, squeezing. He put his hand in his pocket and said, 'Did you think I wouldn't find you? I'll do this with your fuckin' neck,' and he pulled out a poker which he had bent into a horseshoe. Lyn made no attempt to move. Craig bored his eyes into her face, then got slowly to his feet. He spoke through gritted teeth, his throat tight. 'I'm taking my kids,' he said. 'You surely did not think I would let them go, did you?'

Lyn shook her head, unable to speak. 'Mick, start packin', he shouted upstairs. 'I made sure your Irish trash wouldn't win this battle. I brought Mick with me.' It was months later she learned that he had rung a member of the Vice Squad to find out who Lyn's 'Irish trash' were.

Mick was a school chum of Craig's, and Lyn was forced to watch while Mick packed clothes and toys. Every so often, Craig grabbed a fistful of Lyn's hair, saying, 'Watch, slut, watch.'

'Now you keep an eye on her,' he told Mick, and took a pair of scissors and slashed all of Lyn's clothes. 'I'm leaving you with what you had when you met me. Nothing,' he said with the air of a man who had for years provided everything.

Somehow, six o'clock arrived and Craig told Mick to load up the two hired cars they had arrived in. Lyn was sitting on a cabin trunk and Craig knelt in front of her, laughing. 'Well, Lyn, we're leaving,' he said. Lyn lowered her gaze, but made no reply.

'Ha! I hope you don't think you're being left alive to mix with your Dublin trash, do you? Margaret Gaj, that weasel Crummy, fuckin' wankers. Oh no, baby, you've taken too much of my life. You've kept my kids away from me for six months. You'll pay for that. Do you know what you're doing as we're sailing? Answer me! No, you don't, huh? Well, I'll tell you. You're dying. You cowardly bastard. You've got that frightened look in your eyes. You never did have any guts. I'm going to leave you tied up on a chair and you're going to take this bottle of sleeping tablets and when our ship is pullin' out of the harbour, your last conscious thought will be that I've won. I've got my kids back.'

He paused and looked to see Lyn's reaction. She kept her head bent. He punched her in the face and then again and screamed, 'Beg, you bastard! Beg for your life. Beg!' Lyn winced and closed her throat tight.

He dragged her by the hair onto the floor and kicked her. 'I said beg. Beg for me to take you with us.' Lyn lay silent. He kicked her again, 'Beg,' he screamed.

'Take me with you,' Lyn said. He kept kicking. She kept repeating it until it sounded like begging. Then he stopped and made her swallow ten pills, dragged her bodily out to the car and shoved her in the back. She woke at Dún Laoghaire. He supported her up the stairs and onto the boat, smiled as they were boarding and said to the steward, 'She's still drunk.'

He woke her when they reached Holyhead. He did not speak all the way to Nuneaton where they were met by his father. In bed that night Craig started crying and said, 'Lyn, you don't know just how lonely I've been these last few months.'

Lyn cradled him and hushed him, saying, 'Shh, it'll be alright, Craig. I'll never leave you again.' And she meant it. She vowed that she would never take the kids from him again. She was sorry for what she had put him through.

When Lyn opened her eyes next morning she smiled fondly on Craig. Poor Craig, she would never hurt him again. She heard his parents leave for work, and then Craig woke and turned to look at Lyn.

'Get up and feed my daughter, then get back here. I'm going to torture you 'til you tell me every detail of what you've done the months you've been gone.' Lyn backed out of the bed and got dressed. He never took his eyes off her. 'Hey slut, fast,' he said.

Her daughter, Fiona, was in the kitchen playing with her teddy bear. Her little face lit up when she saw Lyn.

'Brekky, Mammy?' she said, smiling. Lyn knelt and kissed her.

'Yes, pet, Mammy will get brekky.' She put the kettle on to boil.

'I said fast, slut,' Craig shouted. Lyn's mouth went dry, her legs shook, her daughter pulled at her jeans.

'Brekky, Mammy,' she said.

'Did you hear me? I said fast!' he roared. 'I want to torture you.'

The shaking got worse. Lyn looked down at her legs, gently prised her three-year-old daughter's hands off her jeans and walked five steps to the back door. She looked back at the little one, opened the door and ran. She ran down the street, kept running for about a mile and as she ran she remembered she had an English £20 note in the pocket of her jeans. She stopped when she came to a shop.

'Where do buses go from here?' she panted at the woman behind the counter. There was a Midland Red bus drawing in nearby. It was going to Coventry. She got in, kept watching for Craig Nelson. Not until the bus finally drove off did she sit up and breathe a sigh of relief.

In Coventry, she rang Margaret Gaj who, satisfied that Lyn had enough money to get to Liverpool, gave her the address of friends. It all worked according to plan. Lyn arrived in Dublin next morning to be met by a group of Dublin 'trash'. They took her home, fed her, someone gave her a warm coat. That night Lyn was back at work.

It was Marie McMahon and Joe Costelloe of the Prisoners' Rights Organisation who gave Lyn the 'right' books. One night at a feminist meeting in Dublin's Trinity College, Lyn was given *The Traffic in Women* by Emma Goldman. It became her bible, much read and dog-eared. She identified with Goldman as an anarchist, rather than a feminist.

Lyn did not have much in common with the feminists she met at this stage, nor did she care for the feminist books going the rounds. For instance, Kate Millet's *Prostitution Papers* left her cold. But Goldman had lived through the violence and poverty and repeated prison sentences. More, she was aware of the complexities of prostitution. Lyn appreciated Goldman's essay as an exposé of liberal and reformist attitudes towards women in prostitution; she did not appreciate that the questions raised by this notorious revolutionary anarchist were relevant to the contemporary international Women's Movement. 'Red Emma' was feared for thirty years in America before she was deported to Russia, where she was born, as the 'Queen of the anarchists, promoter of violence, anarchy, birth control and free love'.

The philosophy of this amazing woman was, as one journalist wrote upon her death in 1940, 'at least 8,000 years before her time.' Lyn swallowed Goldman's ideas whole because they were anarchic. When it was pointed out to her that Goldman's anarchy was rooted in her feminism, Lyn shrugged. She had never met a feminist who spoke like this, never met a feminist with whom she shared this feeling of sisterhood, for Emma and Lyn had a lot of experience in common. The big difference was that Goldman was her own woman. Otherwise, she too had had a violent father, had tried prostitution of necessity, thought little of society's norms, had spent a lot of time in prison. And, to boot, she was Jewish, a bias which Lyn shared with Craig Nelson.

Lyn liked to read Emma's work aloud: 'Woman's development, her freedom, her independence must come from and through herself. First, by asserting herself as a personality, and not as a sex commodity. Second, by refusing the right to anyone over her body; by refusing to bear children unless she wants them; by refusing to be a servant to god, the state, society, the husband, the family. etc., by making her life simpler but deeper and richer. That is, by trying to learn the meaning and substance of life in all its complexities, by freeing herself from the fear of public opinion and public condemnation. Only that, and not the ballot, will set woman free.' The revolution for which Emma Goldman called is still to come.

Meanwhile, Lyn became involved for a while in what she preferred to call politics, about the same time as Dolores Lynch became involved in feminism. She took a job in Gaj's restaurant by day and at night she worked the Canal to save money for a house. Goldman could have told her that the only way to get out of prostitution is to get out of prostitution, but Lyn thought she could get an economic head start.

Craig and Lyn had shared a dream to live in Israel with their children. Now, he wrote and said that if she cared at all for the kids, she would buy them and their father tickets to Israel. She gave it a lot of thought. If she did what he asked, it meant that she would never see them again. On the other hand, she wanted them to have a chance in life. So she sent £1,000 to Craig to cover their air fares. Two weeks later he rang to tell her he had gambled the money away and demanded more. She did not know whether or not to believe him, so she arranged with a London travel agent for Craig to pick up air tickets for the children only. She sent £600 to the travel agents with instructions that the money was to be returned to her and not refunded should they decide not to go. She also had to give Craig legal custody to enable him to take the children out of the country.

He never bothered ringing Lyn to let her know they had actually gone to Israel. She rang the travel agents: yes, they had gone to Israel.

She worked and worked. There was nothing else. She put her money in the Irish Permanent Building Society. One night she could not sleep. After a sleepless week, it hit her: she had lost her children. Jenny, on the Canal, gave her the name of a doctor who handed out prescriptions. She now had recourse to Valium and sleeping pills by the fistful. She started to drink, too.

It was about then that Lyn went public. She and Dolores Lynch did not see much of each other now, but both had become more and more politicised on behalf of prostitutes. They had sought the assistance of the Council for the Status of Women who tried to get an audience about the matter with the then Minister for Justice, Gerry Collins. Their request was refused. Lyn and Dolores met Jim Finucane and planned to establish a centre for prostitutes. Finucane hoped to get Lyn a job counselling the women; she would be paid by the Eastern Health Board. He had faith that Lyn was the one who could get off the game to help other women. Lyn appeared twice on Pat Kenny's radio programme, Politics, had a Saturday profile in the *Irish Times*, and one by Maireád Byrne in *In Dublin*. In 1978, Rosita Sweetman interviewed her for her book, *On Our Backs,* a profile of sexual attitudes in Ireland, published in 1979.

Rosita described Lyn as 'funny and sad and knows she's good at her job.' Lyn told Rosita that it hurt her to think that all she had ever done with 'my human life' was stand on street corners year in and year out, and to end up after all that with no kids, no home, no clothes.

'I'm six months now on my own,' Lyn told Rosita. 'I don't know what I'm going to do in the future. I'm just in limbo. I used to love being on my own, but now I get terribly lonely. I just sort of wander round the house. I can't concentrate on anything. I can't get my brain together after being held down for so long. I always felt I was a complete zombie with Craig. He used to say I was just a bit of flotsam, no good to anyone. Maybe I am . . .'

'I'm a bit disappointed in myself, like in the last four months I've saved £700 and next week I'm putting a deposit on a house. I know if I put my mind to it I can save that in a week, but a house is a material thing. When I get it I'll still be the same screwed up person inside.' She did not get the house because she was the same 'screwed up' person. Perhaps more 'screwed up' than ever, because she was drinking. She found that two double vodkas eased the knot in her stomach – and three were even better.

Down at work one night, the women were laughing, except for Lyn.

'D'you know what it is, Lyn?' said Nella, gasping for breath. 'You're gettin' fuckin' miserable. You used to be great crack.'

'Nella,' Lyn said, 'maybe it's because I realise that this is all there is. What are we laughin' at?' and off she flounced.

She was eating herself up inside, thinking of the kids. The feeling of emptiness was unbearable. 'This ain't for now,' she told herself, 'it ain't for today, and it ain't for just this week. This is it. Me on me own.' She was not to know that Craig would come back from Israel within four months. In any case that relationship was finished; her baby daughter was gone, although she would see the boys again.

She could feel herself sliding. Being on the game was one thing, but now she drank so much she was becoming a slut. 'There's a difference, you know,' she says, not trusting middle-class awareness. 'People started saying: "Lyn's hitting the bottle pretty hard".'

Her new flat in the city centre was lovely, but she started lending it to whomever wanted to throw a party and it became a dump. She hid her daughter's photograph in the drawer. She would have a double vodka and a second, and with the third she sighed relief, the knot inside eased. It went on like that for about nine months. Once or twice she woke up beside a man she never would have chosen if she had been sober, not even as a client.' And then, one morning she woke up to discover a trail of her clothes from the hall to her bed, and could not remember what came before. She stopped drinking.

12

Lyn had achieved the first few steps of her getaway to a 'normal life'. If only those who were helping her had realised that she still lived in a different world from them. The headiness of her activism had calmed, and at the end of the day, all these people had their own lives, homes and families, while she still went down to the Canal and then home alone. And now, she met a man with whom she spoiled everything that had been gained. Down the drain went her savings, followed by her relationship with the Prisoners' Rights Organisation. She eventually ended up with John Cullen, recognised in Dublin's sub-culture as a most unpredictable, dangerous man.

Dennis Black was a small-time crook, ten years younger than Lyn, good-looking and fun. She thought she was in love with him for about three months and when they started to live together he did not want her on the game. But he had no money, so bit by bit she gave him most of the £3,500 she had saved until her account was empty. Quickly, it emerged that Dennis, for all his charm, was trouble, but when she tried to get rid of him he would not let her go. He always carried a blade, and when they were out together he used to stand looking into sports shop windows at the knives.

She had a lot of trouble with Dennis, on and off. She was leaving Gaj's restaurant one night when he came up to her. He was with two other men and he opened his jacket wide, at the same time saying, 'Have a gun, Lyn.' The gun was in his belt. He was just out of Mountjoy where he had been held on the charge of murdering his brother by stabbing him in the back.

Dolores, Róisín and another woman ran back into the restaurant and phoned the police. When Dennis moved off with Lyn, he handed his gun to his mate. The police followed them up to Camden Street, stopped them and asked their names. They asked Lyn if she was with Dennis voluntarily. 'Tell the nice man, Lyn,' Dennis said, smiling as he gripped her arm.

Lyn nodded and the police left. Dennis held her against her will that night and a few days later beat her up. One of her friends at Gaj's advised her to take a High Court injunction against him to restrain him from interfering with her. It worked.

Lyn had been a member of the Prisoners' Rights Organisation for about two years when she met Dennis Black. She had never belonged to a group before and she enjoyed it; going to a meeting every Tuesday gave her a sense of belonging – at least on Tuesdays. She told Dennis things about the meetings, secret things. And then when she was running and hiding from him, he wrote letters to Margaret Gaj and the organisation and disclosed what she had said about PRO members, personal things, little grudges she bore. She was so humiliated when confronted with this that she went away to lick her wounds and never returned to the PRO, lost touch with those friends.

About nine months after she had taken out the injunction, her son Joey came to Dublin to stay with her. Shopping in the city, she bumped into Dennis.

He started a civilised conversation, but the old emotions overcame him and he told her that he knew where she lived and would be round to see her that night.

'I'd prefer that you didn't,' she said calmly and he walked away. Lyn panicked, and on the way home in the bus to Ballymun she planned what she would do to defend herself from Dennis Black's visit.

When Lyn got home she lowered her clothes line over the balcony of her third storey flat to see if it reached the ground. Nearly. Then she barricaded her front door, her son Joey helping her to put her washing machine on top of the table in the kitchen to block the window. They settled down to watch television.

Sure enough, at 11.30 p.m., Dennis started booting the front door in and shouting. Lyn thought he was in the flat. She ran out onto the balcony, stood on the safety rail, grabbed the clothes line and lowered herself over the edge. She got a surprise. It was not like in the movies; the rope cut through her fingers to the bone. She landed standing up, put a foot out to run and discovered that her left foot was broken. She sank down onto the grass in the pouring rain. Looking up, she saw Joey was dangling on the rope.

'Joey, hurry, fetch the cops. My foot is broken,' she called. Joey disappeared over the balcony beneath Lyn's. She dragged herself up against the wall, biting her lip in pain. Dennis walked towards her, a blade glinting in his hand.

'No Dennis!' Lyn screamed. 'My leg is broken. Please, don't hurt me.'

'So's your face,' he said and plunged the blade towards it. She jerked back, but he had stabbed her forehead. She screamed. Someone shouted, 'Leave her alone, you fucking animal.' Lyn screamed louder.

'Please!' she begged. 'Someone please help me.' He stabbed her in her left eyebrow.

'Are you man and wife? Is it domestic?' a man shouted.

'Yes,' said Dennis.

'No,' screamed Lyn. A dirty woman ran up and pulled Dennis off her.

'You dirty animal! Leave that woman be,' she shouted. Dennis paused and looked down on Lyn. He walked away, turned round, came back, kicked her full force in the face and walked away again. The woman looked up at the flats and shouted, 'Go on, ye fuckin' hard men in your shirt sleeves. There's not a fuckin' man among you, all hangin' outa yer windas.'

She tried to help Lyn up, but Lyn gasped in pain. The little woman must have shamed the men into coming down. Two men lifted Lyn and carried her in out of the rain and laid her down in the flats' entrance. Another man brought a pillow and put Lyn's head on it. Another put her broken foot on something. A woman brought a bowl of water and started to sponge the blood from Lyn's face. The police and an ambulance arrived. As Lyn was placed on the stretcher a garda said, 'Do you know the man who did this to you?' She told him Dennis Black's name and address.

As they were putting Lyn in the ambulance, the tiny woman said, 'I'll take care of the child.'

During that time, Dennis Black visited the hospital on numerous occasions to declare his undying love and affection. It reached a climax when he proposed marriage to her. She refused.

He told her she was malingering in hospital, 'fuckin' me about, hangin' on here so that I'll leave you alone, but I won't.' He told her she was coming out to spend a month in his mother's house before she married him. Lyn said that she would do neither. Dennis produced a razor from his pocket, held it to her throat and said 'You are fuckin' going to marry me.' Lyn accepted. The woman in the opposite bed saw all this and went on her crutches to Matron. Matron decided that visiting time was over and cleared the wards.

Next time Dennis appeared, the police arrived at the hospital in full strength, all the top brass. The patients lay helpless, legs in traction, unable to move. And there was Dennis waving his razor. The police were there, now that law-abiding citizens were involved. It was five weeks since Lyn had told them, as she lay on a stretcher, who had stabbed her.

13

Teresa Doyle wanted to see Lyn in hospital. Her pimp, John Cullen, drove her there before dropping her off for her night's work. It was the same Teresa who had been the cause of the trouble between Cullen and Dolores five years previously, but Lyn never thought of that then. She had heard of Cullen; who had not? She had only seen him at a distance before this. He was light of build, with mousy colouring, thinning hair, very thin lips drawn into a permanent leer, and a large nose. And his worst feature was his eyes. Cold, hard eyes. He wore a moustache. He only stayed a minute and the women talked.

Teresa had offered to go on the game for John Cullen because her friend and neighbour had started working for a relative of John's. It was an embarrassment for Lyn to have Teresa visit her in the hospital. Teresa, with her unkempt red hair and ruddy complexion, was always dirty. She was mentally slow and made up life as she went along.

'You know, Lyn, I have a sister looks like you. She's a drug addict. You know her, Lyn, her name's Rita. She used to work with you in London.' Apart from the fact that Teresa had no sister, Lyn had never worked in London.

Now, while her pimp waited outside in the car, Teresa sat by Lyn's hospital bed, making up imaginary people, imaginary places, giving all 'the news' at the top of her voice, and Lyn knew that most of it was invention. Teresa believed everything

128

she invented and the women liked her because of that. She was so totally vulnerable and pathetic, unable to take care of herself. If there was no one to insist that she eat, she went without. She was a traveller*, and lived with her unmarried mother.

Teresa was illiterate and embarrassed by it. She used to pretend that she was reading. Lyn once saw her solemnly mouth words while 'reading' the newspaper upside down. Once when they were held overnight together in the Bridewell jail, Lyn had tried to teach Teresa how to read. She was tired of people teasing Teresa because she could not read, Lyn's own favourite occupation. Teresa said she would like to learn, but when they got down to it, Teresa could not concentrate.

Teresa was crazy about John Cullen, but seemed capable of being nuts about whomever happened to be there. When Cullen got locked up over Dolores, Teresa fell for a traveller. He was from Belfast and nobody ever called him anything else but Belfast. She lived with Belfast on various traveller camps around Dublin for about two years, and had a son with him. She loved being pregnant, but did not know what to do with a baby, how to look after it. She kept that baby with her for a month or so and during that time was extremely distressed whenever she thought of her child.

'I hate the bastard. I feel like killin' him,' or 'I don't want him,' she kept repeating with the frustration of a trapped child. One night Belfast arrived down to the Canal in a temper because Teresa had left the baby on his own in the caravan, cold, unfed. 'Sure I fuckin' fed him yesterday,' she yelled.

A crowd of women, Lyn included, gathered around giving her advice on how to mind a baby and Teresa burst into tears and wailed, 'But I'll never remember that. Jaysus, how can I'.

One of the women, Terry O'Donnell, could not have children. 'I'll mind him for you,' she offered and Teresa gave her the baby. As the years passed, Terry was a nervous wreck trying to avoid Teresa for fear she would remember that she had her baby and might, on a whim, demand his return.

That was Teresa's second child. She already had Jonathan, Cullen's child, whom her mother looked after. Teresa was

---

* 'Traveller', rather than 'Itinerant' is the preferred term used in Ireland

always proclaiming how much she hated Jonathan too, and beating him. Lyn once asked her why she liked being pregnant and Teresa did not know. She just did. When Cullen got out of prison, she took up with him again and tricked him into getting her pregnant. She had another son and neither child was ever properly fed.

Teresa's little house, off the docks, had never been modernised and cooking was done on an ordinary coal fire, though cooking food was rare in that house. Teresa's mother looked ancient, with long tangled grey hair, but 'she had the most amazing, sparkling grey eyes,' recalls Lyn, 'young eyes that looked out of place in her face. When she died, someone said that she was only forty-two years old. I find that hard to believe, but then there were those eyes.'

The woman suffered terrible cruelty at her daughter's hands. Teresa seemed to get a kick out of beating up her mother. Lyn saw this on two occasions. The mother cowered in her chair, crying, and Teresa kept punching her in the face and kicking her on the shins, until she tired herself out with the effort.

'Teresa, stop, for God's sake, stop,' Lyn pulled at her, holding her back from kicking her mother's shins. She could not reach to kick or punch, so she spat in her mother's face. Lyn walked out and sat in the taxi outside the door. Teresa came out a few minutes later.

'What's the matter with you, Lyn? Did I do something wrong, eh?'

Teresa did not realise that the things she did were awful. She would never heed anything anyone said, like a difficult child, which is why the women were so protective of her. She did not seem to need a best friend or friends, though she loved to brag if someone did something nice for her. The women were forever bringing her clothes to wear because she was so shabby and she would brag when she got something nice, bring the item out in a paper bag for a few nights and say, 'Did I show you what so-and-so bought me?' Then she would give the item to someone else. The women got used to giving her clothes that she never wore, but still they gave her things. Terry knitted loads of baby clothes for Jonathan. Teresa showed them around to the women for a few nights and then one morning when most of them had gone home, she said, 'Here, Lyn. Willya take these? What the fuck am I goin' ta do with 'em?' 'Would you not consider putting them on the baby?' Lyn suggested, smiling.

'Ah, fuck it,' said Teresa and threw the bag in the canal. 'Sure, you won't tell Terry, willya?'

Teresa always wore boots. Always. She slept in them whenever they were locked up for the night. She slept in Róisín's flat, before Lyn and Cullen got together, and Róisín said that she would not allow Teresa into bed in boots. Teresa said that was OK, she would sleep on the floor. Róisín pleaded with her to get into bed for a decent sleep, but she would not remove the boots.

Róisín took Teresa to hospital one night when she fainted on the Canal. She kicked one of the nurses when she tried to take off her boots as she lay on the examining couch. When the doctor came, he was very stern and told Teresa that he would not examine her unless she took her boots off.

Róisín flushed scarlet when Teresa unzipped her boots and £10 and £20 notes fell about the place, some sticking to her filthy, sockless feet and legs. The doctor raised his eyes to heaven, but he examined her and said, 'This girl is suffering from malnutrition. That explains the fainting.'

Teresa knew that Lyn liked to read. She brought her a comic, with thought bubbles around the words, when she visited her in hospital.

While Lyn was in the Clontarf Orthopaedic Hospital, the Corporation evicted Joey from her flat, dumped all her worldly goods on the balcony and put up steel doors. Life being what it is, all her worldly goods were stolen and she left the hospital with no flat, no money, nothing. She walked a mile on crutches to the Health Board and asked for a disability allowance. She was told to go to the Tax Office and the Department of Social Welfare and get the forms to prove that she was unemployed and destitute. These places were miles away. She wanted to hit the man inside the hatch, but instead she yelled at him, 'I have no money. None. And I'm unemployed and unless you are blind you can see I'm disabled.' He just repeated the instructions he had given her.

Lyn hopped the mile to Mary's cottage where she was now staying and sank into a chair, furious with frustration. She threw her crutches down. Easier to get money as a prostitute on crutches than beg from one government hatch to another. Better trade than beg. So she went back to work. Lyn got a client five minutes after hitting the streets, but her sense of victory was short-lived because she did not get another the rest of the night. The following night she made no money and the women took up a collection for her. On the third night she went to work prepared. She covered her white bandage with white knee socks, which meant that she was showing no leg. She put on a white tennis skirt. Success. An endless line of cars parked along the Canal all night, waiting for 'yer woman with the legs'. One guy walked up to her, looked from her thighs to her crutches and said, 'Can you, eh?'

Lyn smiled sweetly, 'Can I what, Luv?'

He shuffled, 'You know, can you?'

The women started tittering. 'Can I what? Tell me,' Lyn said.

He looked down at her foot and said, 'Can you still do it?'

'Luv, I don't do it with my foot,' she answered.

Later, Lyn sat down with some of the women on the pavement and gratefully laid her crutches beside her. The Vice Squad pulled up to the kerb and one of them said, 'Well Jesus Christ, I've seen it all now,' pointing to Lyn's crutches and laughing.

'Glad I cheered you up,' Lyn said.

'Didn't cheer me up, though I must say that is what I call dedication to duty.'

'Dedication, nothing. I call it destitution,' Lyn quipped.

'Have to hand it to you, Lyn, you're one tough bird,' he said.

The women had great fun playing with Lyn's crutches, taking turns at crossing the road on them. Some men did not realise her foot was broken. She would position herself on her good leg, just so, then give one of the women her crutches to hide. A car would pull up, terms agreed, then Lyn would hiss, 'Pass the crutches.' Some of the men would gape in astonishment, then disappear in a cloud of dust. And Lyn pioneered a whole platoon of tennis skirted, knee-socked prostitutes.

Mary worked for another Cullen, also a married man. A unique feature of the pimping scene in Ireland is that they are often 'happily' married men, supporting families on the girlfriend's earnings. Many are the nights women have to work harder to get the extra money needed for clothes for the First Holy Communion of the pimp's legal children.

Fintan, Mary's pimp, would call every day at 'pimp's clocking-in time', 11.00 a.m., and stay there until 7.00 p.m. He would then either leave for the pub, go home or take Mary out. Three weeks after she left the hospital, Lyn went out with Mary and Fintan. They went to a hotel on the seafront in Bray where they ran into John Cullen and Teresa.

Lyn got pretty drunk. She agreed to a date with John for during the week, but had no intention of keeping it. However, the following night she was down at work when Dennis Black showed up with a pair of scissors and ordered her to get in his car.

'You're my fuckin' property,' he said. Mary hailed a passing patrol car and as they were pulling in to the kerb, she warned Dennis not to cut Lyn.

'She's doing a line with John Cullen now.'

'Are you goin' with Cullen?' Dennis asked.

'Yes,' Lyn said. Dennis backed off. He disappeared from Lyn's life from that moment on.

Lyn and John Cullen met a couple of nights a week over a few months. Everybody warned her against him. They said he was treacherous, unpredictable, quick with a knife or bottle, but Lyn felt safe with John because other men were afraid of him. And he was affectionate. It took a while to understand his muffled way of talking with a rough Dublin accent, every few sentences strung with 'Dyou know what I mean, like?'

One night, she was chatting to Róisín who asked, 'Are you seein' Cullen?'

'Why?' Lyn stalled.

'Because you keep saying "d'you know what I mean, like". It's driving me crazy. You never used to say that . . .'

John asked Lyn to go to a football match in Co. Dublin. After the match, they all went to a pub. Lyn got politely drunk. Sometime during the evening, John informed her that when she left the pub, she was not going with him. She was to go with one of his mates. Lyn thought he was having her on. There were eleven men in that pub, and he chose the most obnoxious one for Lyn. When the pub closed, John got into his car, a blue Datsun, and Lyn trotted around to the passenger side and tried to open the door. John jumped out in a fury, grabbed her arm and dragged her across the road to the van that the football team had arrived in. He opened the back doors and threw her in.

It was too dark to see how many men were in there; she found that she was sitting on ropes, pickaxe handles and other junk. The minute the doors were closed they drove off at high speed. No one made a move. It was probably due to the pecking order, each one waiting to see who was first, and suddenly a fight broke out up front. Lyn looked out the back window. The road stretched into total darkness and they were in the middle of nowhere. Lyn had spent years trying to out-psych potentially dangerous clients and she resorted to the only weapon she had at her disposal. She played up to the winner of the affray.

She moved closer to him, without seeming to be aware that she was doing it, and begged for protection with her eyes.

'Are you OK' he asked.

'Yes,' Lyn said, letting her voice tremble, 'just so long as those guys back there don't come any closer.' She kept her dainty little hand on his arm.

'Don't worry,' he said, his voice deep with ego. She found out later that the fight had erupted over who was to have first go at her. She had no idea where they were going, but she kept close to her hero, and in her head, frantically tried to figure how she would escape.

Lyn's 'hero' suddenly decided he wanted to have a 'slash'. The driver pulled up on the main road, and a few of the others decided they wanted out too. They piled out, stood facing the wall of a lovely semi-detached house, to urinate. Lyn took her chance and fled. Over her shoulder, she saw the men pile back into the van and drive towards her. They were shouting out of the windows, 'Here, do you want your handbag? Come on back in the van. We'll give you a lift, no messin'.' At that they picked up speed. Lyn ran into the path of an oncoming car, yelling her head off. The car stopped, nice Mercedes with three respectable looking occupants.

'Are you alright, love? Would you like a lift?' the driver asked.

'No, I definitely ain't alrigh',' Lyn said, 'and yes, I would like a lift.'

Lyn always talks when she is excited, and she told them all that had happened. They were sympathetic. She was just beginning to calm down when she realised that they had neared the Bull Wall, and were turning left instead of right. Lyn leaned over the driver's shoulder, grabbed the keys out of the ignition, opened the door. As the car slowed down, the man sitting beside Lyn grabbed her by the hair with one hand and started slapping her around the head with the other. He was yelling at her, 'Give me the fuckin' keys. I'll kill you. Gimme the keys.'

Lyn was screaming, dangling the keys out the open door. 'If you let me go I'll throw your keys back to you. I promise. If you won't let go of me, I'm going to throw them as far as I can. They'll probably land in the sea. Let me go and I won't throw . . .'

He let Lyn go. She jumped out, threw his keys in to him and ran like hell. As she ran out on to the main road, she took a look over her shoulder. They had started the car, put it into reverse and were speeding back towards her.

Lyn stood stock still, screaming, terrified. From nowhere, it seemed, a bus appeared. The driver stopped, 'Jump in quick, love.' There was only the driver and the conductor on board; they were on their way to the depot. They were shocked by her story. One of them was only about twenty years old. 'We can't take you into the depot,' he said, 'or we'll be in trouble, but if you wait in the bus shelter there across the road, I'll give you a lift home on me bike.' Lyn agreed to wait. When he picked her up, he drove like the devil. She had sworn, after seeing so many people in the orthopaedic hospital as a result of motorbike accidents, that she would never get on one. However, the danger was relative tonight. When he dropped Lyn off, he asked for a date later on in the week. Lyn thanked him for the lift, declined the invitation, and went into the cottage. Weary. Even he, polite as he was, did not see her as a person who had just had two very harrowing experiences. He fancied her, that was all. No matter that she was old enough to be his mother.

John Cullen called around to the cottage the next morning to see Fintan. 'How did you get on last night?' he asked Lyn, with that sly smirk of his. He had not seen any of the men since leaving the pub. His car had broken down.

'Sorry to disappoint you, but I got away, didn't I?' she said. 'Your fine friends robbed me.' She left out the boys in the Mercedes and the kid with the motorbike. Cullen called around to Mary's cottage about half a dozen times after that. On each occasion, he was pleasant, kind. He said that he had only been joking when he told Lyn to go off with his mates.

'Why did you throw me into the van with the whole bloody football team?' Lyn asked and he replied she had annoyed him by turning her back to him and talking to his friends. It had made him jealous. He was very sorry; he realised that he had overreacted. He would never do anything like that again. She believed him. If a guy cared anything at all for you, he was bound to be jealous, she reasoned. It was only logical. If he was jealous, of course he would hurt, abuse, humiliate.

'Forget it,' she told him, but it was some time before she trusted him again.

And then one night they went to a pub. 'I am just going over to talk to my mate. Be back in a minute,' he said. As Lyn sat sipping her drink she began to take stock of her surroundings. There were about four of that football team scattered around the pub. She remembers thinking, 'This must be their local.' Another drink arrived via the barman. She looked over at John Cullen who was still deep in conversation. He caught her eye, smiled that smile and nodded to Lyn. She made no attempt to talk to the twit sitting beside her.

Another ten minutes elapsed. Two double vodkas arrived from John. She was meditating on the joys of being on a date with a guy who left her on her own while he spent the night chatting to his mates. She was joined by a middle-aged man who brought her another vodka from John Cullen. He introduced himself. He was the brother of the man sitting to the other side of her. They struck up a conversation and Lyn liked him.

'Do you know what they are going to do to you?' the man said.

'Who?'

He got agitated, glanced furtively in John Cullen's direction and said, 'John Cullen and the guy he is talkin' to.'

'Do what?' she asked, getting that familiar gut-wrenching feeling.

'They are going to set you up for a gang bang. Look, if they knew I was telling you this, they would kill me. But the two of them, plus my brother and two other guys over there, are going to get you. Get out while you can.'

Lyn stood up.

John Cullen was beside her in a flash.

'Where are you going to, love? I'll get you another drink. Sit down.'

She played it cool.

'I am just going to the loo.'

She left her coat behind so as not to arouse suspicion. There were bars on the windows in the women's room. Forget about fire hazards; what about women trying to escape rapists? Lyn stalled, a woman came in.

'Is there a back way out of here?' Lyn asked her.

'No, love, you have to go out the front.'

She tried to stay calm, rationalise. She must not attract attention. She knew that if she delayed much longer she was in trouble. She walked out into the lounge again, sat down, worked out who was sitting where. Could she make it out of the front door fast enough not to be spotted?

The prospective rapists were being careful, casting only furtive glances in her direction. The only one studying her was John Cullen. Did he realise that she knew? She tried to figure out a plan of action. She stared him down. It worked. He had turned his back to her so that she could not lip read what he said.

'Now, Lyn, quick, leave your coat. Don't look back. Just run,' she told herself. The door was just in front of her. Someone grabbed her arm, squeezed it, dug their fingers in.

'Where are you going, love?' She froze and turned to look into John Cullen's face, smiling that smile. She was flanked by the guy he had been talking to all night. Just keep cool, Lyn.

'I was just going for fags.'

'You don't get fags outside. You can get them on the way home.'

He gave a barely imperceptible nod across the lounge. Lyn was quickly surrounded by three other men. John and his mate lifted her off her feet. She shouted, 'I don't want to go home yet. I want to get fags at the bar. I have not finished my drink yet.'

They both gripped her elbows a little tighter. John Cullen glanced around the pub, and said loudly to no one in particular, 'Women. They just cannot handle drink. Come on, love, you'll be all right, d'you know what I mean like? You'll be all right when you get out in the car. A little fresh air and you'll feel better.'

He turned round to give a final shrug of his shoulders to indicate the foolishness of women. He then walked her out of the door, her feet raised about three inches above the floor. Once outside the men quickly bundled Lyn into the back of Cullen's Datsun. Three of them piled in on top of her. John Cullen and his mate got in the front.

The guy who had warned her ran up, banged on the window, 'Let her go, Mylie, let her go. She does not deserve that.'

His brother yelled back, 'Fuck off or you will get your fuckin' skull caved in.'

John Cullen drove off.

14

'Please, will you stop for fags? You said I could get them on the way home,' Lyn tried.

'Shut fuckin' up or I will fuckin' kill you,' John said.

He stopped at a house in Ballyfermot, went inside.

'Please let me go before he comes back,' she begged. Stoney silence.

'Please, I am begging you. Let me out.'

No response. Lyn reached in her handbag, took out her Valium, managed to swallow about ten of them before one of them caught on to what she was doing. Silently, he grabbed the remainder from her and threw them out the window. Then he started to sing the theme from *Mash*, 'Suicide is Painless', smiling at her. She thought, 'Were they all out for the day from the same asylum?' They all did this smiling bit. No talk, just smile. Perhaps they had all been to see the same film and the tough guy just smiled all the time.

John Cullen emerged with a woman. A double gang bang? He drove to another house in Ballyfermot. They all filed out. Lyn was dragged without ceremony into the house, plonked in a chair while records were put on. A glass of vodka was pressed into her hand. Everyone just started up normal chit chat. What was this? Lyn could not understand. She looked at the woman John Cullen had brought. She seemed so cool. Was she used to gang bangs? John Cullen turned to Lyn, 'Go upstairs with Mylie.'

Lyn was starting to feel numb. When she got up to the room she told herself, 'Lyn, pretend this is a client. Just switch your mind off. Think of a good book.' She had just read *The Scourge of the Swastika*. 'Yes, that's it, think of *The Scourge of the Swastika*.'

Mylie was on top of her. Who wrote that damn book? She could not stay in her head. Owen fell out of the wardrobe.

'Fuck off outa the room,' Mylie told him. This was too much. How could she pretend that this was business? Mylie was finished. Another guy burst in the door. He just stood there and looked for a moment before he dropped his trousers and jumped on her. He was ugly. If he pulled up for business on the Canal, she would refuse him. Awful, the smell. Who did write that book? He was finished now. Lyn thanked God she hadn't had a long-lasting client yet. That was £40 she had made. That little fart Owen was next. 'Ah yes,' she remembered, 'it was Lord Russel of Liverpool who wrote it.'

What the fuck? The pig was trying to kiss her. 'I don't fuckin' kiss. Get off me,' Lyn felt sick. Any idiot knew a woman didn't kiss a client. Kissing was personal. Affection. Didn't the little squirt know that? Lyn was screaming at the top of her voice. She could switch off while she was having sex, but kissing?

John Cullen was in the room. Smiling at her. 'Is something wrong, love?'

'You ugly looking bastard, I am going to kill the fuckin' lot of you. You just get me out of here. I don't care what you do to me. I don't care if you all beat me to death. I am not taking any more, and that is that.'

The fixed smile got a little stiffer. 'Who said you could not go? Of course you are free to go. See you downstairs, love.'

When he left, Lyn dressed hurriedly, ran down to the front door. The bloody thing was locked, no key in it. She knew it was too good to be true, started to yell again.

'Open this bloody door!'

John Cullen appeared, smiling, 'Shh, do you want to wake all the kids in the neighbourhood?'

'I can't get out. The door is locked.'

He went back in the room, brought the key, pressed a small bottle of vodka in her hand, smiled that smile. 'Good night, love. I hope you had a nice night.'

Lyn ran down the road expecting at any time to be grabbed again. She looked back, but no one followed. Then slowly the anger boiled over in her. She ran back to John Cullen's car, opened all the doors, got two matchsticks, inserted them into the valves of his two front tyres and ran back to the roundabout. She retrieved the money from inside the lining of her skirt, hailed a taxi and went back to the cottage.

She stood in the shower for ages and ages. At least when she was at work she dictated the terms; no contraceptives, no deal, Mister. Her purse was missing, of course. She sat and waited for Mary to come back from work. She wasn't getting anything out of all the Valium she had taken. Her heart was pounding. Eventually Lyn heard Mary's footsteps. Thank God. If she did not tell someone soon, she would crack up.

The minute she walked in Mary asked, 'What happened with you and John? He came into Gig's looking for you around 3 o'clock.'

Lyn told her the whole story. She was nearly as upset as Lyn. Four of the men had gone into Gig's looking for Lyn.

Mary said, 'Lyn, I told you he was a right bastard. He did the same to Teresa when he was going with her at the start. He let Rory O'Connor and Ronnie Flynn and some others screw her up against a tree.'

They talked some more. Eventually Mary fell asleep.

Lyn sat and watched her, kept thinking through the night of Mary, Teresa, herself and Cullen. Mary had fiery red hair with matching eyebrows and lashes. She was fat like a barrel. Lyn met her when Mary was eighteen years old. Her father was dead; she came from Crumlin and she did not get on with her mother. Mary had a desperate temper. The first man Mary worked for beat her up, so she waited until he was asleep and hit him with an iron bar. And then, just in case he was still in the mood to go anywhere, she went out and burned his car. She had to go into hiding when she cooled down, but nothing could have stopped her rage. She worked for Fintan and was nuts about him. He had five children, and he had two with Mary. Mary's mother kept the first one and Fintan insisted that she had the second adopted. Lyn always wondered when Mary would kill Fintan. She was like a time bomb, her anger over her children suppressed, but murderous. It was palpable. Lyn could feel it and she had never heard a word pass Mary's lips about her personal feelings. Watching her sleep, Lyn remembered the night she saw Mary holding onto the railings as she threw up, three days after a caesarean birth. She was deathly pale, sweating and obviously feverish, but not a moan passed her lips.

'You got to go home,' Lyn said. Mary shook her head.

'I can't. I've got to get money.'

'Look, have this,' Lyn said, holding out the £30 she had made so far that night.

'No, thanks anyway. I'll be OK.'

There were no practical jokes from Mary that night. She was a dedicated practical joker, no one was safe. She would offer a cigarette and it would explode half-way down.

'She used to bake cakes with stones in and dole 'em out to the girls,' Lyn recalls, 'She would give you a present of a frilly handkerchief and you couldn't open it because she had sewn it together. She just loved a laugh.'

Some of Mary's jokes were less than endearing, like pricking holes in condoms and lending them to women who forgot she was not to be trusted. Whenever any one of the women was pregnant, they would say, 'See you borrowed one of Mary's rubbers.' Mary got a lot of stick when this was true, but her vicious temper was reserved for men. No matter what the women said to her, she never got mad at them. She worked seven nights a week and never a night off.

While Mary slept, Lyn thought of what she had said about Teresa who had been 'inspired' by Mary to go on the game. Teresa's work kept Cullen's family in comfort and yet she lived in a hovel. Lyn had been to her home when she stood as god-mother for Teresa's and Cullen's baby. Only one room down-stairs was used by Teresa. It was shared by her mother and her brother, Jimmy, and Jonathan. The dirt must have taken years to accumulate and the place stank. Lyn stood in the middle of the room while Teresa's mother made tea in the grate, and she wondered what sort of man let his kids live like this. Cullen had not even bothered to turn up on the day of the christening. That was Cullen, the way he used and abused people.

Towards morning Lyn decided she was going to kill every man in that gang. When Fintan arrived next morning Mary related all that had happened to Lyn. He smiled and said, 'I told you before, Lyn, you should have picked a nice guy like me. He's a no-good bastard, always was. You should give me your money and I guarantee I won't let all my mates screw you,' he quipped.

Later that day Lyn went and bought a gun used for firing bolts into concrete. When she got back to the cottage, Fintan laughed. 'What do you think you are going to do with that?' he asked.

Lyn was shaking. 'I'm going to walk into that pub, up to each one of the animals who abused me and put the gun to their heads. Then I'll ask them, "Do you feel like laughing now, you bastards? And I'll shoot the bolt into what passes for their brains.'

Fintan thought the idea was hilarious. Eventually, he stopped kidding her and said, 'It is highly unlikely that it would actually kill even one of them. You don't know what you are dealing with. And you're not thinking. You need a good night's sleep for a start. Even if you managed to get one of them, do you think the others are just going to sit there and watch? None of 'em would think twice about giving you a bottle in the face. Don't take my word for it. Wait until you are not so knackered and think about it.' He chuckled.

Lyn was feeling the after-effects of the Valium, apart from anything else, so she went to bed. Next day she was not feeling so brave. She spent the day seething, holding the gun in her hands. She had never thought of herself as a courageous person but she felt that the last stay in hospital after Dennis's attack had knocked the fight out of her. She had completely lost her nerve. She stayed home another night, feeling humiliated by her own helplessness. There was no way that she could retaliate.

Eventually, she forced herself back to work, did her best to blot out the incident from her mind. She had almost succeeded when John Cullen arrived back on the scene.

She lit into him and then, breathless, asked, 'What did I do to you to deserve what you put me through?'

He said, 'Lyn, you think you are better than me. You think that just because you can read books and had a little more schooling than me that you are more clever, y'know what I mean like? Well, that is just where you're wrong. You thought that because you escaped the van that night you had outsmarted me, y'know what I mean? Well, I'll tell you something, nobody outsmarts John Cullen. When it comes to brains I leave you on the Halfpenny Bridge. I had it all carefully planned; I collected Frances, my girlfriend, so that if you screamed rape the cops would know I didn't do anything. I had my own girl with me.'

'Who the hell is Frances?' Seems Frances wanted to marry him, was unaware that he was already married with three children, that he was a pimp and had another two children with Teresa.

'You said that I was free to go, as if I was all along. Why did you do that, to make me think I was nuts?' Lyn asked.

'It could have turned nasty when you started making so much noise, that's why, d'you know what I mean, like? If I had not told them to stop, you would have been badly beaten up, plenty to show the cops. Besides, Frances looked real scared when she heard you scream, y'know what I mean? And then when I got outside and saw all the tyres let down I thought I had you wrong, d'you know what I mean, like? Maybe you were crazy enough to go to the cops. The guys were a little worried in case you tried to do them for rape, went lookin' for you . . . I could have brought them to the cottage, y'know. Hear you're going to polish us all off with a bolt gun,' he laughed.

John Cullen kept calling around to the cottage over the next two weeks and gradually he won Lyn over.

'Who else was I going to meet,' Lyn asks, 'outside of business? You just don't meet nice guys in the pimping game. I managed to convince myself that it was the other guys who had raped me. I know, I know, he was the one who set it up, but he did not rape me.'

In any case, the set-up which evolved between Lyn and Cullen suited her. He did not suggest that she work for him, that came much later. He was married, so he would not want to live with her. Lyn had vowed that she would never live with another man. He had his own girl on the game, so he did not have to rely on her for money. This meant that she could work when she felt like it, keep her own money, pay her own way. This she did for quite a while, even when they went out for a drink. Lyn bought round for round until he said it made a show of him in public, so then she used to buy meals or tickets for the theatre. They went out a couple of times a week. Now and then Lyn felt twinges of guilt over what she was doing behind Teresa's back. She worked alongside Teresa, who talked about 'my John', and no one had the heart to tell her; it was such an uneven competition. What Teresa did not know, it was not their business to tell her. It bugged Lyn. She worked it out by getting at Cullen for the state of Teresa, her home and, above all, her children.

'Teresa lives like an animal,' she said.

'She likes it like that,' Cullen said.

There was one more incident. About four weeks later, Cullen took Lyn out for a drink. Before they went in, he said, 'Give me any money you have on you and I'll hold on to it in case any of those bastards try to dip you again.' She gave him what money she had, skiving off £20 in the process. He fetched the drinks, holding her hand for the best part of the night. She was just beginning to relax when he got up to talk to another man. Lyn was not taking any chances this time. She stood up, picked up her coat and sauntered to the door. He was beside her in a flash.

'Lyn, love, you don't have to leg it. I promise, nothing is going to happen to you. Come back and finish your drink.'

'I'm making sure nothing is going to happen, John. I'll be down the road, waiting for you. I'll be where you can't see me. If you are on your own I will walk where you can see me. OK'

'OK. Promise.'

He went back to finish his drink. Lyn flew down the road, hid in a garden and spotted a taxi. She ran out onto the road and flagged it down. She jumped in and lay down in the back and went down to the Legion of Mary House at 18 Herbert Place.

Lyn, like most of the women, had a love–hate relationship with the Legionaries of Mary, but the house was warm and there was always a cup of tea.

'They were like the worst kind of door-to-door salesmen, although they were all women. Suddenly, one of 'em would materialise as you negotiated with a client,' Lyn laughs. 'She'd just stand there, rabbiting on about sin and Jesus and Our Lady and being saved. It could be a bit of a turn-off, but then a lot of the clients would have come straight from the pub and weren't bothered by them. That's an odd thing about Dublin. You could be on your way to a flat with a client and he made the sign of the cross passing every church.'

Every night the legionaries met, prayed, and then took to the streets in pairs. They would talk to the women and their clients and try to get them back to the Legion House to 'pray'. When they were successful, the clients were taken upstairs; the women were never allowed in the front door, but relegated to the basement. Legionaries from overseas went upstairs, but only four or five volunteers went down among the women in the basement. Women with drink taken were refused admission, though they were adept at disguising that, and there was no drink allowed on the premises. There was always tea and biscuits and chat, even though the conversation inevitably got around to sin and religion. In spite of the earbashing about their sins which the women hated, and having to thread blue string through an endless supply of miraculous medals, they went there to get in out of the cold and have a cup of tea. At the end of the night, around 1.30 a.m., two priests came downstairs to say the rosary. The minute one of the legionaries reached for her rosary, the women always legged it. Dolores, working at the hospital now, had always stayed.

The women sometimes got argumentative, but nothing the legionaries could not handle, until everything started to change in a dreadful way.

It started when Mary, Róisín and Teresa began to go into the house. The older women saw the legionaries as 'pains in the neck', but had a sneaking affection for them. After all, they were always there, trying, in their own way, to be kind. This trio, however, plus a few other youngsters, saw them as 'fuckin' nuisances'. Lyn's lot were grateful for their tea and biscuits; the young ones threw the biscuits in the bin. Two of the legionaries started baking cakes and brought them, wrapped in paper doilies, down to the house. The young women did not want 'fuckin' tea'; they wanted 'fuckin' coffee'. To demonstrate the point, they smashed every cup and saucer in the place. They got coffee. Next, they did not want 'fuckin' cakes'. They smashed things again. They demanded fish and chips. So, every Friday and Saturday night the legionaries would put an enormous mound of fish and chips, bought out of their own pockets, into the Baby Belling to warm until the women came in out of the cold. If Mary, Róisín and Teresa did not get what they wanted, they would upend the table. Lyn could normally see this coming and would hastily pick up her cup and move to the end of the room. Also, before the 'oldies' went into the house, they always changed from their miniskirts as a mark of respect to the legionaries. Not so that trio. They would push whatever legionary opened the door out of the way, prance in, and sit showing off their knickers. The 'oldies' talked small talk, and in whispers if anything about clients or sex came up, so as not to offend the legionaries. Not the young bunch. They were deliberately disgusting. They shouted about spunk, burst rubbers, crabs, VD, what size penis the last client had, anything to upset the legionaries.

They made up a lot of the conversation and the more upset the legionaries became, the worse the rebellious group got. The goal was to get the legionaries to run from the room, crying.

Some nights the trio talked in earnest. Or, rather, Róisín talked. She had a great need to talk about what her dad had done to her and anything else that troubled her. Her personable, normally endearing, way drew everybody else into the discussion. Women Lyn had known for years, and knew nothing about, began to talk openly about themselves. No one wanted to leave. It became their therapy. And, whereas before the Legion House was a place where they went to get warm, now they could not wait to get in. And instead of simply leaving before the rosary, the young ones now refused to let the legionaries say it at all. The women also refused to leave because they were talking. The Legion House had become a Women's Centre. And then it all went wrong.

'I think,' Lyn reflects, 'it had something to do with "unfinished business" in the therapy sense. All sorts of strange vibes were flying. About three weeks ago I bought a book from a second-hand barrel for 10p. It's called *Group Psychotherapy*. I read all the histories of what happened at each group therapy session and it suddenly hit me. That's what happened at the Legion House, group dynamics at its worst, and we had allowed the younger ones to take leadership. All sorts of emotions churned up in the group and we did not have a clue what was happening.'

On that night when Lyn ran from Cullen, Róisín, Mary and Teresa ran in from the street and wrecked the basement. They smashed cups and saucers, the Baby Belling, all the windows, broke chairs off the wall. Teresa hit one of the legionaries and then the trio carried on upstairs to where the other legionaries were praying. They broke up the meeting by kicking each kneeling legionary into standing up.

The head legionary ran downstairs. 'Lyn, please do something . . .' she begged.

'I'm not a bloody screw,' Lyn said to her, and recalls, 'It was a weird feeling. None of the other women were surprised. We all had known, in some strange way, that something was building up. None of us knew why, or how, or what we knew. It was just something in us all.'

The trio were barred from the house that night. Later, Lyn asked Róisín about it and she said, 'We never planned it, you know, Lyn. It just happened. We hadn't even talked about it. We were just in a strange mood.'

Two nights before that final 'wrecking,' the police had chased the three women who ran up the front steps to the door of the Legion House and rang the bell. In spite of their earnest pleadings to let them hide in the hall, they were refused entry. The three were arrested.

All of the women knew the legionaries would not help them escape from the police and accepted it, but the three younger women were furious. After the 'therapy' sessions, the house had become their refuge. Now they had been refused sanctuary. That triggered off the "unfinished business" of early trauma in the three women and erupted in violence.

Lyn felt awful about refusing to help the legionaries, 'but I couldn't go against my own kind'. There are two stories which illustrate the relationship the women had with the legionaries before that fateful night. There was a legionary named Mrs

Kirby, in her sixties, English, married to a Dublin man. She was an extremely kind, patient person and all the women loved her. When she died, they proclaimed her a saint. Lyn was chatting with another prostitute, Brenda, in the Legion House one night. One of Brenda's clients had driven down a laneway, with her in the passenger seat, and parked the car smack up against the wall, so that she was unable to open her door, and pulled a knife on her.

'I started prayin' for me fuckin' life,' said Brenda, 'and it wasn't Our Lady I fuckin' prayed to. Ah no, it was Mrs Kirby. I prayed to Mrs Kirby. I said, "Mrs Kirby, please help me. You helped me when you were alive. Help me now." That woman was a saint.'

The other story concerned Nella Doyle who fell in love with a Mormon who called to her flat canvassing his religion. She later married him, gave up the game. She called to see them in the Legion House about a month after the wedding and had them laughing, telling them how he had refused to make love to her before the wedding. On the wedding night he was so shy he got undressed in the dark. As Nella chatted, an elderly priest in a chair in the corner roused himself from his perpetual slumber. He sat bolt upright, blessed himself and said, 'What did you say, Nella? A Mormon! Sure, they're worse than the bloody Protestants.'

15

The next time Lyn was up in court, she got six months. She appealed and bail was fixed at £500. She was in Mountjoy for ten days, awaiting bail. John Cullen got an uncle of his to stand bail for her. She paid him £80 for the favour.

During the time she was in prison, Lyn hardly slept. This was because the doctor would not give her any sleeping tablets and she was unable to sleep without them. She went home to Mary, waited for her to go to work and took four sleeping tablets and settled herself down for a restful night. The phone rang. It was John Cullen. He said how he had not realised how much Lyn meant to him until she was locked up. He had not thought it possible to miss anybody so much. 'Can I call round now?'

They talked for hours. He seemed a different person. He had thought about all the bad things he had done to Lyn and said that it was because he realised that he was beginning to care for her, was trying to fight his feelings. That was why he had done worse things to her than to any other woman. And then, while she was in prison, he knew he had fallen for her.

'I love you, Lyn,' he said. She not only fell for it, but him too. From then on, things changed. They never went out in company; it was always just the two of them. Another facet of John Cullen was loving, affectionate. Lyn was blissfully happy.

There was a flat coming vacant under Róisín's in Ballymun. Lyn had to move in right away as the people were moving out and the Corporation would put a security man in it to prevent squatting. John and Lyn became even closer, having somewhere of their own. The night before Christmas Eve, he took Lyn for a drink. Lyn got very sloshed and chatted to a friend of Joey's. They gave each other a kiss. When Lyn sat down, someone said, 'You had better watch out. John was watching you.'

Lyn just shrugged it off, feeling very happy with life.

At the end of the night, John was missing and the barman was yelling, 'Time up.' Lyn eventually found John. He was in another room holding a fellow against a wall, smashing his face in. There was blood all over the two of them. Lyn tugged at John Cullen's arm and asked, 'What's wrong?'

John punched her twice in the face. She ran out of the room into the lounge. There was a man lying on the floor, his face slashed all over and the whole place was covered in blood. She ran outside into the road and flagged down a passing motorist who stopped and gave her a lift down to the Canal.

Lyn sat on the steps of the Legion House. She always made it a rule not to work when she had drink taken. She waited for the women to finish work and went with them to Gig's for a meal, where they stayed until about 5.00 a.m., and then got a taxi home.

Lyn was in Róisín's flat when John came to see her on Christmas Day. 'What are you doing tonight, love? Would you like to come to my Ma's with me? You don't want to be on your own for Christmas, do you?'

'I would love to come.'

'Good. I will collect you about 6.30 then.'

Her feet hardly touched the ground on the way up the stairs. After all, married men spent Christmas with their wives and family. She spent the afternoon dolling herself up for him. Róisín was so happy for her and the two of them giggled like schoolgirls. Lyn heard John Cullen putting his key in the lock.

'Quick, Róisín, hide over there. Stop laughing! When he gets right into the kitchen jump on him and we will both start singing "We wish You a Merry Christmas and a Happy New Year", right?'

Róisín hid at the side of the cooker. Lyn stood at the fridge, smiling. She watched him walking down the hall, smiling back at her.

'You would never make a housebreaker, love,' she said. 'The door wasn't locked.'

Smash! One punch sent her flying across the fridge. Bang! Another one on the side of the head.

'Are you trying to make a shit out of me?' he shouted.

He moved swiftly over to the sink, grabbed a butcher's knife. Róisín screamed. He reeled to face her. Lyn ran to him, grabbed hold of the blade of the knife. He was snow white.

'Let go of the fuckin' knife.'

'John, I'm too scared.'

'Lyn, if you don't let go of the knife I'll stick it right through you.'

'John, please, don't hurt me. I'm sorry for whatever I've done.'

Róisín said, 'Let go of it. He won't use it, will you John? Please John, don't use the knife.' She was sobbing. He was looking from her to Lyn. The colour was coming back into his face. The danger was passing.

'Lyn, I won't hurt you if you let go, but you will make me worse if you don't.'

It was a gamble, and the odds were not exactly stacked in her favour. She let go of the blade. He went into the bedroom and lay down and covered his face with a pillow, a gesture that meant he was angry, but trying to control it. She put her hand on his arm.

He said, 'Get your fuckin' hands off me. Don't you dare touch me.'

Lyn followed Róisín into the bathroom and looked in the mirror. Her nose was bleeding, the left side of her face was starting to swell. While Lyn was cleaning herself up, Róisín went to talk to John Cullen. She succeeded in calming him and went into the kitchen to make tea. John had blown up over the night in the pub. He had attacked four fellows who were in the company of the lad Lyn had kissed. He had then driven out to Ballymun, let himself into her flat, waited for her to come home until around 4.30 a.m. He then presumed that she had gone to stay with one of the women. He had waited, fully intending to kill Lyn.

John Cullen had called to the flat at 6.30 p.m. because he knew there would be no one else there at Christmas. No one would have seen him entering the flat; he was right there. Nearly everyone in Lyn's block had gone to visit people. He was going to stab her with the butcher's knife, wait till he was sure that she was dead, then lock the flat after him. It would be days before anyone discovered Lyn was dead. Everyone would presume she had taken off somewhere on her own. John was shocked when he saw Róisín hiding beside the stove. He could not do it with Róisín as a witness.

John talked calmly to Lyn about his plan for her death. He meant it. It was the first time that the full realisation of the kind of man she was mixed up with got through to her. She vowed that she would never cross him again. She would do anything he wanted. She acknowledged, to herself, that if ever she wanted to leave him, she would have to leave Dublin.

John's mood had suddenly changed.

'Come on, my Ma is expecting me up at the house. Forget about what just happened. But after tonight, we won't see each other again. I can see myself ending up killing you.'

Lyn went and changed her blouse, which was covered in blood. Róisín walked with them to the lift. As they were getting in, she said, 'John, please don't hit her again. Will you promise me, you won't?'

'I promise,' he said. 'It's over.'

On the way over to his mother's house Lyn was subdued. She let him do the talking. She was afraid that anything she said might anger him.

Suddenly he said, 'Lyn, I love you very much. Next to my Ma and my kids, I love you more than anything in the world. I never wanted to hurt you. I mean I could have killed you back in the flat and then I would have wanted to kill myself.'

Lyn said she loved him very much, too, and was very sorry for what had happened. They had a pleasant evening together, and arrived back in Ballymun around 3 o'clock promising that they would never hurt each other again.

John began asking Lyn to have her birth control coil removed and have his baby. Steadfastly, she refused. He asked her again and again. She refused, saying that she already had three children and had not done such a good job with them. Another child with no future?

His only argument was consistent. 'If you loved me you would prove it by having a baby for me.'

He had nagged Lyn for a year and after Christmas Lyn went to have the IUD removed. He collected her at her flat, drove her to the clinic, sat in the car while she had the coil removed. After it was done, they were sitting at red traffic lights on Camden Street and Lyn started to cry. She felt so naked. He leaned over, kissed the tears from her face and asked, 'What's wrong, love?'

'Oh John, I'm so scared.'

'It will be all right, love. We will have a beautiful baby, something that is ours alone. No one can take it from us. It will be our future together,' he said, 'd'you know what I mean?'

This did not do much to reassure Lyn.

'But John, you have two kids with Teresa. You don't give a damn about them.'

'Lyn, love, it will be different with us, d'you know what I mean? And you're good around the house and know how to look after kids. I don't give a fuck about Teresa, so how can I feel anything for her kids? I don't even acknowledge that they are mine. I am crazy about you, so it's different. D'you know what I mean, like? Lyn, I would even mind it while you went to work. I have never, ever minded my own kids. Surely that proves how much I want this baby.'

Lyn wanted to believe him. John was not a very intelligent man, but sometimes he could make what, to Lyn, were profound observations. She recalled him once defining what love was: 'Love is how the other person makes you feel about yourself. If someone makes you feel good, you love them.'

One month passed. No period. Lyn was pregnant. She decided to tell John while he was having one of his ritual soaks in the tub. Lyn called the bathroom 'my office'. John could not avoid her there, no distractions, and it was where she got all the information she wanted. She had learned that from Róisín. 'If you want information from a man, grab it while he is in the bath,' Róisín said.

In the full glow of motherhood, Lyn was ready to start the interview when John said, 'Lyn, I am leaving you.'

'What did you say? Don't start messin' John.'

'Lyn, I'm not messin'. I'm serious.'

Lyn's voice started to rise. 'And what the bloody hell am I supposed to do now? I'm pregnant! It was your bright idea in the first place.'

'You can have an abortion.'

'You callous bastard, how can you lie there with that smile on your face, just washing your legs and tell me that? Why are you leaving me?'

'Because I don't love you.'

'John, you look me in the eyes and tell me you don't love me?'

He repeated it but did not look at her.

'I said fuckin' look at me and say it,' Lyn insisted.

He looked at Lyn steadily.

'John, please tell me what all this is about. You say you love me and I believe you do. You could not act the way you do with me if you didn't. You kept on until I got the coil out. Now I'm pregnant. We even have the names picked out and now you say you want out, just like that? I cannot believe that after the last nine months we've been together you don't love me.'

John did not blink, just stared Lyn straight in the eyes.

'Lyn, I was only with you because you were a friend of Dolores, d'you know what I mean, like? As it happens, I do love you, but there is no future for us, so I'm leavin'.'

Lyn was stunned.

'John, I cannot believe you could spend all that time with me just to get Dolores. You didn't need me to lead you to Dolores. Anyway, you know I haven't seen her since before I went to England. I've never known where she lives. She didn't want any of the women to know.'

Lyn, you don't know me. I would spend twenty years with you if I thought it would help me to get to her.'

Lyn could not answer him. She walked out of the bathroom, slumped into a chair in the sitting room. He came into the room with his clothes under his arm and dried himself off with the towel, all the time just staring at her.

When he was dressed he said, 'Come and lock this door after me.'

Lyn walked down the hall after him, silent. When they reached the door he turned, kissed her on the cheek and said, 'I am very sorry, love.' Then he left . . .

Lyn could not figure out what John meant by her being the means of getting to Dolores. They had, in the early days of their relationship, had many arguments over his feud with Dolores. Lyn told John that she had only once seen Dolores attempt to stop Teresa working. Lyn had witnessed that one instance when Dolores had chased Teresa off the streets. If Teresa had said any different, then she was lying to make excuses for her low earnings, Lyn claimed. Everybody knew Teresa made up stories, was a Walter Mitty type.

John always said he did not care; Dolores had got him three years in jail and he was not going to forgive or forget. Even if he had beaten up Dolores because Teresa had lied, Dolores should not have given evidence against him.

Lyn argued. What the hell was Dolores supposed to do, beat him up in return? Her only recourse was to have him charged.

He said, 'Come on, Lyn. You have had plenty of good hidings. Craig Nelson was always beating you. Dennis Black gave you a right going over. He is not half as dangerous as me. How come you did not get him charged?'

'Because I'm not a grass,' she replied.

'You see, now you're admitting Dolores was wrong to get me charged.'

It was useless trying to explain to Cullen that a woman had to yell 'cop' to put an end to being beaten. If women were as strong as men they would not get beaten in the first place and they would not have to yell 'cop'. And that was called grassing; convenient, except for the women. It dawned on Lyn that through all the talks she had had with Cullen on the subject of Dolores, he had been picking her brain. And now he was gone.

She decided to have an abortion. She was not going to bring another child into the world like this. Her whole life was one big mess. She did not need a child, and a child deserved better.

Surprise, surprise! John came back. He reasoned that he had made her get the coil out, and it suddenly hit him that it was not fair to walk out. He was back to convince Lyn to have an abortion.

'My family would take it very hard if they knew you were having a baby, d'you know what I mean, like? So it has to be an abortion,' he said. He meant his mother and brothers. Lyn did

156

not tell him that she had already decided on an abortion. She was just waiting until she had enough money.

'It goes against my beliefs,' Lyn lied. 'After all, it wasn't even an accident.' She could not possibly do it, she said.

'Damn his family,' Lyn thought. They knew that he was married with three kids and they knew he was pimping off Teresa and had three kids with her. Half of his holy bloody family lived off Teresa's earnings and they would take it hard if they found *Lyn* was having a baby for him? She let John Cullen sweat and she enjoyed the next two weeks. He pleaded with her to get rid of the baby. She let him think that he had gradually worn her down until she finally agreed.

Róisín offered to go with Lyn. She had never been out of Dublin and she was dying to see England. They made the necessary arrangements to go to Liverpool. Lyn was irritated at the idea of having to make the trip, 'because the Irish like to pretend that Irishwomen don't have abortions. The unavailability of abortion in Ireland only ever stopped Irish women who could not get the fare,' she said. John arrived over to the flat on the night before they left, saying that as he had forced her to do it, he would stay with her until she got the boat to give her moral support. There was no mention of financial support.

The two of them were settling down to a night's television when Rory Flynn came charging up to the flat. 'John, Willy says to come over to the Penthouse, quick. A guy has pulled a gun on him and wants money from him. He says he's going to move in on Róisín. Willy said to get you . . .'

When John got back, he said he had put the heavy in his place, taken the gun from him and they had ended by shaking hands. John had obviously gotten a kick out of it. Now, he felt so good that he had decided Lyn was not going to have an abortion.

'Go fuck yourself,' Lyn said, for want of anything better to say. They argued. Having flexed his muscles so successfully he did not care, now, what his family thought. He loved Lyn and wanted her to have the baby.

Lyn, who did not give two damns what his family thought, said, 'You change your mind quicker than the weather. Suppose I miss the boat and tomorrow you say, "Well Lyn, I've changed my mind, so ring up and make the arrangements again". Oh no, thanks.'

When they got to the clinic and Lyn was ready for bed, Róisín burst into tears and ran out. The next morning, after the abortion, Lyn was reading the newspaper while the other women chatted. One woman asked if anyone had enquired about the sex of their aborted baby, as she had done. Lyn let the paper drop. A boy or a girl? Dear God. Of course it had to be one or the other. It had been human. She was wide awake now. She had not thought of her condition like that; more like an unwanted growth.

Only one woman answered. 'No, I didn't ask,' she said and turned her head into the pillow, the bedclothes around her ear. A sixteen year old, the youngest in the ward, brimmed up with tears and all the chat stopped. Silence. Lyn pushed it out of her mind.

Where the hell was Róisín? She was supposed to have collected her this morning. When Róisín failed to arrive, Lyn knew that she had overslept. She got her case, left the hospital and walked. Her hotel was only a mile away and Lyn did not bother with a taxi. But she lost her bearings and wandered around in circles for about three quarters of an hour, by which time she felt dizzy and weak and had broken out in a cold sweat. When she eventually found the hotel the night porter was still on duty. He rang Róisín's room and when there was no answer he opened the door for Lyn. She had to shake Róisín a few times to wake her up.

Róisín sat up, crying, 'Oh, Lyn, Lyn,' and she could not stop. Lyn sat on the bed trying to comfort her. She herself felt nothing. They got the train to Holyhead, and Lyn pretended to read a book because every time they talked, Róisín's eyes brimmed up with tears. She was like that all the way over on the boat, too. Cullen met them at Dún Laoghaire and the atmosphere was subdued on the way back to town.

Lyn was in Róisín's flat two days later when there was a fire in the next block. Róisín ran out and arrived back with a small baby, plonked him in Lyn's arms and said, 'Mind him a minute, Lyn. I'm just going to help his Ma get her stuff out,' and she was gone.

Lyn looked down at the small bundle and she was suddenly overcome with emotion. She did not cry. She just felt as if something terrible had happened in her chest. Róisín was soon back, her face shiny with excitement, but as soon as she reached to take the baby from Lyn, her expression changed. She went pale and dropping her arms at her side, said, 'Oh Jaysus, Lyn, I'm sorry, I never thought,' and she searched Lyn's face.

Lyn held the baby out. 'It's OK, not to worry.' Lyn put her feelings to one side.

When she was living with Róisín after Cullen had been arrested, Róisín said out of the blue one night, 'Jaysus Lyn, you know what I was just thinking? Aren't you very lucky you didn't have that baby for John? Imagine the hold he'd have on you now.'

Cullen was cool with Lyn over the next two weeks. He refused to discuss the abortion, just remarked that he would never forgive Lyn for what she had done. He did not have an inkling of what it had cost her physically, and he watched her going down to work when she was not feeling up to it, to pay for the operation and the trip.

About a month later, Lyn heard that Teresa was pregnant. Teresa, a woman who literally could not tie her own shoelaces, had 'tricked' Cullen again. She had gone to the Family Planning Clinic and had her IUD removed. For weeks, it seems, Teresa was telling the other women that she just had to get pregnant.

16

A couple of months after the abortion, John and Lyn were lying on the beach when John said, 'Well, Lyn, are you going to work for me?'

'Are you jokin' or what?' she asked.

'No, I'm serious. Will you?'

'Oh, yes,' she said, 'go out to work for you! While Teresa and I are both down grafting our butts off for you, your wife is at home with her lovely house, sittin' in comfort, minding her lovely kids. Who takes my place? Who is your bit on the side? No, I won't bloody work for you.' Even as she spoke, Lyn was chilled by the menace in the quietness of John's voice.

'Lyn, you remember you once told me that if a man was to beat you very badly, then you'd have to go to work for him?'

Lyn sat up to look at him. 'John, you're not threatening me, are you?'

He turned on his back to look into her eyes, smiled that smile. 'I asked you nicely. Do I have to tell you? Yes or no?'

She recognised an offer she could not refuse. Lyn had vowed that she would never work for a pimp who had another woman working for him. It was bad enough being the girlfriend of a guy who had someone on the game for him. She cringed at the insult of having to work alongside Teresa. She had seen the way women from the same 'stable' had to compete on the English scene. One woman was scared to take a coffee break in case the other woman got more money.

Lyn went back on the game – for John Cullen. He would drop her down to work before he collected Teresa, then drop off Teresa, who still did not know about Lyn. He stayed in the pub until closing time, then picked up Lyn and brought her home. If for some reason he wanted extra cash, he would go to his mother's house after the pub to give Lyn time to get extra money.

This could not last. Lyn had had a taste of working for herself, keeping her own money. Now the pointlessness of working for 'the man' nagged at her day and night. And she nagged John Cullen. His unpredictability was such that she could get away with nagging him for weeks on end and she moaned at him every night she had to work. Tension built up to the pitch where Lyn was expecting an explosion of Cullen's rage, but instead he told her to stop work. In spite of having lost her children, she still drew £55 Unmarried Mother's Allowance as well as having a government subsidised flat. So she could manage without working. She had never learned to spend money on herself. She did not need anything beyond cigarettes and food, in that order, and clothes, which she bought cheap from shoplifters.

The next few months passed peacefully enough. Teresa had her baby, a little girl whom she christened Sally. Now that Lyn could tell herself that John did not want her for her earnings, she felt herself to be more in love with him and became more and more jealous. She resented his wife, his kids, Teresa, Teresa's mother, her kids, his mother, his brothers, all his in-laws. She could not control her possessiveness and she hated everybody else in Cullen's life, anyone who took his time.

One night, John was late. Lyn was busy slamming cupboard doors while waiting for an explanation. He said, 'I was with Teresa. Her mother . . .'

Lyn screamed at him, 'I don't give a damn about Teresa or her mother. I hope her mother drops dead.'

'Teresa's mother died tonight. She got pneumonia.'

Lyn felt weak. Where was all the jealousy leading? And John understood this jealousy. How else could you tell if a woman cared? He was, himself, pathologically jealous. She was not even permitted to go to a pub without him. When he was not there, she stayed at home.

A week later, Teresa's child Paul was taken to hospital suffering from malnutrition. John took Lyn with him to the hospital when he went to see the child. When she walked into the ward, her stomach lurched. The child was the image of John.

'Take him home and feed him up,' John pleaded. 'You know how . . .' Lyn cut him short. No way. Paul was a lovely child, but he was Teresa's. How could John expect her to care for something that he and Teresa had produced when he had not let her keep their baby?

'Alright, don't go on about it. Just shut fuckin' up.'

Paul was taken from Teresa and put into care. Not long after, the new baby, Sally, was taken into hospital with pneumonia. Teresa was relieved; with her mother gone she could not cope at all. Teresa needed someone to take her into care to teach her how to look after herself, but no one thought of that. Instead, she was declared an unfit mother. Still, Lyn, like Teresa, idolised Cullen and Lyn told herself that John could not be blamed for Teresa's state. He was not mean with money, but nothing, not even Cullen, could change Teresa. She was incapable of learning from anyone she knew.

John's relatives came from England for the festive season. 'I'll have to take them out, but I'll be around every night,' he said.

As it worked out, he spent a lot of the days with them, too, and Lyn felt that she was being fitted in for a few minutes here and there.

Lyn had been squatting in her flat, and now she was evicted. She stayed with Róisín for six weeks and on New Year's Day the Corporation gave her the keys to a flat in Coolock. She was overjoyed with the new place. It meant that she was living nearer to John Cullen, but when she told him he was furious. Why hadn't she waited until he had taken her to the Corporation for a flat? Why had she let Willy drive her? He left in a huff, but called back the next day and drove her to Coolock to see that the new flat was OK. It was Sunday, and they usually spent that evening together, but John announced that he was off to his mother's house and then he was taking his wife out. Lyn was livid and jumped out of the car outside Róisín's flat.

'Fuck you and your lovely wife,' she said, slammed the door and stamped upstairs.

Lyn could not take anymore. She was definitely finished with John Cullen. 'That's it, Róisín,' she said. 'He can stay with his lovely wife. I've had it.' John would not hear of Lyn going to a pub on her own but now she was a free agent. Róisín and she decided they would go and celebrate in the Penthouse.

They got there around 9.00 p.m. and stayed until closing time. Then they met Willy outside and went for take-away curries. When they got back to the flat, Lyn made tea while Róisín dished up the curry. Anthony, Willy's brother, arrived with Liam Ryan. They were all sitting at the kitchen table when the doorbell rang. Róisín looked out the window to see whose car was there.

'It's John,' she said, smiling.

Willy let John in. Lyn turned round at the table to watch him walking up the hall. Had he come crawling back? Well, well.

She smiled, 'Hello, stranger.'

He did not answer. Liam said, 'Hello, John.'

Lyn saw the flash of a blade and as John aimed the knife at her ribs, she backed away and fell off her chair. He jumped on top of her, stabbed her, pinning her to the floor with the knife through her ear-lobe. She tried to kick him away, but he threw her legs over his shoulders and lunged the knife at her again. Liam grabbed him from the back.

'John, for fuck's sake, you will kill her,' he said.

John spun from Lyn and she saw him slashing Liam all round his neck. Róisín ran out of the flat and Willy grabbed Lyn by the arm and dragged her up the stairs to the top balcony. Frantically, she tried to get help from the flats, but as soon as people saw the blood they slammed their doors. She looked over the balcony, saw John driving off and ran back downstairs. Liam was lying in a pool of blood and there was thick matter oozing from the back of his head.

Lyn thought he was dead. 'Liam, Oh Jesus, Liam, say something!' she shouted. He flickered his eyelids, his voice barely audible, 'I'm dying, Lyn. Make sure my wife is OK. Tell her how it happened.'

Lyn was crying. Liam asked her for a cigarette and she

crawled around the floor until she found a packet and a lighter. She lit a cigarette and put it in his mouth.

Someone grabbed her arm. 'You know you don't give anyone in his condition a cigarette.' It was the police with the ambulance driver.

Róisín went in the ambulance with Liam. Willy, Anthony and Lyn were taken to Ballymun Garda Station. Willy made his statement, then Anthony, before Lyn was called. They said the reason that she had been held so long was because it was touch-and-go with Liam. There was still a danger that he could die. They knew John Cullen had done it. Lyn denied it. They kept saying that a complete stranger had not walked into the flat and stabbed people. In the end, she said, 'I know who it is, but I will not name him.' After five hours they let her go.

Lyn knew she had not heard the last of John Cullen. Willy was waiting outside with Róisín to drive them home. 'John will be back,' Lyn said. 'He'll be back.'

'Don't be stupid,' Willy said. 'John fuckin' knows that the cops are lookin' for him for Liam.' When they arrived at the flat a uniformed policeman was posted outside. Róisín and Willy went in first because Lyn was so scared. The policeman left and Willy got impatient. 'Come on, Lyn, I already told you. He won't be back.' Lyn knew that he would.

They surveyed the wreckage. How had John managed to do so much damage so fast? The radio was smashed, Róisín's ornaments broken; there were bloody palm prints smeared where Liam had tried to pull himself up. In the kitchen, the table had been upended; curry, tea, sugar and smashed dishes congealed with the contents of a chip pan in the middle of the floor. John had ripped the cooker from its socket. The bathroom looked as if it had been washed with blood. None of them had the heart to move a thing, they were so weary.

In the police station Lyn had been numb, but now she began to feel her injuries and realised that her back was killing her. She had run like hell with Willy, but now she could hardly move.

'Not surprising,' Willy said. 'He smashed that chair over your back.' She did not remember it. Her ear was too painful to touch. When she realised that he had pinned her to the floor through her ear, she started to tremble.

Róisín and Willy got into bed and Lyn sat on the edge of the bed talking to them. Eventually, Willy said he was tired.

'For Jaysus sake, get to bed, Lyn.'

'Willy, I'm scared. I know he'll be back.'

Wearily, Willy dragged himself out of the bed. 'OK, Lyn, if it means gettin' some sleep, I'll take the kitchen door off the hinges and wedge it behind the front door. Anything for a quiet life.'

Lyn still did not feel any safer, but she knew they were fed up with listening to her. She got some sheets from the airing cupboard and made a bed up on the settee. She took three Valium, lay down, and went over the events of the night in her mind. Why had John come into Róisín's flat like a lunatic? Lyn admitted to herself that she had nagged him about taking his wife out, but that was pretty mild compared to some of the nagging sessions she had put him through. Still, she had forgotten that something which anyone else could shrug off could be an unpardonable insult to John. He brooded and brooded over the tiniest thing until, in his mind, it had to be avenged. But what had he avenged this time? Lyn wondered.

Lyn and Liam Ryan had been friendly for years and John knew that, so it could not be jealousy on his part. Could it be because she had gone to a pub without him? And then she remembered John telling her that he had gone with Teresa to visit Róisín some years back and Liam had been in the flat. When they left, Liam had called Teresa back and told her never to bring John Cullen to the flat again. Funny how things slipped one's mind. That was it, Lyn decided.

Bang! Bang! Bang! She knew it. Willy ran in zipping up his trousers, Róisín close on his heels. 'It's him,' he said. Róisín was shaking.

'I told you, Willy,' Lyn said quietly.

Willy hesitated for a split second, then said, 'Róisín, hold this tight. Don't, for fuck's sake, let go of it.' Lyn could not believe it. Willy had dragged the sheet off her bed and was lowering himself over the balcony on it while Róisín held onto the other end with all her strength. He disappeared. Lyn stared at Róisín. He was Róisín's pimp and he had risked going over a fifth storey balcony rather than stay and protect her against John Cullen.

The banging grew louder. The sound echoed through the flat. Lyn could not stand it. She passed Róisín as she stumbled to the door.

'Lyn, don't open it.'

'I have to, Róisín. The noise is going through me.'

'John,' Lyn said, 'push the letter box open.'

'Lyn, open that door, now.' His voice was controlled, soft. She knew that tone of old; it meant that he was ready to go over the edge.

'I'm too scared, John. Push the letter box.'

He did. His eyes were cold, murderous.

'Lyn, open the door. Look, you have to face me sometime. You can't hide,' he said softly, logically.

Lyn stalled for time. 'John, it's best if you call back later Liam nearly died and the cops are looking for you.' They stared, eye to eye, through the letter box.

'John, swear on your Ma's life you won't hurt me if I open the door.' He continued to watch her through the letter box. He was considering.

Eventually he said, 'I swear on me Ma's life I won't hurt you.'

'John, I'm scared,' Lyn's voice trembled.

'Lyn, this is your last chance. Open the door now.' The tone was absolute.

'John, swear on the kids' lives.' Lyn hoped this was too close for comfort; he would not swear on his kids' lives and go back on it. Silence. More silence. Then he spoke.

'I swear on the kids' lives I won't hurt you.'

Lyn lifted the kitchen door, propped it against the wall. She fumbled with the lock and he put his weight against the door. Run, Lyn, she told herself. But she was paralysed.

'Where's Willy?' he asked, one hand in his pocket.

'He's still in the cop shop,' Lyn answered.

'Then what's his fuckin' car doin' outside?'

Lyn could not answer him, her mouth was dry.

He went into each room, out onto the balcony, looked over the side, then back into the box room. He was about to close the door when he caught sight of Róisín, frozen. He gave her a look and then dismissed her. She was no threat.

'Get in here. I want to talk to you,' he called to Lyn. Lyn was not sure where 'in here' was, but she was not going into the kitchen, not in with all the knives. Róisín ran past her and out the front door. Lyn stumbled along the hall, towards the bedroom, and sank down onto the bed.

He was framed in the doorway and had that look in his eyes. As he crossed the room to her, Lyn's mind left her body lying there on the bed. She was completely detached as she noticed that one of his arms hung at a funny angle to his body.

Hypnotized, Lyn watched as he put his left leg up on the bed on her right-hand side. She lowered herself back in slow motion. He brought his right leg up and straddled her, put his right hand into his left inside pocket and withdrew a meat cleaver. Lyn jerked her legs up behind his back, but his weight pinned her down. He raised the cleaver over head, she whipped her hands up and grabbed hold of the flat side of the blade. She was screaming inside her head, but not a sound came from her. She felt her face twist over to one side as it had done before. Was it really a year ago?

'Take your hands off the knife,' he said quietly.

She pleaded with her eyes, the words still would not come.

'I only have to twist the blade and you won't have any fingers left; I said let go,' he said quietly.

She found her voice at last and began to beg for her life.

'John, please, I love you, I'm crazy about you. Please don't hurt me. Please, John, I'm begging you, don't use the cleaver. John, I fuckin' love you, I'm crazy about, please, Oh God please, don't.' He held the meat cleaver absolutely still, without even a blink. With his left hand he reached into his right-hand inside-pocket and drew out a long bladed butcher's knife and raised it in the air. So this was how Peter Sutcliffe's victims felt. She fell off the bed, curled up into a ball and passed out.

John stood motionless, staring out of the window. His back was impassive. Stella, Róisín's neighbour, was standing in the doorway surveying the scene.

'John, love, are you alright?'

He turned to face her, not a trace of colour in his face.

'I'm OK, Stella.'

Lyn sprang to life. She jumped up, picked up the cleaver and the knife from the floor, ran out down the hall and out the door.

She threw the weapons over the balcony and made a run for Stella's flat. Cullen was beside her like lightning; he grabbed hold of her dressing gown.

'Get back in the flat.'

Lyn tried vainly to wrench free. Stella came to the rescue.

'Lyn, John isn't going to harm you. He's alright now, aren't you, John?'

Lyn would not let go of the door jamb. Cullen pulled a bunch of Lyn's hair and wound it around his fist and dragged her towards the open door. Lyn looked at Stella and mouthed, 'Don't leave me.'

'Tell you what, John. Lyn, why don't we all go into the flat and I'll make a nice cup of tea? The neighbours are all out to see what's going on.'

John let go of Lyn's hair. The colour was starting to flood back to his face. That look had gone. Lyn felt safer but she shook all over. He walked her down the hall to the sitting room. He lay down on the settee and closed his eyes and told Lyn to sit down beside him, but 'don't say a fuckin' word'.

Stella came in to say that she was unable to make the tea in Róisín's kitchen because of the mess; she would make it in her own flat and bring it in to them. Lyn knew that Stella was going to tell Róisín and Willy the danger was over.

All the time Stella was gone, John was silent. He just gripped Lyn's hand tightly. Lyn knew he was fighting the demons inside his head, the way she had seen him do so often. When he came to terms with his mind it would be time to talk, so in silence, she waited with him.

Stella bustled in. 'There John, love. Lyn, is it strong enough? I have to get my lot off for work. Will you two be OK now? No more fighting? See you later . . .'

John let her get her cigarettes from the bedroom. When she got back he was sitting up drinking his tea. She knelt down beside him, their eyes locked. Lyn was still afraid. He pulled her towards him, pushed her head down onto his chest and cradled her. They stayed like that for what seemed an eternity to Lyn, locked in their separate thoughts, no words spoken. She did not have a clue what John was thinking. Relieved, she felt a surge of forgiveness for him. But at the same time, she knew that theirs was a disastrous relationship. There was too much insane jealousy. And suddenly, she realised what it was; they were obsessed with each other. She realised that, in a way, they were two of a kind. Lyn had never been jealous of a man in her life, but now she understood her jealousy with John. She had taken a perverse pride in the fact that no man could get inside her mind. Her body was present, her mind always cut off. This, she realised, was the fascination that John held for her. She could not get inside his mind either. The difference between them was that John's mind was dark and dangerous, vicious, while hers was cloudy, grey, cynical.

Finally, John spoke. 'I'm going round to me Ma's to see if the cops have been lookin' for me about Ryan. That's the reason I came here so early, d'you know what I mean? I mean if Liam was dead I would have finished what I started before they lifted me.'

'What do you mean, John, love?'

'Forget it. We'll talk about it later,' and he ordered her to be ready with all her stuff packed to move into the flat in Coolock. He would be back later. She was not to stay in the flat with Róisín and Willy.

Willy arrived back immediately after John was gone. Willy had got into the flat underneath from the balcony below. When he heard Lyn's screams, he knew John was there and had taken the chance to run up the stairs to Stella's flat where he sat drinking tea till it was all over. Lyn could not be bothered to talk to him. The gutless wonder, she muttered to herself and to him she said, 'Don't worry, I'm leaving later.' Her sarcasm was wasted on Willy.

Lyn packed and cleaned up Róisín's flat. It was hard work; her back was giving her hell. She dreaded moving to Coolock where she would be completely alone with John. No Róisín to call on, no Stella to protect her. She had been so happy when she finally got the flat from the Corporation. Once again, her dream of a home had gone sour. Lyn knew that her relationship with John was doomed.

17

It was moving day and the pain in Lyn's back was almost unbearable. She had not slept since Saturday after the ordeal of the stabbing, five hours of sitting in the police station, waiting to hear if Liam was dead, plus the dawn raid from John Cullen, followed by cleaning up Róisín's flat. Now Lyn packed, moved, unpacked, hung curtains in the new flat, laid carpets, shopped for food. And when all that was accomplished, at 11.00 p.m. John arrived from the pub as though he had spent a pleasant, but tiring weekend. 'Hello, love, what's to eat?'

Lyn was on the point of asking him if he had had a good day at the office, but deciding against irony, she said, 'You look jaded, love,' before she set about making him comfortable. The flat seemed too quiet after the endless din in Ballymun, and Lyn felt isolated with just the two of them as they spent the night in the usual way, him sprawled out on the settee, her waiting upon his needs. And then she sat hunched, running her fingers through his toes.

There had to be silence while John read the paper. It was only when he was finished that Lyn was permitted to speak, and he decided on the topic of conversation. Some subjects were taboo. Tonight, he was tired, he'd had a hard day. He dismissed Lyn's services earlier than usual to go home to sleep. After John left, Lyn lay staring at the ceiling. She hated the flat, and felt utterly alone there. 'I should have stuck it out in Ballymun,' she told herself. 'At least I had someone to talk to there. I'd only to bang on the ceiling with the sweepin' brush and Róisín would come down and we could lift our spirits slaggin' men, especially married men. And their lovely wives.'

Lyn's solidarity with Róisín was the most important thing in her life at this stage. She could not think of another positive thing, and realised that she should never have moved away from Róisín. They were in the same situation, both bound to men who had 'lovely wives', 'lovely children', 'lovely homes', 'lovely incomes' from their 'lovely husbands.' The backbiting Lyn and Róisín did was a safety valve, and when they reached the stage where they imagined lovely homes wallpapered in gold, and lovely wives bedecked in diamonds and furs, with lovely children who attended private schools, they were in gales of laughter.

Lyn knew that, without Róisín, the laughing days were over and she was facing unrelieved reality. She would have to be ingratiating to John until whatever it was that had freaked him out was out of his system. Lyn hated grovelling, but from experience, she had learned that it did wonders for the male ego. She planned to carry on grovelling until she felt on safe ground.

Tuesday, Wednesday and Thursday brought the same old routines: clean the flat, shop for John's dinner, read for a couple of hours, work on the Canal for a few hours and then home to prepare a meal for John who arrived at 9.30 p.m., after which he ate, and he read the newspapers while Lyn soothed him through his toes. There was a bit of talk before John went home to his wife, and Lyn got into her lonely bed, took sleeping pills, did a crossword, read and fell asleep.

On Friday, Lyn opened the curtains to discover that she was snowed in. The contents of the 'fridge consisted of one bottle of milk, a bit of butter, a small piece of cheese. She made a cup of coffee, washed and got back into bed to keep warm. There was no coal. After the central heating in Ballymun, the flat was freezing, and there was nothing for it but to wait for 'superman' to come ploughing through the snow. Night fell. No superman, and every time Lyn looked out of the window, the snow was deeper. She was cranky, willing to bet John had made it up to Teresa to collect his money so his lady wife would have plenty of coal to keep her home fires burning. 'I hate pimps,' Lyn said out loud. Her reverie was interrupted by a knock on the door. It was a pal of John's.

'Oh, hello, Patsy,' Lyn said.

'I thought I should come and let you know John is locked up in Mountjoy. He was arrested this morning, something about a stabbing.' Not another one. Lyn sank onto a chair and thought for a moment.

'But how could that be, Patsy? It's just not possible. He didn't leave me 'til 2.00 a.m. What time was he lifted? Who could he have stabbed from here to Kilbarrack?'

Patsy answered, 'I don't know, Lyn. We got a call from John's wife to say he was arrested for stabbing someone called Ryan. She wasn't too clear on it, so I came to see her, but I thought John would want me to let you know. There's bail fixed on him. We'll try for it on Monday.'

When Patsy left, Lyn thought about what he had told her. Why had John only been arrested now? If Liam had wanted him charged, it would have been done the next day. Perhaps the police were pushing, pressing charges? In that case, Lyn thought, there was no need to worry. Liam would not go ahead with it; he would not be pushed into court to charge John. She wanted to ring Róisín; she'd know what was happening. Lyn put on her slippers, a pair of socks, jeans, fur jacket and went out to the call box up the road. It was freezing and the snow was ankle deep. Lyn had never owned a pair of boots, hated boots. She dialed Stella's number.

'Hi, Stella, it's Lyn. Could I speak to Róisín, please?'

Lyn could hear her footsteps as she ran down to knock on Róisín's flat, footsteps coming back. Thank God Róisín wasn't out.

'Lyn? Willy here. Róisín is in the bath. Something wrong?'

'Hello, Willy. Patsy just called and said John was up in the 'Joy over stabbing Liam. Did you hear anything?'

'Yes,' said Willy. 'Liam signed himself out of hospital and marched into Ballymun station and demanded to know why John hadn't been charged.'

'So they charged him, eh? When is he up in court again? Is there bail on him?'

'Yes, Patsy said they were going over to the court on Monday to try for it.' Willy said.

'Do you realise what John will do if Liam persists in this?'

'Don't worry about that, Lyn. Liam won't go to court,' Willy said. 'Never.'

'Willy, what's it like over there in Ballymun? I'm snowed in here. It's freezing and I've no coal for the fire, the shop across the road from me is closed and I've no food. I haven't even any milk for the coffee. Do you think the snow will last for long?' Lyn asked.

'You've no food at all? Why don't you come over here and stay with Róisín? I can collect you. It may take me a while to get there, the roads are very bad. It took me an hour to get across town to Ballymun this morning,' he said, 'but at least you'll be warm here.'

Lyn closed her eyes. She could feel the heat.

'No, I can't, Willy. If John found out he would kill me.'

'How the hell can John find out if he's in the 'Joy?'

Lyn replied, 'Willy, you know perfectly well that Mountjoy has a telecommunications system second to none. He would know I had done it before I did it. Thanks for offering anyway.'

Lyn made her way back through the snow. She could have taken the chance and gone to Róisín, but she knew she was in enough trouble over John being in the 'Joy. She thought longingly of the warmth seeping up through the floors in Ballymun, the lashings of hot water, the food, and above all, the company of Róisín. She got back into bed to keep warm. So Liam had got John nicked. Well, who could blame him? He had come up with Anthony to visit his brother and have a cup of tea after the pub, and had ended up fighting for his life. But did Liam know what he had started? They would all pay dearly, or John Cullen was not John Cullen.

Lyn had, tentatively, tried to tell John that she had made a statement on the night of the stabbing, but that she would not name the man who had done it.

'What the fuck did you go and do that for?' John fumed at her.

'Does it matter? You know Liam won't charge you.' She tried to make him understand that when she made the statement, she

173

thought Liam was dying. 'If Liam died, how could he get you nicked?' Lyn asked, and thought that John seemed convinced because he had calmed down. Still, he said, 'Shut fuckin' up about it. So I won't be charged, it's not the point, d'you know what I mean like? Even if it had ended up murder, you should know to say fuck all to the cops.'

'Sorry, John . . .'

Now the fat was in the fire. God, what would he do when he got out. She would be classed like Dolores, public enemy number one. He might even kill her for it. Lyn imagined John lying there in his cell, thinking: 'She's a danger to me. I'll have to get rid of her.' What could she do? She hit on the idea of writing him a long, loving letter, contrite over any part she had had in what happened. She wrote that she was heartbroken at the thought of him locked up, and realised how stupid she had been, how she never dreamed when she made the statement that Liam would get him nicked.

Lyn knew that the letter would not reach Mountjoy until John was out on bail, and it would be sent back to her, but she was sending it in case he did not get the bail. Then he would have the letter, compliments of Mountjoy. When she came back from the postbox, she got back into bed and figured that the trip out in the ice would be worth it if the letter got her a reprieve.

The minute she opened her eyes on Monday morning, Lyn had all her usual stress symptoms; sweating, fast heartbeat, knot in her stomach and the pain in her jaws made her eyes water. She jumped at any small noise. Would he get the bail? 'Please God,' she prayed, 'don't let him get the bail and I'll try to lead a good life from now on.' All morning, she waited. Then it was afternoon and no sign of him. Perhaps his bail was refused. It was not that she did not love him, but she was sure that he would walk in with a knife. 5.00 p.m. He definitely was not out on bail or he would be there. She could not stand this any longer and went out to phone Mountjoy.

'Hello? Could you tell me have you got a John Cullen there please? I'm his wife. He hasn't been home in three days. I've rung all the hospitals . . . Yes, I'll hold on.'

Lyn's heart was beating so fast she thought the man outside the kiosk could hear it. Seconds ticked away.

'Hello Mrs Cullen? No, he's not here. I've checked the list. He was here, but he went up to court this morning, and he hasn't come back.'

Sweet Jesus, Lyn thought, why did you do this to me? She bent her head against the wind and made for the flat. If he got the bail this morning, was he waiting till it got dark to come and kill her? Dare she go home? But where could she run to?

She turned the corner and John's car was parked outside the flat. Lyn faltered. 'Don't,' she told herself. 'He may be watching you from the window. Run to him. You're so happy he's home.'

She ran to the front door and put the key in the lock, took a deep breath, braced herself and pushed the door open. He was lying on the bed, smiling. 'Hello Lyn, baby. I've missed you.'

Relief flooded through her. He reached out his arms to her.

'Oh, John, I've missed you, too,' Lyn said.

She hugged and kissed him.

'When I rang the 'joy just now and they said you were out I was so happy. I wrote a letter to you in case you didn't get the bail. They'll probably send it back to me. John, I'm sorry about the statement I made to the cops.'

'Shh, don't worry about it, love. Liam will never reach the court.'

He said he wanted to kill her for going out without him and when he saw Liam Ryan sitting at the table, he was further incensed. 'Don't you know I hate that bastard?' John asked Lyn. He had aimed for Lyn's heart with the knife, John reminded her, but she had fallen off the chair. He had tried to plunge the knife into her back, but because she was kicking him, he could not get at her properly. Liam jumped on his back and pulled him off. That angered John. Anthony grabbed the knife and pulled Liam into the bathroom. John had taken two knives and gone looking for Lyn. When he failed to find her on the stairs he went back to the flat and Anthony was in the hall, trying to drag Liam out. John attacked Liam with the two knives.

'Why did you stop?' Lyn asked.

'I thought Liam was dead,' John said. And he had gone home.

John could not sleep. He kept brooding over how Lyn had

175

made a fool of him by getting away when he was trying to kill her. He figured Liam was dead and the Murder Squad would be up on a dawn raid. He got up, washed, shaved, selected the sharpest implements he could find and went back to Ballymun to finish Lyn off. If he was doing life for one murder, he reasoned, he might as well go up for as many as he could fit in. He had decided that if Willy was there he would kill him, too. He was furious when Lyn would not open the door. He intended giving Lyn five minutes, and if she did not open it, he was going to get a gun and blast his way in. But then, when he took the butcher's knife out of his pocket, Lyn passed out. John said that her face was all twisted and he could not stab her while she was unconscious.

He said, 'You know, Lyn, you wouldn't have recognised yourself, d'you know what I mean, like? Your face was that distorted.' He kissed her tenderly, 'You won't ever have to be scared of me again. You can ask any question, talk about anything, and we'll work it out together. Right?'

He was tired and went home early. Lyn was happy that things were shaping up for them. She had only nagged him because she was insecure. Now she felt safe. She believed all the promises. When they kissed goodnight, he paused and looked over his shoulder. His eyes went cloudy. 'Of course Lyn, if Liam does persist in getting me nicked I would probably get seven to ten years for attempted murder.'

'John, love, don't be so silly,' Lyn's heart thumped. 'You know he won't do it.'

'I don't know about that. Lyn, don't get me wrong. I'm not worried about doing time, d'you know what I mean? It just means I will have to get Dolores. I keep putting it off, and putting it off, but if I know I'm going in I will have to get rid of her.' He stared out into the yard.

'Come on, love, it's not going to happen,' Lyn said. 'John, I'm freezing with the door open. You go home now, love, and have a good sleep and you'll feel better. I'll see you tomorrow.'

Lyn made a cup of coffee and got into bed. She took her sleeping tablets and lay waiting for them to take effect. Where was all this going to end? All her fears had been dispelled and she had felt at peace. Now, she was in knots again. With his parting words, John had shattered everything. Was this to be the pattern of her life, always, Lyn asked herself: peace at three o'clock and devastation an hour later?

The next five days passed without incident, except for what happened on Sunday. During those five days, Lyn read Linda Lovelace's autobiography, *Ordeal*. When John Cullen relaxed he was easy company. Relaxed, he read the newspapers while Lyn read a book. *Ordeal* got to Lyn, she wanted to cry when she read some of the things Linda was forced to endure. Lyn identified with her. It could have happened to her, she felt, and she got so upset reading *Ordeal* that she could not keep the book to herself. She kept interrupting John: 'John, listen to this.' John would look up from his paper, listen to what Lyn read out, sympathise and share Lyn's revulsion at the things Linda had suffered as a sex slave. When John went home at night, Lyn thought of him fondly. After all, compared to the men in Linda Lovelace's life, John was not the worst by a long shot.

With things going well between them, John and Lyn went out for a drink. John Cullen is an epileptic who has to take six tablets a day. He was not supposed to drink alcohol. He could never handle drink, getting drunk after three pints. Lyn did not realise the effect that alcohol could have on an epileptic. He held her hand that night and told her how much he loved her.

Lyn was not the world's greatest drinker either, and anyway, *Ordeal* was on her mind. She started to cry. 'John,' she said, 'I don't understand how any man could put a woman through all that. She was completely degraded.' John reached over her, opened her handbag and took out some tissues and proceeded to wipe the tears from her eyes.

'There, love, don't cry. You have someone who loves you. She didn't. There's the difference. You know what I mean? That's all that matters.' People in the pub stared at them.

Lyn was Linda Lovelace then. And she felt that any of the women she knew on the game were like Linda. Where could a woman run to, she asked herself. Who would help a prostitute? Who would hold out a hand in friendship, Lyn, in her cups, asked herself. Except that Lyn forgot there had been those who had tried, hard, to help her. None of those friends came to Lyn's mind as she wallowed in the awful story of *Ordeal* and gulped some more vodka. An alcoholic had AA, Lyn told herself; there was help for a drug addict in therapy centres. But who would help a prostitute? If someone had asked, 'What about the supervisor at Dolores' hospital, or the people at Gaj's restaurant?', Lyn's self-pity might have turned to angry denial. But nobody asked, and Lyn just got sadder, clinging pathetically to John Cullen's hand.

When they got back to the flat, they got into bed to keep warm, whereas in Ballymun they would have watched TV, played a few records, cooked some food. Here, it was too cold. Lyn fell into a drunken stupor. She was dreaming that she was in a shower and she was being strangled. She told herself to wake up, the way people do in a nightmare.

She opened her eyes. John was kneeling over her, urinating in her face, smiling. Her hair was drenched. She jerked her head to one side. 'You dirty swine, get fuckin' off me,' Lyn screamed at him. He was still urinating over the bed. He stopped smiling, grabbed her by her hair and rammed his penis into her mouth. She felt the urine trickle over her tongue and she closed the muscles in her throat, tried to lie absolutely still. If she moved, she would be forced to swallow. She fought to lie still, just lie there. It seemed to go on forever. She could feel urine trickling out of the corners of her mouth, into her ears, saturating her hair. At last he stopped, but continued to kneel over Lyn, grinning. She stared back at him. 'Now, will you get off me, you perverted bastard?'

She could hear the humiliation in her own voice. 'Don't let the bastard see you cry,' she told herself. She did not cry. He got off her and wiped himself on her remaining dry pillowcase.

Lyn made for the bathroom, banging the door behind her. She washed and washed and washed, her neck, her face, her shoulders, her hair. Then she cried. Silently. She would not give him the satisfaction of hearing her. She picked up a bottle of Dettol and smothered herself in it. She gargled with the Dettol, stormed back into the bedroom, and at sight of John Cullen, threw the bottle right across the room. It hit him.

'There, you bastard, you need it more than I do.'

He was up in a flash. He threw her face down on the bed and

before she knew what was happening, he was grabbing her tights and bra off the chair, and had her arms tied to either side of the bed.

'John, I'll kill you, you bastard. You touch me and I swear I will fuckin' kill you!' She was screaming as he banged drawers open and shut. 'I fuckin' hate you,' Lyn yelled.

He gagged her with a scarf. She was still yelling, but all he could hear now was muffled sound. She felt him tying her legs to the end of the bed. He had her spread-eagled, tied to the four ends of the bed. Whish! She tried to turn around but could only see the wall by her side. Oh God, the pain. He was lashing her buttocks and thighs with his leather belt. Lyn screamed louder, louder, but no one could hear her with the gag. Cullen was loving it. As long as she screamed, he thought he was winning. Lyn used all her willpower to stop screaming. No noise came from behind the gag, but it carried on in her head.

She was still squirming, but could not escape the belt. He stopped. Her flesh was raw. He did not speak, came and stood at the top of the bed and looked into her eyes. He looked at her body to assess his handiwork, looked back into Lyn's eyes, steadily. She would not cry. His eyes slanted. She knew what was flashing through his crazy mind. He thought there was still fight in her. He knelt on the bed and untied the scarf from her mouth. She could see his limp penis coming towards her face. He yanked her head back by the hair, looked into her eyes and smiled. He pushed the thing against Lyn's mouth. 'Suck it.'

Lyn would not move her lips. She just lay there. He leaned over the side of the bed, retrieved his belt and lashed her again. 'I said fuckin' suck it.'

Lyn could not. She just could not. She started to cry, debased. It did not matter if he knew he had won. She sobbed, tears ran down her face. He grabbed her hair tighter. Her whole body shook with uncontrollable sobbing.

'Look at me, Lyn.'

Lyn closed her eyes. She could not bear him to see the humiliation in her face. He jerked at her hair again. 'I said look at me, Lyn.'

Lyn opened her eyes, wishing she could die. Through her tears she saw something she would never have believed possible.

It was like a shadow passing across his eyes, recognition that he had won. He was satisfied.

Neither of them spoke for a long time. She turned her head away from him, stared at the wall and lay exposed in all her misery. She did not care. She heard him moving around the room. She did not have the heart to turn and see what he was up to. It did not matter. And then, Lyn felt his cold hands on her red, raw skin. He was rubbing lotion into her wounds. She did not stir. He lay down beside her, turned her head to face him, kissed her eyelids and said, 'I'm sorry.'

She felt so empty, 'Why, John, why?' and the tears started again.

'Lyn, love, don't cry. You know I love you.'

Cry? Lyn could not stop. She heard his voice droning on and on, explaining, but it just did not matter any more.

'Lyn, you know when you were reading out bits of that what's-her-name's book? You know that *Ordeal* thing? Well, I wasn't paying much notice to you, but I started thinking of it later, d'you know what I mean like, and I got a hard on. I kept thinking of it, and I wanted to do everything I could to you. It's not my fault, Lyn, it's yours. You always make me feel that you're looking down your nose at me, that you're too good for me. I can understand why men beat you up. It's the way you look at them. D'you know what I mean like? I don't blame them, you push them into it. When I look at you, I never know what's going on in your mind. Well, I want to own you, to make dirt of you, to do things to you that no one else has ever done. Can you understand all I'm saying to you, Lyn? What do you mean, no? Look, you're always reading those fuckin' books. You shut me out. I don't like that. I want to get into your mind. I want to do like the fellows in that book. I want to do all that can be done to bring you down. Are you listening to me, Lyn, d'you know what I mean?'

Lyn did not answer.

'Look, Lyn, I wasn't going to whip you. I just wanted to make dirt of you. I just got mad when you came in and fucked the bottle of Dettol at me. I wanted to kill you. You know what I'm like, Lyn? You were dicing with death. I only whipped you because I love you. I didn't want to harm you.'

180

Nothing about John Cullen could shock Lyn now. She gritted her teeth and said, 'John, if you want to debase a woman, if you want to whip a woman, if you feel you have to piss on a woman, will you just go home to your lovely wife, or go to Teresa and do it to them? Just leave me alone.'

'Lyn, d'you know what I mean? It's pointless talking to you.'

He was exasperated. 'Look, I'll tell you once and for all, it's you I love, so it's obvious it's you I want to do things to. I don't love them, so how could I do it to them? You're supposed to be the one with the brains, don't you see . . .'

Lyn did not answer.

'Fuck you, Lyn, you're just being bloody awkward. I'm going home.' Leaving, he slammed the door after himself.

18

'Lyn,' said Willy, 'would you ever stop parading up and down? This room is like a matchbox. Sit down, you're making me dizzy.' He and Róisín had come to talk about Liam's court case against Cullen. Lyn was not listening; she was preoccupied with her backside. Róisín was watching Lyn closely and followed her into the kitchen.

'Lyn, what's the matter?' Silently, Lyn lifted her skirt to waist level and turned around. Róisín gasped, 'Oh my God, Lyn, did that headcase do that?' Lyn nodded, blushing with humiliation. Róisín turned Lyn this way and that, all the time exclaiming, 'Oh Jaysus. Oh Lyn. Lyn, are you not terrified living here on your own with him?' Lyn nodded.

'Willy,' Róisín called, 'come and look what that mad bastard did to Lyn.'

'No, Róisín,' Lyn said, pulling her skirt down in a hurry. Róisín described the state of Lyn's buttocks and thighs and Willy said the appropriate things. It did not mean anything to Lyn. All the noises of sympathy proved was that Willy was not a brutal pimp, but Lyn thought him a sly snake in the grass. A slither. She would rather not have given him the satisfaction of knowing what had happened.

Róisín and Willy set about trying to convince Lyn to leave John, pointing out that the relationship was bound to get worse and he might even kill her.

'Of course, I'm off,' Lyn said. 'John Cullen will not know when or where I am going. The only sure thing is that I'll be leggin' it.' The other positive conclusion Lyn had reached was that she no longer loved John, was free of her obsession with him. She had wanted to get inside his mind and had partly succeeded, but it had disgusted her. She wanted out.

The next few weeks saw a rapid change in their relationship. Lyn made the most of every weal and welt and drop of blood on her backside. Sorry John, can't do the shopping. Sorry, can't cook. No, sorry, I can't run my fingers through your toes. Why? Because I cannot sit down. It was true because it was three weeks before she could sit. She had to sleep on her stomach and, through it all, she despised him. Her hate fed her courage. Whenever he looked for sex, Lyn snapped, 'Don't touch me.'

Through her years with Craig Nelson, Lyn had got used to nagging. John Cullen never nagged. He brooded. Discussions other than trivia were verboten, the promises he had made on his release from Mountjoy forgotten. He made no reference to the whipping or her debasement. She told him that she would never drink with him again, and that if he wanted to go to a pub, it would have to be with 'your lovely wife, or some of your lovely friends'. Mostly, she was quiet. It was months before John asked Lyn to go out again. Although, in the meantime, if he noticed that she had changed, he made no reference to it.

Whatever it was that had attracted John to Lyn in the beginning, did not matter any longer. He thought that she was beaten, and that now Lyn was his property. If her spirit was broken, all the better; it meant he would have more freedom to do whatever he desired and she would not dare to question him. It did not occur to him that she might leave him. He had won the war. Lyn knew the way his mind worked. What he did not realise was that while she had become terrified to answer him back, she seethed in her head. As a prostitute, she could have forgiven the whipping; she accepted the urge to flagellate. But she regarded herself as John's lover, not his prostitute, and the episode had brought her down.

John still came to Lyn every day for seven hours. She was polite, dutiful, but she no longer communicated with him. He pretended not to notice. If they had still been having sex, Lyn would have understood his silence over their changed relationship. Most men she had known would not notice if a woman was suddenly struck dumb as long as they got sex. They spent the nights with him reading the newspapers, Lyn reading her books. He no longer minded Lyn reading all the time he spent with her, and Lyn often glanced at the clock, wishing the hours away for him to leave. She thought that John continued to spend time with her out of perversity, because he enjoyed knowing how much she had grown to despise him.

One day John Cullen announced that Lyn would have to mind Jonathan, his son by Teresa. Since her mother had died, Teresa had trouble getting childminders, and John's pocket was suffering. He smiled as he said it, which meant it was another offer Lyn could not refuse.

Lyn worked on the streets until 10.00 p.m. when John collected her with the child in the car. He drove them to Lyn's flat and stayed until it was time to go home. The following morning, he would take Jonathan back to Teresa. And so it went. Lyn was bitter at the way her slavish life had expanded to include childminding. This schedule also meant, though, that John was having to do something for his money and he did not like it. Also, Liam Ryan's case was drawing closer, and John grew more anxious. He was paranoid over what Liam had done to him. Whenever he mentioned Liam, he had a new solution to what he called the 'Ryan hassle'. Lyn was not interested and John knew it. At the same time, he began to brood about Dolores. Word of this must have reached Dolores, now working in St James's Hospital as a maid and absorbed in charitable deeds, for it was around this time that her sister remembers she became more and more nervous, anxious about coming home from work alone. Her sister, Kathleen, always picked her up in the car.

Hardly a day went by now that John did not mention Dolores. 'How,' he raved, 'did she have the nerve to get me nicked?' Lyn was not interested. She could not be bothered to point out that he had not served three years in Mountjoy Prison for bible punching.

Every night of his three year sentence, John Cullen had lain on his bed and plotted how he would 'get' Dolores. He told Lyn that he had got an erection when he imagined torturing Dolores in preparation for killing her. He was incensed when, just before his release from prison, his brother Paul had come in to start a three year sentence after a pub fight with Tony, Dolores' boyfriend. Paul's sentence had delayed John's revenge. He knew that if he killed Dolores before Paul was released it would impede his brother's parole.

When Paul had served his three years, John was caught up in his affair with Lyn. Now, he told her, 'I will get seven to ten years for stabbing Liam Ryan. That's nearly a life sentence. I may as well get Dolores Lynch before I go in, I couldn't do a stretch knowing she's breathing. Anyway, she smokes so much she could die. I can't let her deprive me of the satisfaction of killing her!' He talked about violent death in a completely detached way: 'See Lyn, I've already decided that I'm going to kill you before I go to prison over Ryan.'

Lyn imagined she could hear him thinking, 'M-m-m-m, yes, now that we're on the subject, d'you know what I mean, like, I may as well do it now.' He would kneel beside her, smiling, his hands round her throat, smiling, squeezing, smiling, tighter, smiling, until she was dead, then gather his belongings, comb his hair, smile at his reflection in the mirror while he hummed and thought, 'that's that done with'.

'John, please stop; it's not funny,' she said.

'Lyn, love, it's not meant to be funny. I'm deadly serious.'

Lyn knew that she was only trying to defuse the situation. He shifted his gaze from a point over Lyn's shoulder, looked into her eyes and said absent-mindedly, 'Relax, I'm not going to do it tonight. I love you and I want you around. I'll do it a day or two before the court case.'

The following night he started an argument over something trivial and threw dirt about past lovers. Lyn kept silent, but did not take her eyes off him. He stopped arguing as suddenly as he had begun. He jumped up. Lyn flinched.

'Jonathan,' he yelled, 'get dressed. You're going home to your Ma.'

Lyn did not move, even though she knew that John would not hit her in front of the child. He had told Teresa that his sister Bertie was babysitting. Jonathan would tell his mother that

Daddy had hit Bertie. He slammed the door on his way out. It was still only 8.00 p.m., which meant he had ample time to collect Teresa from work, drop her and Jonathan home and head for the pub. John Cullen, like all pimps, was loathe to forfeit a night's money, so taking Jonathan back showed his anger had gone beyond control. Lyn knew he would return. When he walked out without speaking, John was plotting destruction, like the time in Ballymun when he sat brooding in the pub, and then had gone home and collected his sharp knives. Lyn whisked around the flat in a panic. She hid everything that could be used to inflict pain on her and then she thought of running. But where? Who would protect her against John Cullen? Whoever said that there was nothing to fear but fear itself, Lyn decided, could not have known what it felt like to wait for their own murderer.

Lyn swallowed twenty Valium before she realised that John would come back and find her unconscious. She was terrified of waking to face him with a knife. Smiling. And what might he do to her dead body? She reminded herself that it did not matter what happened to her body when she was dead, but she could not escape the thought of his defiling her in death. He was capable of anything. The idea was more than she could bear, so she ran out of the flat. She had been taking Valium for years and sometimes it did not work on her at all, but this time it hit her all at once. She remembers hitting the pavement. In her mind, John was ramming his penis into her mouth, hitting the back of her throat, worming its way down to her stomach. Lyn tried to sit up, but she felt so sleepy. Hands pulled her back, soft voices. 'Lie down, it's alright.'

Lyn opened her eyes, angels smiling at her. In white. No, humans standing over her pushing something down her throat. She sat up, tried to push them away. She was pushed gently, firmly, back onto the bed. 'Just lie still,' a voice said.

A nurse held her arms down. The tube was removed. Lyn cried. Did these people not know what they were doing, what they had saved her for? She slept till 7.00 a.m. and was brought a cup of tea by a smiling nurse who asked her if she felt strong enough to go home.

What could she say? 'Well actually, if I go home, I'll probably be murdered by my pimp.'

Lyn went home. A state of severe shock hit her when she reached her flat and she lay in her fur coat on the settee, shivering constantly, for three days. On the fourth day, Geoff Mason, a friend of John's, called. Lyn had not washed since leaving the hospital.

'What happened to you?' he asked, taken aback by her appearance.

'John left me,' Lyn said, 'and I took an overdose of Valium.' She knew anything she told Geoff would go straight back to Cullen.

Two hours after Geoff left, John Cullen was standing looking down at Lyn on the settee. Smiling. 'I've brought Jonathan,' he said. 'Will you look after him? I'm going for a drink with a guy.'

Lyn sighed. 'I can't be bothered to look after myself,' she said wearily. He left Jonathan, who played with his toys and watched television until bedtime. Then, without even giving him a wash, Lyn fed him an overripe banana, a bag of crisps and white lemonade and he fell asleep on her bed. John came back when the pubs closed. He sat down beside her.

'Here, chips and a hamburger. Geoff said you hadn't eaten for days.' She looked at the food, but did not answer him, started to pick at the chips, and suddenly she was ravaging the lot. John switched on the television and said, 'Take my shoes off love, and run your fingers through my toes.'

John fell fast asleep without mentioning the last few days. Questions whirled around inside her head. Had he come back to the flat the night she overdosed? She was certain he had not come back into her life, calmly, out of any feelings of remorse. Perhaps he just needed her to mind Jonathan? No, Lyn decided. John was too stubborn to give in to that. She guessed he wanted her suffering to continue. 'Perhaps,' she thought, 'I am guilty of dumb insolence and must be punished.'

Craig Nelson had told Lyn about the 'screws' in Reading Borstal. They used to punish the prisoners for looking the wrong way, called it dumb insolence. Lyn recalled John Cullen telling her he had never had an argument with his wife. His mate, Geoff Mason, told Lyn that John's wife acted like a Geisha girl, obeyed John's every whim and fancy. 'Well, that's probably why you love me,' Lyn said, 'I have a mind of my own and I certainly have a mouth.'

To her astonishment John Cullen replied that he hated women who had opinions, or who 'think they do. Women can't think. They are for the bed and the kitchen. In that order. When a real woman gets an opinion, she keeps it to herself . . .'

When John woke up, he started talking about his fantasy. He had seen a film years ago called *The Collector*, where the central character collected things; butterflies, stamps etc., until he saw a woman he wanted to 'collect'. He lured her into his house and when she tried to escape she discovered the windows were bricked up. Lyn listened, palms sweating, heart thumping. She had still not recovered from the overdose.

'That's my fantasy for you, Lyn. I would love to lock you in a deserted house. Keep you tied up on the bed. I would come to you every three days. I'd screw you first, then feed you like a dog. You'd learn to rely on me completely. I'd be the only person in the world, d'you know what I mean like? Then you would fall crazy in love with me . . .'

People have their fantasies, but when John Cullen had one, Lyn paid attention. The practicalities struck her.

'What happens when I want to go to the loo?' she asked curiously.

'I wouldn't let you. You would have to lie in it,' he said, a distant look in his eyes.

'You mean you would still want to screw me?'

'Yes,' he said, 'I want to see you reduced to the level of a dog. A dog in chains. It would turn me on.'

He had mentioned this a few times and now Lyn was getting worried. Since Liam's stabbing, John's state of mind had got worse and worse. All the dark thoughts and fantasies he had kept locked in his head had become priorities to put into action. She pleaded severe nausea, having eaten hamburger and chips on an empty stomach, and he left early.

A week later, Teresa's son Jonathan was taken into care. John was very relieved. It bothered him that his *legitimate* children would one day meet the boy and discover that they had the same father.

It was 16 March. John was flying to Birmingham the

following day for a nephew's wedding. They went to visit Róisín and Willy. Róisín asked John's permission for Lyn to stay with her. 'No, Róisín,' he said, 'I am chaining her to the bed while I'm away.'

Róisín knew about *The Collector*. 'But John, what about the people next door? They'll hear her.'

'No, they won't. I'm going to gag her,' John said. Lyn flickered her eyes at Róisín.

'What about her grub?' said Róisín.

'I'll feed her tonight. That should do her till I get back,' he said, leaning over to kiss Lyn. 'You'll be longing for me to come back, won't you, love?'

Lyn smiled back at him nervously. 'Don't mind him, Róisín, he's only messin'.'

Róisín was not convinced. After about an hour John told Lyn to hurry herself. He wanted his dinner. Róisín came to see them out. 'Bye John, Lyn. Have a nice time at the wedding, John.'

While Lyn was cooking dinner she had a flash of inspiration. 'John, can I see you off at the airport? I'll miss you so much.'

He considered. 'Hmmm, I suppose so. Me Ma will be with me.' Another battle won. Lyn was not going to become a collector's item!

Lyn looked forward to three days of peace. She floated into a taxi at the airport.

'Ballymun, please,' but Róisín was not there. She had been arrested the previous evening and was sent to Mountjoy Prison for seven days. Lyn decided it would be wise for her to leave the flat. John would be furious if Lyn remained with Willy. As she was leaving, Liam Ryan called to see Willy. She had not seen him since the stabbing and she fled into the kitchen, embarrassed to face him, but he followed her. They talked about the stabbing and she told him that her life was in danger if he insisted on giving evidence against John. Liam's wounds were still visible. He was going on about Willy's desertion of him on the night of the attack.

'Liam,' Lyn said, 'you're not listening. If you charge John he'll get you for it. He won't let you get away with it. Look how many batterings poor Dolores got and he said that if you do nick him he'll kill me before he goes in.'

189

Liam considered. 'No, sorry, Lyn. Someone has to put a stop to him. I still have nightmares over it. I wake up sweating; it's affecting my wife and kids. I even sent a message with Willy that if Cullen made an apology and reimbursed me for my clothes he ruined when he stabbed me, I'd forget about it, but the bastard wouldn't even do that. I don't want you to get hurt Lyn, but I won't let him off the hook.'

Lyn could not argue with that. Liam was right.

19

The day John was due back from Birmingham, Lyn was doubled up with 'mysterious' cramps in her stomach. They eased when she took a few Valium. They had arranged that he would come a day earlier than his family expected him and Lyn met him at the airport. He was glad to see her. The next morning, he asked her to account for her movements of the past few days. She told him and then shook as she finally said, 'Liam insists on giving evidence.'

'So, the bastard's getting smart, is he? Well, I'll fix him. I'll also have to speed up getting Dolores; I was waiting to get the wedding over. I'll get her in the next week or so.' Lyn was silenced.

The next few days passed without incident, no reference was made to Liam or Dolores. John was brooding. He called early one afternoon in a marvellous mood.

'You're very early,' she said.

He smiled. 'I've good news for you. I found out where Dolores lives.'

'Why is that good news for me?' Lyn asked.

He was exasperated. 'Look, dummy, it means I don't have to get her at the hospital where she works, d'you know what I mean like? I can get her at the house.'

John Cullen had been for a drive with Teresa when he realised he was in the vicinity of where Dolores lived,

Clanbrassil Street. A child was playing in the street and he asked her if she knew where the Lynches lived. The child answered, 'Yes, in that house there.' He described Dolores and the child said yes, that was the right house. Cullen was so excited he dropped Teresa home early and drove straight out to tell Lyn the news. What reaction did he expect? He had probed and probed over the past eighteen months, sometimes in such a subtle way that Lyn had not noticed. She told John that when she was friendly with Dolores, Dolores had lived in flatland like the rest of the women. Lyn had never asked questions of Dolores regarding her home or her family. The women on the game respected each other's privacy. They understood Dolores' shame and effort to protect her family's identity. Lyn had never wanted to know more about Dolores than the younger woman volunteered, which was very little. To Lyn, Dolores was just Dolores. The fact that they had drifted apart did not mean that they had lost affection for each other.

John Cullen could see Lyn did not share his happiness over discovering where Dolores lived, and that she did not seem to be taking him seriously. He stalked off in a tantrum. He made no reference to Dolores the following day. The day after that, he did not show up. When he arrived the next day he was trying to get around Lyn, a rare occurrence.

'Don't get narky, Lyn love. I wasn't up to anything.' He meant that he had not been with another woman. 'I went to Dolores' house last night and set fire to it. I've just been round now to have a look and the fuckin' thing didn't work. The fire must have been put out,' he said with disgust. 'I done it with firelighters in the letterbox. It was dead easy. The letterbox was down near the ground. I waited down the road to see it, it was going great, but there was nothing on the news today. So I drove 'round there. The front door was open and people were comin' and goin'.'

So he had really done it. Lyn felt an enormous relief. At least it was over and nobody was hurt.

In spite of having failed to burn the Lynches' house down, John was happy. He asked Lyn out for a drink. She said it would be nicer to stay home. He was in good form that night and as Lyn relaxed she asked, 'John, now you've set fire to her house,

will you let it go? I know what it's like to live in fear of your li
Dolores will know it was you who did it and she'll be terrified.'
He lay for an eternity debating the wisdom of what Lyn had
said.

'Suppose so,' he said eventually.

Lyn was reading a book called *The Lady Killers,* histories of
women who had met violent deaths over the last two centuries.
Jonathan was asleep. John was scouring the newspapers. Lyn's
palms sweated so much she had to close the book. 'What are
you thinking about, Lyn?' John asked. Lyn could not think of
something else on the spur of the moment, so she said, 'I was
thinking of the women in that book. I would hate to die a violent death. It scares me.'

He stared at a space over her shoulder. 'Mmmmm,' he
mused. 'I'll say you probably will though, Lyn. I can't see you
living much longer.'

'Don't say that, John.'

'But it's true, Lyn. What's more I will probably be the one to
kill you.' He was still staring at that space over her shoulder. Lyn
had always felt that she would be murdered, if not by a client,
then certainly by a pimp. John talking about it, calmly, as
though it was inevitable. It caused her mouth to go dry.

John did not talk about Dolores for two weeks, but his anger
with Liam Ryan increased. Messages were still coming via Willy
O'Donnell. One week, Willy did not think Liam was going to
give up and then again, he might drop the charges. Lyn knew it
was getting to John. At around 3.00 a.m. on a couple of nights,
John said, 'Get dressed.' and drove them out to Liam's house
where they sat in silence. He never spoke, just stared at the
house. It was intended to intimidate Liam.

John still made regular promises to kill Lyn before he went
to court. He did not threaten her. He took great pains to let her
know how much he loved her, but he knew that she would not
wait for him while he was in prison, so, he promised. If he had
not whipped and debased her, Lyn believed that she would have
waited a lifetime, because prior to that Sunday, she was crazy
about him.

John Cullen loved his three legitimate children, so Lyn pointed out that if he killed, he would get life and his children would

193

they grew up. His reaction was predictable for a
r that matter, a lot of decent citizens. 'I wouldn't
ng you, Lyn, d'you know what I mean? Not when
nd out that you were a prostitute.'
also figured that if he got seven years for Liam, that was
all a life sentence with time off for good behaviour consisted of
anyway. If he had to face a long sentence, he planned to tell his
wife to carve out a new life for herself.

Lyn grew more fearful every day that passed, felt headed
towards breaking point. She was going to visit her sons, Chris
and Joey. Chris was doing a three-year prison sentence in
England. Her fifteen-year-old son, Joey, was in a young offenders' home. Joey had gone back to England the previous year,
and his father had beaten him for treason, which meant living
with Lyn. Joey ran away and the English police had picked him
up, fished out an old warrant for robbing cars and Joey was
placed in a home.

Lyn decided that when she went to England she was not
coming back. She got very excited about it, but at the same
time, she was scared that John would suspect her intentions. So
she went into a major 'grovel' for a week before she was due to
leave. John suggested that she take Róisín with her. He would
have gone himself, he said, but he was having trouble with
Teresa and had to stay to direct operations. Teresa had heard
rumours of John's affair with Lyn.

Róisín was delighted to go with Lyn. Mary said she would go
too. Lyn had £300 in the bank and she worked for a week on
the Canal and saved another £300. It was not easy. John liked
her to be available whenever it suited him, so it meant that the
hours she was free to work were limited.

The night before they left for England, Lyn got a taxi home
from work, grabbed her fur coat, her briefcase containing all her
personal documents and her four treasured books; Jimmy
Boyle's *A Sense of Freedom,* a copy of *Our Bodies, Ourselves,* her
Roget's Thesaurus and, of course, Emma Goldman's essays. She
deposited the stuff in Róisín's flat. Willy had gambled the money
Róisín had put by for the trip and asked if Lyn would lend her
£300. She did not have the heart to refuse.

Lyn made it back to her own flat just ahead of John. She was 'all over him' that night. When he drove her to Róisín's flat, she was trembling with her secret so much that he looked at her keenly and asked what was wrong. She broke down. 'I don't want to leave you for four whole days. You know . . .' she sobbed. He promised to make it up to her when she got back.

Róisín and Mary arrived home from work at 5.00 a.m. having made enough money for their pimps as well as to cover their four nights in London. The three women were giddy with laughter as they boarded the 'plane. Lyn's laughter was partly an act. She was expecting John Cullen to grab her by the arm at any moment and say, 'Where the fuck do you think you're going with all that gear for a weekend?' If it happened, she told the others, she would ask for political asylum. When they were on the 'plane she forgot to be scared of flying. And when they arrived at Heathrow they were still laughing.

Lyn had lived in England for years, but for Róisín and Mary it was a novelty. They insisted on doing the tourist bit. They were like naughty schoolgirls, insisting on going around the red light district, visiting porn shops. They visited Chris and it was a happy time for them.

Lyn phoned Joey at the young offenders home. They arranged for him to 'walk out' and Lyn telegrammed him money so that he could get from Liverpool to London. Now, Lyn ran out of cash and if she stayed in England, Joey would be caught. She phoned John and asked him if she could bring Joey back to Dublin, omitting to say that Joey at that moment was inspecting the hotel corridors. John agreed at once. He had always got on well with Joey, but being consulted made him feel important. John was very loving on the phone. 'Hurry home,' he said. Lyn did not have much choice. Besides the lack of cash, and Joey, Róisín and Mary would suffer if they went home without her.

There was one sticky moment getting Joey through Heathrow. Lyn was ahead of Joey and she looked back in time to see a policeman talking to him. 'Come on, son, stop dawdling,' she bluffed in her exasperated mother's tone. The policeman saw the boy was with her and motioned Joey on.

When they landed at Dublin Airport, Willy and John were waiting. John was in high spirits, chatting to Joey all the way home. His good mood continued all evening with him and Joey discussing football. As Lyn cooked dinner she was surprised to find herself singing. Perhaps, she thought, things might change. She was so happy to have Joey and knew that John would not get violent while Joey was living with her. Joey idolised John and was loyal to him, as Lyn would find out. Joey had seen so much violence that John's friendliness was a marvel to him. Joey had changed. In the past he had resented her for leaving his father, no matter that she had been consistently battered; he thought all parents acted that way. And then when his father had given him such a bad beating in Liverpool, Joey had withdrawn his love and loyalty.

The following weeks were idyllic. Joey's resentment towards Lyn had gone. John Cullen was spending more time with her and they were getting along well. John called early in the morning and they went out for a drive in the country. On a nice day, he and Joey would play football for a couple of hours. They shopped, went home for dinner. John took his bath before going to collect his takings from Teresa. Each day he gave Teresa £10 with instructions to get a meal and a taxi to work. When he went back to Lyn, they passed the evening reading, watching television and talking. They never went out. Joey loved this set-up. It gave him a feeling of security.

Lyn also enjoyed things as they were. She had given up any thoughts of escape. She could not have stayed in England anyway, because of Joey. And where else could she go after sixteen years in Dublin with a police record? When she had talked to John on the phone and asked him if Joey could come home with her, she had told herself that perhaps she expected too much from life and was being soft. If you were on the game, you had to expect to be beaten up, humiliated. And she had felt so futile in London. The glimpse the women had got of the red light district was obviously even worse than it was in Dublin. And John Cullen would never harm her with Joey in the flat, so she should just try to make the best of things. If she could handle John Cullen, she was laughing. Well, not quite. But John had changed. Now, he was more human. Lately, whenever he got randy, he would whisper in her ear, 'Can I tie you up and whip you, Lyn?'

Lyn would jump up. 'Don't touch me, John. I'll scream. Touch me and I'm gone, I swear it.'

He knew she meant it. Lyn knew he would not take 'no' for an answer forever. Sometime when Joey was out?

John had given up going to collect his takings from Teresa on Sundays and stayed with Lyn instead. He went to Teresa one Monday expecting a double night's takings, but she was not there. The woman who lived across the road said that Teresa had not been home since Saturday.

Lyn was secretly delighted. Imagine Teresa having the guts to walk out on John. She knew it was killing him, that he was thinking 'how dare Teresa leave him'. He hunted his prey. Lyn shivered to think of what John would do to Teresa when he caught her. He was down the Canal every night interrogating the women, then sneaking into Teresa's house at odd hours hoping to catch her, but Teresa was not to be found.

20

Lyn knew it was coming. With Teresa missing, she had to go back to work for John. One night as he drove Lyn to work, John told her he thought Teresa might be staying with another prostitute, Scotch Sheila. Teresa had told him that she and Sheila were great friends. Lyn doubted that, but John was now in pursuit of Sheila. He drove to her flat in Rathmines and as he was parking the car they saw Sheila entering her flat with a client. John got out and followed them. When he came back, he was raging. He got into the car and drove around the block, got out and picked up a building brick. He got back in and drove back to Sheila's flat where he left the car again and threw the brick through her window. Sheila ran out shouting after John, who cursed at her and jumped back into the car grinning, and drove Lyn off to work. Lyn did not ask what all that was about. She was relieved to be down on the Canal in the relative sanity of her working situation.

Later that night John was still going on about Sheila. She had got lippy when he barged into her flat. He pushed her aside and searched for Teresa. Sheila screamed at him, 'How dare you walk into my flat!' John did not hit her in front of the client, a potential witness if she yelled 'cop', hence the brick through the window. Next afternoon, John and Lyn went for their drive past Sheila's place where a man was putting in a new pane of glass. Her car was parked outside. John drove around the block, stopped and got out, leaving the engine running. Seconds later, Lyn heard women shouting and screaming. John reappeared, smiling, inspecting his knuckles, silent. But ten minutes later, he said, 'Did you hear the row?'

Lyn shot a look at him. He was grinning. She nodded. He laughed. 'When I got to the house there was a woman coming out. I pushed past her and went into Sheila's flat. The bitch, she started yelling about her fuckin' windows. So I gave her a few digs. That slag of a girlfriend, Toni, jumped in so I punched the head off her as well.' It had obviously cheered him up. He was smiling and singing along with the radio all the way home.

A week later he told Lyn that his car insurance had expired. Would Lyn do a double shift? When he picked her up at 3.30 a.m. she had earned £260. Cullen was delighted, actually stayed with her until 5.00 a.m., an hour later than normal. Lyn took her sleeping tablets after he left and lay waiting for blessed oblivion. 'The way to a man's heart is not through his stomach,' Lyn claims. 'It's through his pocket.'

She was awakened by a persistent knocking at 6.00 a.m.

'Who is it?' she shouted.

'Me,' came the reply. Lyn staggered out of bed, pulled back the bolts, opened the door.

'Jesus, John, you've only been gone an hour.'

She got back into bed, pulled the duvet up and closed her eyes. He dragged the cover off her and said, 'Come on. Up. Get dressed, quick.'

'I've only just taken my tablets,' she told him.

'Do as you're told,' he ordered, and went out to wait in the car. She got dressed, went out, and sat wearily in the car, too tired to speak.

'Lyn, I couldn't sleep when I got home. I don't know why, but I've a hunch Teresa is in her house and I want to catch her. She won't be expecting me. I was up there last night while you were at work. There were signs she'd been in, d'you know what I mean like? I knew because I'd set traps. I figure she more than likely goes in very late when she thinks I'm at home with me wife. She won't dream I'd go up at this time of morning.' When they neared Teresa's house, he left Lyn in the car and walked. Seconds ticked by. Lyn closed her eyes. She awoke to the sound of running footsteps, sat bolt upright. John jumped in and started the car with a screech of gears. Lyn was wide awake now. Trouble.

'Did anyone pass here?'

'What?' she asked, stupidly.

'I caught them in the bed. I battered the pair of them. His taxi was outside the house. They ran out. I don't know where he went.'

He was screeching round corners. Lyn did not know what he was talking about with his face white, perspiration beading on his forehead, his tongue protruding and a ticking in his top lip. He was not just talking crazy; he looked it. They rounded another corner and clipped a parked car. The next turning they took they barely missed running down a milkman who had put his crate of bottles on the ground. They were screeching up and down streets, around corners. Here was the milkman again. He had lifted his crate from the back of his float and when he saw them he dropped it with a bang. As they passed, Lyn threw a look at his face. His mouth was hanging open. Another turning, John aimed the car at a low wall.

'John, for fuck's sake, you'll kill us,' she screamed.

No, it was not the wall he was aiming at, but a young man who had hurdled it. He was clad only in trousers. He had the rest of his clothes under his arm. John slammed on the brakes and stopped an inch from the wall. The young fellow jumped and made a run for it, but John was on top of him, kicking and punching.

'John,' Lyn screamed, 'Leave him, please, John, no.'

People were hanging out of windows, someone shouted that they had rung for the police. The young man lay motionless. John jumped back into the car and put it into reverse, his foot right down on the accelerator.

'John,' Lyn was hysterical now, 'no, don't drive over him. No-o-o.' She tried to grab the steering wheel but he gave her a left jab into the face.

'John please, everyone's watching.'

They heard sirens coming nearer. The young man sprang to life, grabbed his jumper and shoes and ran. John put the car in forward gear, skidded round a corner, brakes screeching. There was the milkman again. He had just placed his crate on the road and this time he did not bother to look back before he abandoned the crate and tore across the road and scaled a garden wall.

The siren sounded nearer. John slammed on the brakes, cut the engine, pulled Lyn over to him and pretended to neck with her but looked over her shoulder. The siren faded. Colour flooded back in his face. Lyn had to ask. Surprise, he answered her!

'She hadn't bolted the door. I crept up the stairs. They were both fast asleep in bed. I grabbed the chair and smashed their heads in. I got tired. I went downstairs to wash the blood off me hands 'cause I couldn't keep a grip on the chair. No one makes a shit out a me, so I went out the yard to get the axe to finish them off. I heard a noise, and when I looked back in the house I saw him run out the front. I ran out after him and I saw Teresa legging it down the road with only a skirt on. He ran the other way. I lost the bastard. I think she ran into the bus station. We'll head for there.'

As John drove to the bus station they saw an ambulance driving away from it. He turned around to trail it when they spotted a squad car following. John slowed, let the patrol car pass and then followed them at a distance. He stopped the car and threw a bunch of keys to Lyn with instructions to hide them. Lyn got out and hid them in some bushes. Then he took up the trail again. The ambulance drove to Dr Steevens Hospital and John parked nearby. The keys Lyn had hidden belonged to Teresa's fellow.

'You know, Lyn, I didn't think Teresa had the nerve to cross me, you know what I mean, like? I didn't believe the English birds when they told me she was having it off with a fellow. If I had believed it, I would have gone into the house tooled up. Lyn, how dare she cross me?'

Lyn mumbled that she did not know. 'Poor Teresa,' Lyn thought. She was unfortunate to get caught.

John went into the hospital to warn Teresa against having him charged. It occurred to Lyn that he might have another go at Teresa with the scissors he had on his key ring, and before he left, she asked him to leave the keys in the ignition. A few minutes later he was back, grinning. He had passed two policemen before he found Teresa in the third cubicle. She was lying on a couch, being tended by a doctor. When she saw Cullen she jumped and screamed and tried to sit up.

'Is that the man who attacked you?' the doctor asked.

'Hello Teresa,' John said in a soothing voice. 'I heard you had trouble. What happened to you?'

'No, doctor,' Teresa said, 'he didn't do it. He's me brother.'

'Her arm's broken,' Cullen told Lyn, 'and her face is in a mess. Her scalp is wide open. She looks like it's a wig she has because her whole forehead is all kind of pulled back.'

He was happily excited and handed Lyn £10. 'You take a taxi home and I'll see you later.' He was going to hang around the hospital with Teresa in case she might be tempted to tell the police who had attacked her.

Lyn went home and tried to sleep, but the sleeping tablets had worn off. Once again, she felt that sense of relief that the 'something terrible' that had happened had not been to her. To Lyn, at this stage, watching disaster was not like seeing an accident and feeling sorry for the victims. She was simply thankful that, once again, it was not her. And never more than now that she was aware that the war was on again, and that John Cullen had embarked on a long, violent campaign against his enemies.

He called to the flat at 5.00 p.m. and took a bath. Lyn followed him and sat probing. He told her that Teresa had thirty stitches across her forehead, her arm was broken in two places. The arm had been set in plaster, but she would have to go back at a later date for an operation. They had given her painkilling tablets and released her into the care of her loving 'brother', John Cullen. While he was waiting in the hospital, Teresa's boyfriend came in for treatment. John told him that he could have his taxi back if he paid £200 for the keys. He arranged to meet him that night.

When the time neared for John to meet Teresa's boyfriend, he told Lyn to get ready, she was going with him. They drove down to the Grand Canal at Baggot Street. John pointed to a fellow sitting on a bench on the far side of the canal. 'Ask him his name and if he says Liam Kelly, get the £200 off him and come back to the bridge.'

Liam Kelly refused to hand over the cash to Lyn until he got his taxi. 'Look, I'm only followin' John Cullen's orders, right? At least let me see the money,' Lyn said. Liam flashed it. Lyn walked back to the bridge to wait for John who drove by several times, smiling. Lyn simmered. He was setting her up to see if the police came. Two young men approached and asked was she looking for business.

'No,' Lyn snapped. 'I'm waiting for a bloody car to run me over.' Eventually Cullen pulled in to the kerb. She nearly took the hinges off the door as she slammed it behind her.

'Where's the cash?' he asked. Lyn explained and John drove around the block a couple of times, thinking. He toyed with the idea of burning Liam's car, but decided on the cash instead. Liam had to pay for having sex with Teresa, John fumed.

They drove to where Liam was waiting. Then the elderly man Lyn had noticed hanging around near Liam ran up shouting, 'You bastard, look at my son's face. You did that, you animal. I've a good mind to fetch the police. How dare you charge him for his own car back? He hasn't got £200. That's my money and I've worked bloody hard for it.'

Smiling, eyes slanted, John said, 'Look, your son raped my girlfriend, d'you know what I mean? She will stand up in court and say that, so if you still want to call the cops . . . Either he pays me the money or I burn his car. It's up to you.'

The Kellys knew they were beaten. Mr Kelly said he would drive Liam, but John insisted that Liam come in his car. As they were travelling to where the car was hidden, John started small talking as if they were on a picnic. Lyn was not paying attention to the conversation until she heard him say, 'Tell you what, then Liam, if you think you fancy Teresa, I'll sell her to you for £5,000.' Lyn whipped around to face John. He was smiling that smile. Liam did not answer.

'Liam, are you listening to me? £5,000 and she's yours.' Liam remained silent. Lyn stared incredulously.

'Teresa can earn that in a matter of months. Tell you what. Give me a deposit of £1,000 and you can take her off my hands. You can pay me the rest in installments, over say, mmmm, six months, what do you say?' It dawned on Liam that John was serious.

'I wouldn't be able to raise £1,000,' he said. It was also dawning on Liam that Teresa was a prostitute. In her world of make-believe she had woven a tale about herself that he believed. Although they met in an all-night café he had not guessed that she was on the game. Teresa looked even younger than she was and had an openness and vulnerability which people found attractive. She introduced him to her 'friends', two English prostitutes and explained that she babysat for them while they worked.

'Sure you wouldn't hold it against them?' she is reported to have asked, all innocence. Liam believed that her parents had died in a 'plane crash without naming her as a beneficiary, hence her reduced circumstances. She had also told him that she was waiting for her English divorce to come through; she had been married to a singer. Now, Liam did not want Cullen to know that Teresa's occupation was news to him so he said, 'I wouldn't be able to raise £1,000.'

'That's a pity. Oh well, at least I offered. If you do manage to scrape it together, the offer still stands.'

As they neared Liam Kelly's car, John asked for the £200. Liam said that he wasn't handing over the money until he got the keys. An argument developed and Lyn sneaked a look at John, guessed he was about to snap. 'Liam, please,' Lyn said frantically, 'give him the money. You don't know what you are dealing with. I promise I will make sure you get your keys.' He handed her the money.

Liam's car came into sight. John told him to get out and wait until he came back with his keys. Mr Kelly's car pulled up behind and he got out and started yelling at John. Lyn's 'lovely pimp' drove off grinning.

'Where the hell are his keys? You promised . . .' Lyn began.

'Shut fuckin' up. The keys are in me Ma's house. He's not getting them back.'

She would not shut up. 'You listen to me! I don't give a damn about you. Your word means nothing, but I gave my word. I want those car keys, John. Why should that poor young fellow pay for his own car back?'

She did not notice that they were driving to his mother's house. Without a word he slammed on the brakes, stormed into his mother's house, got back into the car and tossed a bunch of keys in Lyn's lap. Before they reached the street where Liam waited, John braked, leaned across and opened Lyn's door. 'Right! Out! You think that little prick should have his keys, well, you give them to him,' he said.

As he drove off, Lyn yelled 'Fuck you, too.'

Liam walked towards her. Lyn smiled nervously and handed him his keys. 'I'm sorry he didn't give 'em straight off,' she said. He smiled back. Lyn was about to turn and leave when she heard a bloodcurdling scream, and two young men jumped over the garden wall where Liam had been standing. Lyn saw a knife glinting, gasped, but could not move. The one with the knife charged at her. Liam grabbed Lyn, but his father circled his waist to pull him back.

'No, son, don't touch her. It's not her fault, it's that bastard Cullen.' She ran around a corner, into a garden and sat down behind a wall, crying hysterically. She heard a car screeching, travelling in the opposite direction, and presumed it was the Kellys. She stopped crying and just sat, huddled. She thought, 'I should have joined a circus, teamed up with a knife thrower. At least I would have been paid for it.'

The two men who had leapt over the wall were the two who asked Lyn if she was looking for business as she waited for John to pick her up on the bridge at Percy Place. They must have hidden in Mr Kelly's car. She waited for about an hour, then sneaked out of the garden and walked down to the main road in the hope that John Cullen would come looking for her. She could not go anywhere. She had no money.

John Cullen drove by two and a half hours later, smiling. She jumped into the car and slammed the door.

'Everything OK?' he asked. She ignored him. He drove in silence for a while then slid his hand onto her knee and squeezed. 'Sorry I was late,' he said, smiling. Lyn flipped and slapped his hand away.

'While you were gallivanting, a guy came at me with a knife. If I'd been stabbed, I would have been well dead in the two and a half hours it's taken you to come back.' He stopped smiling.

'Shut fuckin' up,' he said. 'What the fuck do you expect?'

'I'm payin' you seven hundred pounds a week to protect me,' she yelled back. 'I don't expect to get bloody stabbed.'

She could not believe it when she saw he was heading for the Canal, dropping her down to work! When they got there, he leaned over to kiss her goodnight, saying, 'What time do you want me to pick you up?'

'Forget it,' Lyn snapped and walked off, leaving the car door open. 'I'll get a taxi home. Then if a guy comes at me with a knife perhaps the taxi driver will be man enough to help me.' Even as she said it, Lyn expected him to run her down. He just smiled.

John did not go near Lyn for days. It suited her. She docked some money for herself, and when he did turn up she told him business had been slow. When he came along two nights later, Lyn was waiting with her friend Gemma. The Vice Squad were making arrests, so John agreed to give Gemma a lift home. On the way out to Tallaght, Gemma remarked on the smell of petrol in the car. John said that was why he had been late. He had run out of petrol and had to walk to a garage and get a can. The minute Gemma got out, John said, 'I thought we would never get rid of her. I spotted Sheila's car parked along the Canal. I'm going to set fire to it. I only hope the bloody thing is still there.'

He had been brooding over Sheila, and was on the rampage. They drove back down the Canal and Sheila's lovely sports car was still there. John took his can of petrol and some rags and went to Sheila's car, opened the door and poured petrol all over the seats. Then he lit the rags and threw them onto the front seat, closed the door and ran. As he was about to drive away he swore, 'Damn, it's not burnin' very well.' He ran back and opened the door. Whoosh! Flames shot out as the breeze fanned them. He smiled all the way home. Lyn sat silent.

Two weeks later, John Cullen put Teresa back to work on the streets. Her stitches had been removed, but her face was still in an awful state, her arm in plaster.

'How can you expect her to work in that state!' Lyn asked. His reply was typical of a pimp.

'Teresa is left-handed, she can work with her right.'

Lyn had been referring to Teresa's face, which was a frightening sight. She could stand on the streets all night and never attract a client. John would not listen. Teresa had to be taught a lesson. She was going out to work, and that was final.

Besides, John had a plan. Teresa must not be allowed to grow out of the habit of work because in the future he wanted her money to support his family. He and Lyn would open a joint bank account, keep Lyn's flat going out of her money and the remainder would be put into the bank. Except that Lyn dug her heels in. She refused to work while Teresa was out in that condition. The argument flared for days. Besides, Lyn knew that John only had to threaten her and the 'joint' account meant nothing. They agreed to open an account from which each one could withdraw money. Lyn stopped docking money. It seemed pointless to dock on herself. She worked harder. They were going to save £10,000 and apply for a loan to buy a house in Lyn's name. Then they would repeat the procedure and purchase a house in John's name. Lyn did not believe that these plans would reach fruition, but at least she would have some money saved.

Four weeks later, Teresa went missing again. She had been seen with Liam Kelly. A black cloud loomed over the Canal. John rang Mr Kelly who informed him that he had washed his hands of his son. With no satisfaction coming from that quarter, John went wild with rage. He brought Teresa's music centre, electric kettle and gas heater to Lyn's flat, saying Teresa was getting nothing. That was all Teresa had to show for six years' work on the streets, and Lyn had given John the heater for Teresa because she could not light a fire with a broken arm. He had smashed Teresa's table and chairs with an axe.

A few weeks went by with John Cullen brooding. Not a word filtered through about Teresa. One night when John picked her up after work, Lyn smelled petrol. 'I set fire to old man Kelly's taxi. It's completely gutted. He won't be earning any money for a while.'

On the way back to Lyn's flat, John stopped beside a phone box and told her to go inside with him. He dialed a number. 'Mr Kelly? Your car was only the start. I told your son you don't fuck with John Cullen. I want Teresa or I want £5,000. Tell Liam that. I will ring again tomorrow.' He was quiet when they got to the flat, ordered Lyn to sit on the settee and run her fingers through his toes, 'and don't fuckin' talk'.

John did not phone Mr Kelly as he had said. On second thought, he figured, the police might have the Kellys' phone tapped. 'If Liam wants to protect his family he can ring me Ma's house. Teresa will give him the number.'

The night after that, John announced as she got into the car that he was going to burn down the Kellys' house. It was said calmly, matter of factly.

'John, you can't, not the house. You can't set fire to the house. John, for Christ's sake, there are young kids in there.' She started to sweat.

'Shut fuckin' up,' he said and hit her in the face, Stay quiet, Lyn told herself and she leaned back in the seat and closed her eyes. He parked down a side road, went around to the boot of the car and took out a packet of firelighters and a can of petrol.

'Give me your lighter,' he said. Lyn handed it to him. 'Get into the driver's seat and keep the car going. If you see the cops have me, get a taxi up to me Ma's and tell them to be over to the court in the morning.' He handed her £10 for a taxi. Lyn could not drive and she struggled to find which pedal to push. The engine kept cutting out. It must have been heard revving miles away, but Lyn was scared to ease her foot off the pedal in case it stopped.

She watched him pour petrol over the Kellys' front door. He paused, looked left and right, then went straight over to the car. She could imagine that crazy look in his eyes. He lit a firelighter and threw it at the door and stood watching it until the blaze took a good hold. Lyn saw a face peering out of the upstairs window. A car passed, slowed down and reversed. Lyn panicked, forgot to keep her foot on the pedal. The engine cut out. John sprinted back and into the car. 'I told you to keep the fuckin' thing going,' he shouted. He got the car started and drove home, had a bath and once again ordered her to sit on the settee and run her fingers through his toes. She was desperate.

'John, where is all this going to end? It's not the Kellys' fault that their son went off with Teresa.'

'It won't end until I either get Teresa back or the five grand.'

'I found out where they are. Well, not exactly where, but I'm gettin' warmer,' John said when he arrived at nine o'clock the next morning in a state of excitement. He handed Lyn a letter from a hospital in Waterford. It asked for Teresa's medical card, saying

208

that she had been in a road accident. John had been unable to sleep, got up early and went to inspect the damage caused by the fire at Liam's house. He was annoyed to find that only the front door was burned. Then he drove to Teresa's house to see if she had sneaked in there. That was when he found the letter. Now, he dragged Lyn out to a phone box to ring the Kellys. Mrs Kelly, Liam's mother, came on the phone and pleaded with John to stop it all. Liam was the eldest of her family, she told him, and there were small children who were terrified. She would hand Teresa over herself if she knew where she was, said Mrs Kelly. 'Listen, Missus,' said John, 'I know they are in Waterford. If I don't get Teresa or £5,000 by tomorrow, it's going to get worse,' he threatened and slammed down the phone.

Back in the flat he got undressed and into bed and presented his toes for Lyn's attention. She sat on the end of the bed for four hours, soothing him through his feet, while he stared at the ceiling, brooding. The angrier he was when Lyn started this, the longer he took to calm down. When he said, 'OK, get into bed,' Lyn was exhausted, but she knew he felt calmer.

'John,' she said, 'no more fires. Please. I can't stand any more. I feel like taking every tablet I have.' She had given up threatening to leave him; the man knew she had nowhere to go. He believed that she might kill herself; she had taken pills before and he knew women did that. He did not answer, just held her closer.

After Lyn's work that night John headed the car towards the Kellys' house. 'John, I meant what I said today,' Lyn's voice was almost inaudible and she thought that he had not heard.

'Relax, Lyn,' he said. 'I'm not going to set fire to it, but I'm fucked if I'm lettin' them away with it. I'll just fuck a brick through the window.'

'Leave me home first. I'm not feelin' so hot.'

'Shut fuckin' up,' he ordered.

They parked in the same place as before, and he sauntered up to the house. All the lights were on. He threw the brick through the downstairs window. Lyn saw a man jump up quickly. It looked as if he had been sleeping downstairs. People ran out of the house. As he ran towards the car, John turned and shouted, 'Don't say I didn't warn you.'

Not one word passed between John and Lyn for the rest of the night. When he was leaving, he kissed her on the cheek, smiled and said, 'Goodnight, love. I'll be up early in the morning. I have a few plans.'

Joey was in Liverpool at a match. Lyn got into bed, took a double dose of sleeping pills and thought about the uselessness of being alive. Every day was a nightmare which she ended with drugs. Upon waking each day, she felt panic, fear. The knot in her stomach was permanent now, as was the pain in her jaws from clenching her teeth. All day long, she took Valium to relieve the tension in her jaws, the pain in her ears.

If Cullen had battered Lyn every day she would not have been as frightened or dispirited as she was now. She would have made excuses, as she had done for years with Craig Nelson. Living with John's evil, intense, brooding thoughts and actions had her terrorised. And she felt so isolated. She lay awake worrying about John's plans for the following day before the sleeping pills took effect. She did not wake until four the next afternoon. John had not called, and his absence made her more panicky. It was easier when she knew what he was up to.

John Cullen was always so fastidious that when he arrived unshaven that night, Lyn knew something was wrong. Without preliminaries, he lay down and told Lyn to tend to his feet. As she soothed him, he unfolded his story.

He had been searching for Teresa when he noticed a plain-clothes police car following. The driver motioned him to pull in to the side of the road. He and his car were searched. In the course of questioning, the police mentioned that the Kellys had made a complaint against him. If there was one more incident in connection with the Kellys, John would be arrested. John went home and brooded, furious with the Kellys, but he cheered up when he realised that they had not pressed charges against him. 'You know, Lyn, I've won. They are too scared to get me nicked,' he said.

'John,' Lyn said, 'you've been warned. You go near them again and you're sure to be arrested. This is a big deal to the Kellys, violence isn't an everyday thing in their lives. They are ordinary, frightened citizens . . .'

He listened, but Lyn knew she was not getting through. He drove her to work.

The Vice Squad were active that night, so the women went to a café in O'Connell Street. Lyn was deep in conversation with Róisín when one of the women muttered that John Cullen was outside the café. Trouble. Lyn left and got into his car. He did not speak, but as they were driving through town she asked where they were going.

'Home. You can take the night off.' Lyn shot a look at him, afraid he was annoyed with her, but no, he was relaxed. She did not dare ask why. When they got home and she was making sandwiches, he put his arms around her waist and nuzzled her neck. It must be good news. She waited. Eventually he enlightened her.

Liam Kelly had been in touch with John. The men had talked. Liam's affair with Teresa had come to an abrupt end. A few weeks of endless arguments had finished with Teresa grabbing the steering wheel of Liam's car as he drove at seventy miles an hour through Waterford city, and they had hit a brick wall. Teresa had signed herself out of the hospital, got back to Dublin and was now plaguing Liam Kelly and his family with phone calls, declaring her undying love for him. Liam no longer wanted Teresa. She was a terrible liar, he told John, and to think that he had wanted to marry her!

The Kelly family were living in fear of John, and Liam wanted to negotiate an end to the blitz. He agreed to bring Teresa to John. Liam rang Teresa at the convent where she was staying and she was delighted, agreed to meet him. John was ecstatic. 'See Lyn. You always say you don't believe in God. Perhaps you will now. Teresa crossed me and Liam crossed me and look what happened to them, d'you know what I mean, like? Liam's car is a write-off. I don't think he was insured. His family want him out. Teresa's face is cut to ribbons and she's lost the only thing she wanted – me. See, God is on my side.'

Lyn got the next night off too. There was victory news. Liam and Teresa were in the café, where they had arranged to meet, when John walked in. When she caught sight of him, Teresa screamed and attempted to stand, but John gripped her arm and pushed her back down on the stool. Her bowels opened.

The smell was awful. John gloated. Fingering the scars on her face, he said, 'See what you get for leaving John-John?' Teresa was unable to answer. Liam looked peculiar. 'Well, Liam,' John asked, 'what do you reckon? She's pretty ugly now. If you still want her you can have her for £1,000 flat. She's useless to me. She won't earn a penny now.' Liam asked John's permission to leave.

John could not have gotten greater satisfaction if he had killed the pair. He ordered Teresa into his car and dumped her home.

'Well, Teresa, I hope you've learnt your lesson. Tomorrow you are back to work. You get your own shopping, coal and contraceptives. Don't fuckin' dare to ask me to do anything for you. All I want is me money. I'll call twice a week for it. If you are out, leave it here.'

Teresa was back at work. Most nights she would not earn anything. Other nights, she would stand freezing for eight to ten hours and finish up with £10. Lyn saw Teresa one night, and had to look away from her face. Teresa did her best to avoid John Cullen, and periodically he would hunt her down on the Canal to make her account for her loss of earnings. Every time she saw him approach, her bowels opened and she had to go home and change her clothes. What had happened to Teresa was a constant reminder, to the women in Dublin prostitution, of the power of a pimp.

Lyn begged for Teresa. She pleaded that she had suffered more than enough. And then she tried the common sense approach: Teresa was earning so little, she was more trouble than she was worth. No answer. Lyn resorted to the ploy that never failed, stroking his ego. She said she was jealous of his association with Teresa. He let Teresa go. Her nerves and health began to improve. Teresa gave up the game, helped by the nuns.

John seemed to settle, treating Lyn with consideration and above all, tolerance. When her periods were due Lyn became unbearable. In the past, John steered clear of her for a few days every month because if he was around at that time, it always ended up with him threatening her and storming out of the flat. Now, he just laughed off her irritability, cuddled and kissed her until her mood changed. They went everywhere together. If

Lyn was tired, she got the night off work and still their joint account grew in the bank. She wanted the flat redecorated and John got a fellow in to do it. But it was too late. A year ago, Lyn would have been the happiest woman on the beat. Now, too much had happened.

21

One night, they were watching television when John announced that he could make a proper petrol bomb. He told Joey to watch, reminding him, 'Remember what I told you, Joey. Never let your enemies off. Watch this. It may come in useful when you grow up.'

They watched, fascinated, as Cullen demonstrated. Lyn was impressed. So much for adult education. The incident was forgotten as the World Cup Football took over their lives.

Joey videotaped every match and they had football for breakfast, dinner and tea. When he grew tired of watching the video, he would go out in the yard to kick football. He was forever hitting the windows with the ball and Lyn often shouted to him to get offside. A few times, he came in furious after arguing with the guy upstairs over the noise. The man called him an 'English bastard', and told him, 'I'll break your fuckin' neck if I catch you playin' football outside this flat.' Lyn did not pay much heed, but John Cullen told Joey, 'Tell him to go fuck himself and mind his own business.'

One Friday night John said he was feeling under the weather and went home after he dropped Lyn off to work. Lyn thought it was an opportunity to work longer hours, especially since it was Friday when business was always good. When she strolled down the path of the Canal, she found the streets deserted, so she figured the women would be in the Legion House nearby.

Gemma came in a few minutes later. 'Joey's lookin' for you,' she told Lyn. 'The poor kid got beat up by the fellow who lives upstairs from you, and he's after smashin' your windows, too.'

Lyn ran from the Legion House, hailed a taxi and toured the district but failed to find Joey. She did not know what to do. If she went home alone, her neighbour might beat her up, too. She would have to get John. She chatted to the taxi driver, told him that she was seeing a married man and was in a spot of trouble and needed to get the man out of the house without arousing his wife's suspicions. Lyn offered him a fiver if he would go to the house and ask for John Cullen while she waited around the corner. The taxi driver chuckled, 'Women,' he said, and agreed.

Lyn spotted Joey then. He sat in the taxi and told her what had happened. The man upstairs had watched John and Lyn driving off, then ran down the stairs and battered Joey around the head with a hurley stick. When Joey fought back, the neighbour went berserk and smashed all Lyn's windows. He yelled at Joey, 'I'll get you lot out of that flat, you English bastards. I'll kill you and I'll kill that fuckin' black bitch, too.' He meant Lyn, with her black hair.

Lyn told the taxi driver to drop them at Kilbarrack and Joey knocked on John's door. If his wife answered he was to say 'Me dad wants to talk to him.' He was to say the same if John answered, in case Judy overheard him.

Lyn said to him, 'Joey, don't, for Christ's sake, mention me, right?'

Lyn waited around the corner. Five minutes later, John and Joey drove up. John laughed when Lyn got in the car. 'Jesus, Lyn, when Joey said "me Dad wants you", I thought Craig Nelson was in Dublin, and Joey never said, when he got in the car, that it was you.' Joey is a fellow of few words.

Now Joey told John why they had been looking for him. He listened and stopped smiling, his face set.

As they walked towards Lyn's flat, the glass was crunching under their feet. John stood staring at the broken glass in the door; all four panes were smashed. He went to the airing cupboard and took out the hammer and then sat on the settee, tossing the hammer from one hand to the other, silent, staring at the floor.

'Right!' Lyn jumped. He had reached a decision. 'Go upstairs and ask him to give you the money for the glass.'

Lyn went up and knocked on the man's door with John on her heels. 'Knock louder,' he said, and stood back out of view. Lyn knocked again. The man was expecting trouble; he opened the door half-way. Lyn could tell by the way he stood that he had something in his hand. 'Are you going to pay me the money for the glass?' she asked. He stuck his chin out.

'Why should I?' John threw Lyn aside, kicked in the door, grabbed the fellow with his left hand and hit him over the head with the hammer.

'You fuckin' broke the windows didn't you,' he said, hitting him with the hammer again. The man screamed, 'OK, I'll pay, I'll pay.' The man's wife ran out screaming. Their two little children came into the hall in their nightdresses, crying, and got in between the legs of the two men. The people next door were out on the balcony. John pulled the man out of his flat and pushed him backwards over the balcony railings from the waist, blood pouring from his head onto the ground floor.

'Are you going to pay for the fuckin' glass?' John kept repeating, and struck him again.

Lyn yelled at him. 'For Christ's sake, John, he's already said he'll pay.' The man was unconscious.

John held him for a few seconds more, the hammer still raised in the air. He jerked him up from the balcony railing and dropped him onto the concrete. Then Cullen walked slowly back down the stairs and into the kitchen where he washed his hands and the hammer very carefully. Lyn's next door neighbour knocked on the door to say that the police had been called. John decided they had better leave the flat. As the three got into the car, an ambulance pulled up. They passed a squad car with its siren blaring. John was cool, calm.

It was best if Lyn stayed with Mary for the night, John said. They drove down to the Canal to collect her keys, then back to Ballymun. John was in great humour. He asked Lyn to sort through Mary's videotapes and put on a film. Lyn could not concentrate on the film, kept seeing the blood from the man's head dripping over the balcony. John left at around 3.00 a.m. Joey and Lyn sat up waiting for Mary to come home from the Canal. Lyn could see that Joey was upset. He must have been doing a lot of thinking because he said, 'I was thinking of John. Mam, he is a bit mad, isn't he? Did you see him with the hammer, Mam? He was trying to kill him. If you have trouble with someone, you just fight them. It's a bit much to smash their heads in with a hammer.'

Poor Joey did not know the half of the trail of havoc his idol had left. When Lyn had sent for John she had wanted protection, not a bloodbath. The stabbing of Liam Ryan and herself, John's merciless treatment of Teresa, his ruthless campaign against the Kelly family, the attempt to burn Dolores' house, the burning of Sheila's car and now the incident with the hammer attack. Joey said John was a 'bit mad', but was furious with Lyn when she took the suggestion seriously.

John decided Lyn was to move back to Ballymun in case the man died of his injuries. It was easy to hide in the warren of flats in Ballymun. John sent someone 'round to board up the broken windows to secure the flat until Lyn got her furniture stored. It was eight days before she could arrange for a removal van and she left her home in Coolock unoccupied with only a piece of plywood protecting her things. The word must have got around: 'Don't touch that flat. It's more than your life is worth. It belongs to a nutter.'

When Lyn moved into the new flat she started hiding the cutlery again. She first hid it after Liam Ryan's stabbing, but had taken to leaving things in the kitchen drawer since Joey came home. The hammer incident changed that.

John always ate a lot of fruit and one night, from his horizontal position on the settee, he ordered Lyn to fetch him an orange and a knife. She threw him an orange, then went into the kitchen and opened the drawer. Oh Christ! There was no knife. She forgot that she had hidden them. The damn things were two feet away from where he was lying. Lyn stood in a state of panic, wondering how she was going to get the knife.

'Just as I thought.' Lyn jumped. She had not heard him sneaking up on her. He pushed her back against the kitchen wall and opened the cutlery drawer and he turned to face her.

'Where are all the knives?' he asked. Lyn's legs trembled. She opened her mouth, but could not speak. 'Lyn, I'm leaving you,' he said quietly. 'I told you before that I wouldn't harm you again, d'you know what I mean like? This ain't the first time I've looked for a knife or something else, and you had them hidden. I never said nothin' because I knew you were scared then, but I haven't laid a finger on you for six months now. It's no fuckin' use to me if you're that scared of me. Look Lyn, I keep telling you, I love you, I fuckin' love you very much. It will kill me to leave you, but I have to do it. I can't live like this.'

Lyn felt cold in the pit of her stomach. She knew that if he left her he would go away and brood. He would then come back and carry out his promise to kill her. She pleaded, 'I know you haven't hurt me, John, but I can't help it. So much has happened. It's been downhill since Liam. I mean Teresa and the Kellys, the attempt on Dolores' house, Sheila's car and taking a hammer to that man's head.' The words were running out of her, she could not stop. 'I feel it's as if you've tasted blood and you want more, you can't stop. I know in the end you'll turn on me.'

He listened very carefully to her. When Lyn stopped he looked at her for a while longer and then took her by the hand into the bedroom. He told her to lie down, then lay down beside her. 'Lyn, it's time we had a good talk.'

She settled down and listened to his oration, a long one for him.

'What more can I do to prove how much I love you an' I'll never hurt you again, Lyn? D'you know what I mean, like? I've given up all me friends for you. I gave up playin' football.' Only because he fell for Lyn after setting her up with the team. 'Teresa is gone. I let you nag me, d'you know what I mean, like? I don't bother you for it. I put the money in both our names so that you'd have something put by. I let you bring young Joey to live with us. No other man would do that. I let you go to visit Chris whenever you like. I don't mind about the loss of earnings. I haven't looked at another woman since I fell for you.'

'Liar,' Lyn thought.

'I definitely haven't screwed another woman. You went mad over me wife givin' me love bites and I had to tell her to stop and that wasn't easy. I give you good working conditions. I let you take a night off if you're not well. I let you buy what you like out of the money. I let you have Sundays off.' He was not finished.

'I'm very, very patient with your moods. I'd have killed any other woman for slamming doors and answering back. I love you, Lyn. I love five people in this world, me three kids, me Ma and you and I don't hurt people I love, d'you know what I mean? Don't interrupt! I know I've hurt you in the past, but that was because I was jealous. I know you're mine now, and you're not into other men. I believe you wouldn't do anything to make me mad enough to take a knife to you. I'd only stab you if you went with another man or grassed me up. All your other faults I can put up with. If you start naggin' I'll walk out and come back when you're over it. Now Lyn, will you put the knives back and start afresh?'

Lyn was not convinced. She knew he loved her. He loved her the way she had loved him, a mixture of insecurity, obsessiveness and jealousy, and she knew that any slight on her part could bring his wrath down upon her head. She smiled at him. 'OK, John.' He kissed her. In spite of herself, Lyn was touched by his mammoth effort to communicate and agreed to try again. She told herself that she still 'sort of' loved him except when he acted crazy and terrified her. Any woman who has lived with a violent man will know that feeling. Lyn was accustomed to much more violence in her life than the majority of women.

The next few weeks were quiet. Three things changed that. Joey started going to Liverpool for football matches every weekend. John's wife had to give up the birth control pill for a few months. And Liam Ryan was pressing charges against John.

John had been up to court again over the stabbing. The book of evidence had been served on him. He brooded over that and resented Lyn having made the statement. The trial was listed for October. He believed that he had always been unlucky in the courts in that month. Liam Ryan had been warned not to give evidence against John. Liam dug in his heels and let it be known that he would not be intimidated. Cullen was going to pay for the stabbing.

The deterioration in John Cullen was visible. He lost his appetite, got irritable over the slightest thing and started drinking heavily. He started to mention Dolores again. He was not satisfied that she was scared over his attempt on her house, or, if she had heard about Teresa. It wasn't enough; he wanted to see her eyes when she knew she was going to die. He started wanting kinky sex again.

After the tie-up that Sunday he had asked her many times could he do the same thing again. Now his demands intensified. He asked her every day. Can I do this? Can I do that? She either said 'no', point blank, or if he was in bad humour, she made excuses.

Lyn suffered from a lot of mysterious ailments over those few months. She hid everything that could be used for a tie-up, tights, scarves etc. She got up at night when he had gone, did the washing and hung it out, then made sure to bring the line in before he arrived next day. When Joey was at home and John looked for sex, Lyn said she was not in the humour. He did not push the issue. He did not want Joey to hear them arguing. He could get his sex at home. Then he told her his wife could not have sex because she was not taking the pill, so Lyn would have to step into the breach.

'Careful John, me back's killin' me.' 'Don't lean on my chest, I've a lump in my breast and it hurts.' She had a cyst. 'No, I can't do it that way.' Her best ploy was to sit up quickly and talk in earnest. A little 'intellectual' conversation always floored him. She had learned a little trick in handling some of John's deviations: clinical discussions turned him off. Not being very bright, he would try to control his temper and attempt to look intelligent while Lyn prattled on. Then he would say that he did not want her to do it that way every day, just once.

Lyn would reply that they had tried it; it was too painful; hadn't he promised he would never hurt her again?

When Joey was away for football matches Lyn had to lick John's boots. She was above reproach. Then she had a brainwave.

'John, you know how you said I will have to go into hiding to avoid the subpoena for Liam's stabbing? Well, we are going to need money to cover my loss of earnings, right? I'll know when because Róisín will tell me when she gets her subpoena. So, I think I should work a double shift on, say, Fridays and

Saturdays. What do you think?' That would cover the nights Joey was away at football matches. It would mean John would not collect her; she would make her own way home in a taxi.

John beamed at her. 'You're a great bird, Lyn. You're always thinkin' ahead. I'd been thinkin' myself you'd been off for a good while, but I didn't like to ask you to work longer hours.' That still left the day time.

'John, I'll be jaded after a double shift. Will you call a bit later in the day? I need my sleep.'

'Right, love,' he replied. 'You have a good rest and I'll be up in the afternoon.' John went missing the odd day and Lyn knew he was hunting for sex.

22

John Cullen was missing for three days, during which Lyn was attacked at work by a bunch of skinheads. When he did arrive, she was furious. 'Don't walk in here grinning like a bloody Cheshire cat. Come for your takings, have you? My hero! Where the hell were you when I was getting my head caved in?'

'Your head looks OK to me, other than your big mouth,' he replied, smiling.

'Listen,' Lyn said, 'four guys followed me down a laneway and one of them got out and smashed the windows of the car I was in. The guy used a bloody iron bar to do it. If I hadn't ducked I wouldn't *have* a bloody mouth. I wouldn't have a head on my shoulders at all! And another thing. Those guys came at me because of you. It was you they were out to get, someone you've crossed, probably someone connected with the Kelly family.'

He snapped, 'Shut fuckin' up. I had work to do.'

'Work?' Lyn yelled. 'Since when the hell did you ever do an honest day's work?'

He wasn't smiling. He was trying to control his temper.

'Listen, you dummy,' he said softly. 'I went to burn Dolores' house again but there were too many people around so I had to knock it on the head.' 'You are a bloody liar, John Cullen,' Lyn yelled. 'I know you were out with some tramp.'

He lost his temper. 'Listen you, you fuckin' idiot, I don't have to lie to you, d'you know what I mean? I don't have to lie to anyone. No one fuckin' owns me. If I was with a woman, then I was with a woman. There is fuck all you can do about it. I wish I was with a woman. You're drivin' me to it. I said I went to Dolores' and you just better fuckin' take it that that is where I was.'

Lyn was still seething over the attack, her pimp's absence. 'Don't you call me a fuckin' idiot. I've got more brains in my little finger than you've got in your head. You're the idiot. You! Only a bloody imbecile would keep on about something that happened seven years ago. You're sick in the bloody head, John Cullen. Well, I'll tell you something. I've listened to you for the last two and a half years. Dolores this, Dolores that. Every time you go missing for the night you come up the next day, – "I was up at Dolores" ' – a load of crap you're giving me. You had your chance with Dolores, and you promised you'd leave it at that. I don't want to hear the name Dolores again, do you understand? In fact I don't want to hear anyone's name again. If you want to get somebody as you say, well don't tell me about it.'

Lyn knew that she was pushing her luck. She did not care. She was in bits over the incident with the skinheads, and had something to flaunt: her legs were all cut.

John Cullen pushed her back on the bed and put his hands round her throat, his voice was even, controlled. 'If Joey wasn't in his room, I would snuff the life out of you. You are a fuckin' liberty taker. If we were on our own, you wouldn't dare to talk to me like that. I'm going out on my own for a drink. I may pick a woman up, I don't know. Just remember one thing, Lyn. I won't forget this.'

He left. He turned up a few days later and acted as though nothing had happened.

A week later Róisín was served with her subpoena and said that the sergeant had asked where Lyn was living. Lyn went to work that night. She did not know it then, but it was to be her last night on the streets. To avoid the subpoena she ignored any knock on the door for weeks. John went up for trial, but it was put back. He had undergone another change. He brooded all the time now and had stopped taking Lyn into his confidence, would not discuss the stabbing case at all.

Some days Lyn was physically sick with nerves. She did not know what was going on in his mind, and she let her imagination run riot. Perhaps he would kill her before he went to court. Perhaps he would kill Joey, too. She wondered whether he would kill them both together. How would he do it?

John kept moving Lyn to different flats in Ballymun to avoid the subpoena. She kept her own flat where Joey stayed to mind her furniture. Christmas came. Lyn persuaded John to let her go and visit her mother, explaining that the pressure of hiding and moving to different flats was getting her down. She needed the break. The real truth was that his court case had once again been put back until January, and Lyn knew the waiting would get him down. She feared what John might do. After the two previous Christmases, which had ended with Lyn at the point of a knife, Lyn was afraid of Christmas in Dublin.

John rang her a couple of times while she was in England. He told her that he had driven up to Liam Ryan's house three nights running and just sat and watched it. Liam had looked out and seen him. John hoped it freaked him out. The next time John rang, he told Lyn that he had beaten up an English prostitute. He said, 'I was depressed over you being away. I had nowhere to go. It's no use going to our flat if you're not there, d'you know what I mean like? So I decided I felt like giving it to a bird. I picked up a black woman off the square. She said she wanted £25 in the flat.'

When they got to her flat John lay down, and she told him to get his shoes off the bed. John smiled at her and said, 'You take my shoes off for me.' She got pretty lippy then, John said on the phone, 'so I jumped up and punched her in the face. She opened a drawer and took out a knife and I really lost the head. I took the knife off her and beat the hell out of her. Some fellow came up from the flat below and asked what was going on. I told him to get back downstairs or he would get the same. She ran into the kitchen and took up another knife. I just laughed at her and twisted her wrist till she dropped the knife and I gave it to her again then for her nerve.'

'I suppose you bloody screwed her before you beat her up?' He got angry. 'I wouldn't screw a black bird.'

Lyn arrived back in Dublin alone on 1 January, Joey having travelled on to Liverpool. Bizarre as it sounds now, Lyn hoped that 1983 would be a better year than 1982. John met her at the boat. He was very subdued, different. She could not put her finger on the difference. He was affectionate, tender, asked her how she had enjoyed the holiday; told her, repeatedly, how much he had missed her, but his mind was elsewhere. He stayed with her until 4.00 a.m., their usual time. Lyn had been nervous about coming home without Joey, but John was preoccupied, and Lyn wondered what had happened to him while she had been away. Something was on his mind. If his name was not John Cullen, she would have sworn that he was feeling guilty!

Lyn knew that he had been in the flat while she was away. Róisín had taught her all the traps that she used to set to catch Willy out. She would sprinkle Harpic in the toilet bowl. A man would just flush the toilet without thinking. She would leave a wire clothes hanger on the bed, and if he was getting in with a woman he would throw it on the floor. Her party piece was leaving little notes in between the sheets: 'He's a married man!' 'He's a pimp with three women on the town', or 'He has VD.'

When Lyn was head over heels in love with John she had told him all Róisín's traps because she thought that she would never have to resort to that with John. Now things had changed. He had changed. Before she went to her mother's, Lyn had set traps, subtly. She folded the towels in the bathroom, just so. Almost every article that would be likely to be used she placed strategically. When she asked him who he had brought to the flat, he replied, 'I was only up once to take a bath. Anyway, that's the end of the matter. There is something more important to think about. I want you to go up to Liam Ryan's house and get him into his car on some pretext, d'you know what I mean like? Get him in the car, ask him for a lift somewhere, then go to the police and say he raped you. I want him to go before the jury handcuffed to prison officers.'

'John, do you think I can just walk into a cop shop and say Liam raped me and they will fly out and arrest him? D'you not know that they would have me examined by a doctor?' 'I've gone into this very carefully, Lyn. I'll screw you just before you go and rough you up a little, a few bruises. D'you know what I mean, like, nothin' too bad. Now, when you get Liam in the car, make a play for him. Pretend you want him to screw you, get his trousers undone and grab his pubic hairs. Then you can mix them up with your own before you go to the police. Now, what do you think?'

Lyn was at eye level with his hair transplant. It looked like pubic hairs and she was bursting to laugh. She thought of Liam, of all people!

'Think? I think it's bloody hilarious! I could just picture Liam's face. He would have a coronary. Liam is just not into women. I've known him years and I've never heard even a whisper about another woman. He's one hell of a conservative guy. If he didn't die of a coronary, do you honestly think he is going to sit there and watch me pull a handful of his pubic hairs out and do nothing? He would probably kill me!'

Lyn collapsed laughing, tears and mascara streaming down. She could see the blood draining from John's face, but she just could not control herself. At least she would die laughing.

'Look,' he said, 'every time I get a good idea you take the piss out of me. I don't see what is so funny about what I've just said. Even if he does beat you up, so much the better. Are you going to do it? Yes or no?'

'I'm sorry, John, I just keep seeing Liam's face. He would think I'd lost my marbles if I dropped my hand on him. Ask me again tomorrow, it may not seem so funny then.' She tried to placate him.

'Right, Lyn, perhaps it does sound a little crazy, but we will talk about it again. I still think it's a good idea. If the jury see him in custody, they won't take his word on anything.'

Joey arrived back from Liverpool the next day and John and Lyn met him at the boat. There was no more mention of Liam and the staged rape. In the next week John missed four days coming to see Lyn. When he did arrive, it was around 11.30 after the pubs. He promptly fell asleep until she woke him to go home at 4.00 a.m. His trial was listed for 11 January and he called to Lyn after the court hearing to tell her it had once more been put back until 1 February. He was as high as a kite. Liam Ryan had gone to court that morning and Willy had approached Liam on John's behalf and asked him to say that he was mistaken; it was a stranger who had stabbed him. Liam refused.

'See, I told you, Lyn,' Cullen said. 'I said he would get up in the witness box and point me out. And you kept saying he wouldn't when the day came. Well, we all thought the trial was going ahead this morning and the rat was there. February the first gives me three weeks. I'm going to sort Liam out, and there is one other person I have to make sure is dead. She's not getting off scot free.'

Dolores again.

'Look John, I keep saying it to you over and over again. I know Liam. I know how his mind works. Do you seriously think he will stand up in a public court and point you out? How will he ever live it down, being called a grass? He just wants you to suffer. He wants to make you sweat till the last minute. When they say to him, "Is this the man who stabbed you?", he wants your nerves to be at screaming point. He wants you to look at him and then he'll say, "No, that's not him." You can't blame him, John, for wanting you to suffer. You did nearly kill him.'

Lyn knew he was not convinced, but he let the matter drop. On the day of the Lynches' death, John arrived at half past four in the afternoon. He was always a little late on Saturday because he spent time with his children when they were not at school. Lyn wished she could have kept Joey from going to the football match in Liverpool. John was in such a weird humour, she would have to lick his boots. He watched television. Lyn cooked dinner. Lyn talked in a bright voice, but John was unresponsive. As the night passed, Lyn grew more uneasy. He brooded, staring at the television, but she knew he was not seeing it. Even in his bath, she did not learn anything from him. There was a terrible heaviness in the flat, like the presence of a serious illness.

Because there were no thermostats to control the heating in individual Ballymun flats, it was always oppressively hot, but Lyn was not sweating because of the heat. She wished John would say something. 'John I'm going to have a bath. I feel very sticky. Will I put a film on the video or are you going to read the paper?' The television had finished. He stared vacantly at the ceiling.

'John?'

He shifted his eyes to look at Lyn. 'I heard you. You can put a film on and hand me the paper.' She sorted through the films, and opted for a three-hour recording of the World Cup Highlights, thinking, 'Find something kinky in that, John'. Then she went into the bathroom, locked the door and sank back into the bath with relief, her eyes closed.

When she had fallen madly in love with John, they had always taken their daily bath together. He would get in first and when he had washed, he would tell her to get in with him. She always had the tap end. They joked about that. Lyn said that if ever women got equal rights, they would have to take it in turns for the taps. Nowadays, Lyn took her bath alone, with the door locked. She had a good reason for that. John Cullen had bought her a book, *Crime in our Century*. In Chapter Three, 'A Question of Suicide', there was an account of the trial of John Joseph Smith who was the accused in the 'Brides in the Bath' murders. He married four women, took out insurance policies on each one and then drowned them. The pathologist, Bernard Spilsbury, could not ascertain how the women had been killed as there were no marks of violence on the bodies and no excessive water on the floor. It was only when the trial was in progress that the inspector in charge of the case discovered how the murders were committed. The bath was an exhibit in court. The inspector asked a woman police constable to don a swimming costume and get into the bath. He tried holding her head under water. Strong as he was, he could not hold her under water for more than a few seconds and water splashed everywhere. Then he picked up her legs and pulled. She went unconscious. A shocked court watched as it took half an hour to resuscitate her. She explained that the shock of the water going up her nostrils was what had caused her to pass out.

Lyn had read the chapter to John. He laughed and said, 'That's a very good idea you've just given me, Lyn. If I ever wanted to get rid of you I could wait till you were in the bath, then pull your legs from under you.' So now, she locked the bathroom door.

Lyn lay soaking in the bath that night, 16 January 1983, not wanting to get out, delaying the moment when she would have to rejoin her tense, silent, brooding lover. She dreaded whatever the night held for her. Even now, she often wakes up at approximately the same time as the nightmare happened and, sweating, relives it all, hears the screams. She relives standing in a garden watching John Cullen put a fire bomb through the open window onto the floor of Dolores Lynch's home and remembers how three women died because a young prostitute had, seven years earlier, dared to stand up to a pimp.

23

'Well, Lyn, you have been a free agent for almost twenty-four hours,' said Róisín. 'Will you come for a drink?' Free. And still afraid to go for a drink with a woman friend. Lyn felt guilty about thinking of going for a drink. John would hate it. She felt him as still a part of herself, or herself a part of him. She had to keep reminding herself that she had helped to put him behind bars. In John Cullen's eyes, she was no longer a person. She was an object of hate. She was wracked with guilt for grassing. No matter that she had just confessed her own guilt which consequently included John. She had wanted to pay for her weakness. Pay for letting the awful thing happen. She did not have the heart to go for a drink.

The next day was Saturday. At teatime, Róisín and Willy set to work to persuade her to get out of the flat, celebrate her freedom from John. He had done so much damage, she could not say that she was not relieved to be free of him. And yet, she missed him.

For Róisín's sake, Lyn agreed to 'celebrate'. They went to the Penthouse. Lyn had not been there since the night of Liam Ryan's stabbing. She sat and looked around. Nothing had changed. They were upstairs, which was as large as a major warehouse with its pin-ball machines, snooker tables and men huddled over playing cards and dominoes. It looked better than middle-class with all the well-dressed women, their gold

sovereigns and charm bracelets. A closer look revealed the battle scarred faces of both sexes, the men scarred by each other
and the women by their men. And of course, the tattoos. A
stranger might only notice so many beauty spots under one
roof. The Borstal spot on the face is the universal hallmark of
the ex-convict. When Lyn tattooed the spot on her own cheek
years ago, the face looking back at her from the mirror smiled
acceptance. 'It's not the temperature in the Penthouse that's
hot; so are the clothes and the jewellery bought from the local
shoplifters and robbers,' says Lyn.

Willy and some friends were down the other end of the pub
playing snooker. A man Lyn did not know walked over to them
and said he had visited a friend of his in Mountjoy and the
friend had asked him to get a message to Lyn from John Cullen.
John said he loved her and asked if she would go up and visit
him.

Lyn went to pieces, overcome with pity and guilt. Róisín took
her hand, squeezed it and said, 'Lyn, I would feel the same way
if I got a message from Willy from Mountjoy. But you know
yourself, John's different. John would probably attack you in the
visiting room.'

Lyn knew that Róisín was right. He was crazy enough to lure
her up to Mountjoy and attack her in full view of the prison
officers.

They were knocking back vodkas, but Lyn was so depressed
that she was still stone cold sober. Willy and his friends joined
them. One guy sat next to Lyn. She noticed that he was drinking lemonade. He was extremely good-looking and under different circumstances Lyn would have been interested, but he
just sat staring at her without speaking, making her feel uneasy.
Róisín and Lyn were talking about John in an undertone when
the guy said suddenly, 'You know, you look like Joan Collins.'

Lyn broke off the conversation to look at him. He was not
smiling, he had a very serious expression on his face. Lyn smiled
nervously and answered, 'I don't know whether to take that as
a compliment or not. Everybody tells me that. Personally, I
think she's awful.'

He didn't acknowledge Lyn's reply, just stared a while longer
and said, 'I was asked to do a job on you last night.'

'What do you mean?' she asked. 'I was offered £5,000 to exterminate you,' he said coldly. He continued that weird stare and eventually he asked, 'How would you like to go?'

'You can shoot me,' Lyn said, 'in the back of the head, so I don't know it's coming.'

He still stared, 'Mmmm, I don't know. My boss was approached to do it, but he doesn't need the money, so he put me on to it. I'll have to think about it.' He stared at Lyn for a while longer, then got up and went to the bar and asked over his shoulder what Róisín and Lyn were drinking.

Willy leaned over the table and said softly, 'Lyn, don't take the piss out of Terry O'Brien. He means what he's saying. He was offered £5,000 to kill you. Put the charm on. I think he fancies you.'

Róisín heard what Willy said and started to cry. That did not help Lyn. By the time Terry O'Brien came back with the drinks, Róisín and Lyn were in tatters. He sat back down beside Lyn. She did not turn on the charm as Willy had advised because she could not find any, but she treated him with due reverence. He was still staring at her, but now she knew that he was a hit man, Lyn wondered what he was thinking. Was he measuring her like the hangman does for the noose? He knew Lyn was uneasy.

'You don't know me, Lyn,' he said, 'but I know you. My boss knows you.'

'No,' Lyn said sweetly, 'I've never seen you before. What is your name?'

He pulled his stomach in, puffed out his chest. 'My name is Terry O'Brien. My boss knows you, says you're a nice bird. Now I've met you, I think so, too. I don't know whether I will take the contract or not.' He got up and left.

'Lyn, I'm not going back to the flat,' Róisín said, and started weeping again. Lyn tried to console her, although she was as bad, not crying, but in a state of terror. By closing time, Róisín was adamant that she was not going back to the flat. Willy tried arguing with her, but she refused to listen, so in the end he said, 'Right, come with me.'

The two women followed Willy into Ballymun Garda Station. He asked to speak to the sergeant in charge, who was also the sergeant in charge of the Liam Ryan stabbing. They spent about an hour talking to him. Willy demanded protection from the police for Róisín and Lyn. He said he had been told by a man in the Penthouse that there was a £5,000 contract out on Lyn. The sergeant was unimpressed. He told them to go home and stop being melodramatic. Róisín sobbed uncontrollably.

Willy said, 'Look, you give me permission to carry a gun and I will protect the two of them.'

Lyn caught the sergeant's eye and raised her eyes to heaven in mockery behind Willy's back. The sergeant laughed and so, did Lyn.

'Willy,' she said, 'he can't give you permission to carry a firearm. Don't talk so stupid.'

The sergeant said if Róisín and Lyn went home, he would get someone from the Murder Squad out to visit them. They were not very happy about it, but they had to leave it at that. They left the station and Willy drove them home. Róisín was still crying. She begged Willy to stay in the flat with her. He refused, saying that he had stayed away from his own house for four days.

Willy ferreted the gun from its hiding place. There were three bullets in it. Lyn used to go for target practice in England and became a pretty good shot. Lyn told Willy that if she had to, she would use the gun. Lyn was taken aback when he said, 'You won't need it, Lyn. I'm taking it home with me.'

'Willy, it's me the bloody contract is out on!'

'Lyn, you heard Terry say that he would think about whether to take the contract or not. I don't think he will now that he has met you. If anyone is going to get killed, it'll be me, so I need the gun for my protection.'

Lyn sat up all night keeping watch and waiting for the Murder Squad to call. They never came. Although Terry had said he was not sure if he would take the contract or not, Lyn knew that even if he did not, someone else would. There were men who would kill for less than £5,000. Lyn felt hurt, but not surprised, that John wanted her killed. It numbed any feelings of guilt or pity she had for him.

Willy called at around noon with his gun. When he learned that the Murder Squad had not come, he said he would wait until the evening and then call them himself. Róisín and Lyn were too terrified to walk across to the shopping centre to the phone in case they got hit on the way. Lyn was furious with the police. They had given great assurances while they were getting the statements, but now she felt thrown to the wolves. At 8.00 p.m. Willy was done up like a dog's dinner, going out for a drink. 'Willy, you needn't think you are just walking out of here,' said Róisín. 'I refuse to stay in this flat tonight. I told you that. It's OK for you, you're walking around with a gun in your belt, while me and Lyn are sitting here like two stoolies.'

Willy banged the palm of his hand on his forehead. 'Christ, I forgot! I will ring the Murder Squad the minute I get in the pub.'

Their hero walked out the door to go to the pub with his .45 in his belt.

Thirty minutes later, two detectives from Kevin Street arrived and agreed that the women should be moved out of the flat at once. Róisín left a note telling Willy they had gone with the police. The men checked their guns before they opened the door to go out, checked the stairs, then decided it would attract less attention if they walked over to Ballymun Garda Station in two pairs. Lyn set off with one detective, Tom, whom she knew from way back and liked. She used to see him in the patrol car when she was down on the Canal.

Tom said that Willy's phone call was the first they had heard of the threats. The sergeant from Ballymun had not phoned them and the two detectives made a few phone calls before driving the women to a hotel for the night. Róisín wanted to ring Willy to let him know where she was. 'No, Róisín, I would prefer if you didn't,' said the detective. 'Pressure could be put on Willy to tell where you were.'

'It wouldn't take much pressure,' Lyn thought. Róisín insisted on ringing Willy in the pub anyway. She told him that they were being taken to a hotel and she would contact him in the morning.

'Well, that's a worry off my mind,' said Willy.

The detectives left them at the hotel, advising them not to go out that night, as if they needed advising. They watched television in the lounge, then took coffee and sandwiches up to their room. They giggled like school girls. Róisín was always giddy and the atmosphere in the hotel was such a relief from all the tension of sitting waiting for some lunatic to boot the door in.

In the morning, they went downstairs and Lyn paid the bill. Róisín had no money and it left Lyn with one pound, but at least she had slept. The same two detectives brought them to the station to tell the whole story to the Murder Squad. They were put under the twenty-four-hour protection of the Special Task Force.

24

When Lyn was under interrogation by the Murder Squad, she had been subpoenaed as a witness in Liam Ryan's case against John. On 1 February, 1983 she was outside the courtroom waiting for the case to begin when she saw John Cullen walking towards the court, handcuffed to a prison officer. Lyn hid behind a uniformed guard as John swaggered into the courtroom.

Lyn bowed her head as she entered the tightly packed court and stood just inside the door, ready to make a run for it should John try to get at her. John's barrister was mumbling and Lyn kept her eyes fixed on the judge until she became aware of Róisín.

'Lyn,' she whispered, 'John's trying to attract your attention. He's pointing at me to tell you to look at him.' Lyn darted a look in John's direction. He was gesticulating and miming the words 'come here'.

'I can't,' she mouthed back.

He shook his head furiously. 'Come fuckin' here!' he mouthed angrily. Lyn was faint and clutched Róisín's arm for support before a firm hand took her arm and steered her outside. The detective said, 'I saw him raving at you. You shouldn't look at him. Stay there.'

Lyn walked unsteadily over to a table and pulled herself up to sit on it. She was not there for more than five minutes when Róisín and a detective came out of the courtroom.

'It's put back again till 4 February,' said Róisín.

'Oh no, Róisín, I can't go through this again.' Lyn turned to the detective. 'What the hell's going on?' Lyn asked.

'It's only three days; he's up on Friday. We've fresh evidence. He admitted the stabbing when we had him in for the murders. We'll be in touch with you before then.' Willy was going on about John wanting to talk to Lyn in the courtroom.

'His actions were like a cry from the heart,' Willy said. 'You could see the pain in his eyes, Lyn. He needs you.'

Róisín thought differently. 'You must be joking, Willy. He looked like a bloody madman. I was terrified. I think if Lyn had gone over to talk to him, he would have just closed his hands around her throat. And by the look in his eyes, it would have taken a good few cops to get him off her. What do you think yourself, Lyn?'

Willy watched Lyn in the driving mirror. 'I don't know,' Lyn said simply. She did not know what to think. She did not know how she could face John again on Friday.

The uniformed policeman was on duty on the balcony outside Róisín's flat on the fourth floor. It was so cold that they were only working in two hour shifts. Willy had forbidden the women to have them in the flat. His mates would not like it. Róisín's neighbour asked the policemen to sit in her hall and gave them hot soup and tea. The men were unarmed, no hindrance to an armed killer, with just a walkie-talkie for protection. Lyn felt sorry for them.

Róisín wanted to go back to work. Lyn kept arguing with her that it was not safe since John Cullen knew it was she who went to the police about Dolores. But Róisín and Willy were broke, so Lyn gave Willy £100, telling him that it would cover her food for two weeks. She could not eat with worry, but at least the donation would keep Róisín safe a little longer.

By 4 February, Lyn had not heard from the Murder Squad about the stabbing trial. She presumed that she had got the dates confused. Róisín and Lyn followed Willy over to the Penthouse that night. Terry O'Brien came in and sat down to talk to Lyn, who waited for him to make a reference to the £5,000 contract on her life.

Terry said that he had heard from Willy that she was having aggro with Joey. 'He can come and live with me if you like. I have a way with lads of that age,' Terry told her. 'I'll keep him under control.'

Lyn reflected that it would take nothing less than a hit man to make Joey civil, but she said, 'He'll be alright. He's just a kid. It's all a bit much for him,' and she thanked Terry O'Brien profusely. He didn't say he was passing on the contract to someone else, but he told her to consider him a friend.

'If you need anything at all, come to me.' Lyn thanked him profusely again and Terry then introduced Lyn to his brother Bill, from which another problem for Lyn developed. Bill O'Brien never took his eyes off Lyn the whole night. She could feel him staring at her from right opposite and she looked everywhere but at him and could still feel his eyes on her.

At the end of the night, Róisín and Lyn went in to the shopping centre for a take-away curry. Willy O'Donnell and Bill O'Brien stood at the door of the car having a heated discussion. They could not hear them, but Lyn sensed it was about her. When they got the curries, they were on the way to the car when Terry O'Brien came running to Willy and whispered something urgently. Lyn watched Willy take his gun out of the waistband of his trousers and hand it to Terry. Willy reached into his trouser pocket, withdrew his car keys and gave them also. Róisín, Willy and Lyn set off on foot, with Róisín putting out a barrage of questions. Why had Willy given the keys and the gun to Terry? Terry was going to do a job. He would drop the car and the gun back over to Róisín's flat in one hour.

'What were you and Bill O'Brien arguing about?' Róisín asked.

Willy said, 'Oh stop! He was raving about Lyn. He fancies her. He wanted us to have a party in the flat so he can get off with her. I had a hell of a job putting him off. I kept saying, "You don't know what that bird has been through. She won't go with you. She's in tatters after the murders and the arrest. She needs a rest." He wouldn't give up. I had to more or less promise him that you'd go with him in a week or two, to shut him up.'

Róisín was already fast asleep. Lyn envied Róisín her ability to sleep. She took her sleeping pills and settled herself down with a book. She was drifting off to sleep when there was a loud thumping on the door. 'Who is it?' Lyn asked.

'Lyn?' She recognised Terry O'Brien's voice. 'Is Willy there?'

Lyn yawned. 'Are you on your own, Terry?' Lyn asked.

'Yes,' came the reply. Lyn opened the door. Terry smiled sheepishly and stepped into the hall saying, 'Sorry to disturb you, Lyn.' She padded down the hall in front of him, sat down on the settee trying to wake herself up.

'Do you want a cup of tea, Terry?' Lyn asked sleepily.

'No, Lyn. I'm in a hurry. Tell Willy his car is over at Ballymun Garda Station. Here's the gun,' he said, pulling it from inside his overcoat and handing it to her.

Lyn put her hand over her mouth to stifle a yawn, then asked, 'What happened, Terry?'

He laughed. 'I was driving around the roundabout at Ballymun when I spotted a police roadblock. So I slowed down and put the gun at the side of the road, then drove on. The cop at the road blockflagged me down and when he asked me my name, I said, "Willy O'Donnell". He started yelling. He said, "Don't get fuckin' smart with me, Terry O'Brien, you're under arrest!" I've been locked up for four hours. I'm up in court in the morning. Tell Willy I'm sorry about the car. I'll go now, Lyn. Sorry for getting you out of bed.'

Lyn locked the door after him, got back into bed and tried to sleep and then it hit her. She started to laugh until she could not stop, tears streaming down her face. 'Oh God! Who is it? Terry O'Brien. Are you on your own? Yes. Open door. Please do come in, Mr Hitman. Would you like a cup of tea before you shoot me? Here's the gun, Lyn. Yawn. Thanks, Terry. Yawn. There's a cop outside the door freezing his balls off to prevent me getting hit and I invite the hitman in!' Lyn laughed herself to sleep.

Róisín was horrified the next morning. 'Lyn, were you not scared?'

Lyn giggled. 'Róisín, I was so bloody tired it never dawned on me. I'd have opened the door to the devil himself. "Are you on your own, Terry?" And they laughed.

Willy called about 9.30 a.m., in a bad mood over Terry and the car. He brightened considerably when Lyn told him that the car was in Ballymun Garda Station yard, and that Terry had left the gun. When Willy was leaving to collect his car, Lyn said. 'By the way, Willy, thanks for putting Bill O'Brien off last night. I think I would go crazy if anybody even attempted to make love to me just now.'

He gave her a penetrating look and said, 'I know, Lyn. Your whole personality is kind of wound up. I can see it in you. You're ready to explode.'

Lyn became deeply depressed as the day wore on and decided not to go to the Penthouse. It was only asking for trouble. She realised that she was doing what she always did in an emergency, attracting the toughest guy in the pack to protect her from John Cullen's fury. Bill was not a pimp, but he was the hardest man in the pub. He would become a pimp, and he had a reputation as a woman beater.

She had just gotten rid of the most dangerous pimp in Dublin, and the time had come for her to go it alone. Friday 4 February marked another milestone for her. That was to be the day she unconsciously turned her back on the old life.

It was only a matter of days before she did it physically, too.

John Cullen was sentenced to three years' imprisonment for the stabbing of Liam Ryan. Lyn was overjoyed that she had not had to give evidence. His trial had originally been listed for hearing by a judge who had an awesome reputation for handing out severe sentences. Instead, John had pleaded guilty in front of Judge Neylon. He had admitted the stabbing when he was being interrogated about the Lynch murders.

Lyn now felt an overwhelming release of tension. There was no fear of John appearing in the doorway and she would be safe for at least two years. But Lyn still had another problem. She had not told the police everything about the night of the fire and it weighed heavily on her conscience. Three days later, she went into Kevin Street Garda Station and gave them the full account. They listened in silence and when she had finished, one of them demanded to know why she had not told them everything when she was under arrest. Lyn wanted to explain that she felt safe now that John was doing a three year stretch, but decided to let them figure it out for themselves.

'No matter. She's telling us now. She was too scared before,' one cop said. They drove Lyn out to Portrane to show them where John had dumped his clothes the night after the fire. They clambered over the cliff and found some shreds of clothing, but there was a fierce gale and they had to abandon their search. On the way back to the car, Lyn caught her heel and fell headlong, exactly as she had done that night with John. They said they would send the forensic boys out later in the day, and remarked that Lyn looked peaky and ought to go home and get some rest. She was shattered by having to return to Portrane, but slept well, relieved. The next day the unarmed police were removed and the Special Task Force was assigned to protect her. Lyn realised that what she had told the Murder Squad was dynamite. She was a vital witness: she had seen everything.

Róisín went back to work. The first night she started back, Lyn waved goodbye from the kitchen window and was stunned to see the Special Task Force cruise along behind her. Panic.

Lyn hung out of the window for half an hour, watching and waiting until she realised they had not simply escorted Róisín to the taxi rank. Róisín returned at 5.00 a.m. 'The STF followed my taxi to work and they parked opposite while I stood on my beat,' Róisín laughed. When she got a client, they followed her and parked at the top of the laneway until she had done the job.

'Great,' Lyn thought, 'they are making sure Róisín is safe at work while their prime witness is a sitting duck. Now what?'

On Monday 4 February, Róisín and Lyn had tea with a nun they had met at the Legion House. They spent an easy afternoon talking out their fears and hopes. The nun had been a great help to Róisín in relation to the time she was raped. 'She just talked to me, Lyn, and asked me questions and after a while I began to believe what she said, that I'm worth something. I'm not just a bit of dirt. I'm Róisín.' Lyn was surprised to hear the giddy Róisín talk like that. But the nun, because she was a nun, had never succeeded in getting through to Lyn.

'She was a nice woman,' Lyn recalls, 'but still a nun. They all get around to religion eventually, don't they? When they started in about Mary Magdalen, I always switched off.' Lyn and Róisín took a taxi back to the flat and Róisín went off to work, followed by her escort.

For nine days after that, Lyn never moved outside the door. She was feeling the pressure of living in somebody else's space. She longed to sleep in a bed. She had slept in Róisín's bed the first two nights and had woken in the middle of the night drenched, when Róisín wet the bed. Lyn supposed it was Róisín's nerves and moved onto the settee. Also, there were endless visitors in and out of the flat. Lyn hated that. She longed to be alone.

Two of the Murder Squad arrived at the flat. They did not search it, but they asked Willy for his gun saying that if he handed it up he would hear no more about it. It was common knowledge that Willy was carrying the gun and the police said that they were in a lot of trouble over it. Willy insisted that he was not actually the owner of the gun, that he had only had it out on hire at a cost of £200 and it had been given back to the owner. They did not believe him, but let it lie, probably hoping to catch him off guard with it. Little did they know that Willy had been walking around Ballymun with the .45 tucked into his trousers, armed as he passed the Special Task Force with a smile and a wave.

When the detective left, Willy became very morose. The gun was under his bed at home. He sent a fellow to retrieve it in case his house was raided by the police and told him to put it in a safe place. Willy said he did not feel safe in his own house now without protection.

'I'm not very happy about Róisín going to court when I can't carry the gun,' Willy said.

'I fail to see what being unable to carry a gun has to do with Róisín going to court,' Lyn said. He knew Lyn was upset, so he let the matter drop.

Lyn could not let it drop. 'You're only worried about your own skin, you're a gutless wonder,' Lyn yelled at Willy. 'You should have thought things out a bit before you went to the police about the fire. It's too late worrying about your skin now. The Cullens know you grassed.'

Willy grinned sheepishly. Then Lyn turned on Róisín. 'Remember one thing, Róisín. Willy will leave you one day and when he does, you'll have to live with what you've done. He only cares about his own skin. You think I don't know you're backin' off and leavin' me on my own?' Lyn flashed at her.

Róisín did not answer. Lyn stormed out of the flat. She passed the Special Task Force car. It was the first time since they had started the 'protection' that they had seen her outside the flat. They looked bemused and Lyn could see that they were undecided about whether to follow her. She was the main witness, but stubbornly, Lyn did not turn her head as she passed them. Fearfully she entered her own flat and after searching it, barricaded the door. She looked out the window. No Special Task Force. Probably on the walkie-talkie right now, she thought, panic stations: this one's left, do we follow or stay outside Róisín's flat? Instructions please?

Night fell, and still no police protection. Lyn sat up in a chair all night waiting for her assassin. When daylight came, she snatched two hours of dream-filled sleep. The day passed as she tried unsuccessfully to read or watch the television. That night, Lyn sat up again till daybreak, her nerves tuned to screaming point, waiting, listening. She was too scared to move outside the flat. She knew her executioner lay in wait. Three days and nights, Lyn sat in that flat waiting for the guardians of the law to come to her aid. Where the hell were they, she wondered? Had the outside world ceased to function? That night Lyn sat up with pots and pans of water on the stove, simmering at boiling point. Dolores had told her that this is what she had done, when she went to bed at night during her trouble with John Cullen seven years ago. Lyn had laughed when Dolores had told her that, little knowing that seven years later, she herself would be sitting waiting to scald the executioner who had been paid by Dolores' executioner.

On the fourth morning Lyn broke. She knew that she could not take another night like that. She dressed and walked over to Ballymun Garda Station at 8.45 a.m. She had to risk getting hit on the way. Lyn asked the sergeant if she could make a phone call to Kevin Street Gardaí. She gave her name and said, 'Look, I have been over in my own flat for the past three days with no protection whatsoever and the Special Task Force are following Róisín around like imbeciles. Do you not realise that she will not give evidence when the trial comes up? It's as simple as this; I am not leaving Ballymun Garda Station until I get police protection. My nerves are shot to hell worrying, waitin' for someone to blow my head off my shoulders.'

She could hear the hysteria in her voice, but she was unable to control it. The voice on the other end spoke soothingly. 'Calm yourself, Lyn. There must have been a mix-up somewhere. Go back to your own flat and wait and we will call out and collect you. I give you my word. You will be alright going back to the flat in daylight, OK?'

Lyn pondered this for a minute then reached a decision. 'Right,' she said. 'I will go back to my own flat and wait. I'll wait until 6.00 p.m., that's when it gets dark. If you are not out to me by then I will be arriving in your station bag and baggage, and I won't leave there. I mean it. I will move into Kevin Street until you give me protection.' She hurried back to the flat.

Lyn waited. At 5.30 p.m. the Special Task Force had still not arrived. She packed a suitcase of clothes, selected some books, unplugged her portable television set, and was gathering toiletries from the bathroom when there was a knock on the door. She shouted, 'Who is it?' Back came the answer, 'Gardaí'. Lyn looked out of the spyhole and recognised the two detectives. She opened the door and looked at her watch. It was 5.55 p.m.

'Your deadline was nearly up,' she said. They told her to leave her gear behind; they were taking her to Kevin Street. Their guns were visible as they walked down the stairs. Outside, Lyn moved automatically to the back door of their Renault van, and one of them said, 'No, Lyn. You get in the front. I'll hop in the back.'

Lyn giggled. The tension was leaving her. 'This is highly irregular. I am used to being hauled off in the back of police vans!'

There had been a breakdown in communications. When the Special Task Force had been put on the post to protect Róisín and Lyn, they had seen that Lyn never moved outside the flat, so their policy was to follow Róisín. It had thrown them when Lyn left the flat. They could not follow two people in different directions, so they had reported to their superior that Lyn had left the flat. But the word was not passed on to the Murder Squad. Kevin Street was unaware, until Lyn's phone call, that she was back living in her own flat. She spent about three hours in the police station where she was given endless cups of tea and treated with consideration. During that time, a detective she had known since he was a rookie doing point duty on the Canal came in to talk to her.

'They are fixing you up with protection,' he said. At around 9.30 p.m. they announced that they were taking Lyn home and that she would have twenty-four hour armed police protection. There would be a male driver and a policewoman. When she got back to Ballymun, Lyn went over to talk to the driver of the car that was to be used for her escort. The driver was a policeman she had known when he was detailed on anti-vice duties. He had never arrested Lyn because she had always left the beat whenever he had warned her. They spent a while just reminiscing over the good old days. Then she took her leave, climbed the stairs and clambered wearily into bed where, without the aid of sleeping pills, Lyn slept solidly for ten hours.

Joey arrived back from Liverpool the next day. He nearly had a fit when he found that the police were outside the flat twenty-four hours a day. He started off again, calling Lyn Mrs Black and Supergrass! 'You are going to have to lump it,' Lyn said wearily.

25

Lyn did not go out during her first ten days under police protection. She was withdrawn and depressed. Joey went to the shops for anything they needed. The escort worked eight hour shifts. At each change of shift, one of them would knock on the door and ask Lyn if she wanted to go out. Having spent twenty years trying to evade the police, she presumed they were only being polite and would hate her to say 'yes'. On the eleventh day, a policeman named Tom knocked and asked Lyn if she wanted to go for a drive. She was overjoyed to see him. She had met him when she was in the Orthopaedic Hospital recovering from her wounds after Dave Black stabbed her. She declined to go out, but asked Tom would he like to bring the policewoman up and she would make them tea. Over their tea, Tom and Lyn reminisced about their original meeting.

In the course of that afternoon with Tom and the policewoman, Lyn realised that each shift had been hoping that she would venture out, anywhere, even just around the block. They did not care about her reputation; they just wanted to pass their shift hours as quickly as possible.

The following Monday, Lyn's electricity was disconnected for non-payment of £225. She sent Joey over to Willy O'Donnell to ask him for the key to the electricity fuse box. The fuse boxes for the flats in Ballymun are situated on the balconies. ESB supply to a flat is disconnected simply by removing its main fuse. People in Ballymun are very enterprising. Some locksmith had forged a master key that would open any fuse box and Willy O'Donnell had it in his possession at that time. Willy sent Lyn the key and also a man who would rig up the electricity for her. At around 8.00 p.m., on his way to the pub, Willy called to see if Lyn's electricity had been turned on. She told him that the man had called, but was unable to connect the supply as he needed some tools and had promised to call back later to complete it. At around 11.30 p.m., Willy called to the flat on the pretext of seeing had the guy come back to fix the electricity. Lyn pointed to the light bulb and said, 'What do you think that is? It's not a star!'

Willy said, 'Lyn, I have something serious I have to say to you. I don't want you to think that I am a sleeveen on the day, but Róisín is not going to give evidence against John.' He had the grace to look embarrassed.

Lyn looked at him in disgust, smiled condescendingly and said, 'I don't know why you think you are making a declaration. I never for one moment thought she would give evidence. It's OK. I won't suddenly think you're a sleeveen on the day. I have always considered you a slither, as Róisín would say. But while we are on the subject, state your case. Why isn't she giving evidence?'

Lyn enjoyed watching his squirming discomfort as he answered her. 'Róisín and I had a good talk about it last night and she's afraid that if she gave evidence she'd spend the rest of her life looking over her shoulder. I agree with her.'

'You make me sick, Willy. You and Róisín went to the police about John. Not because Dolores was dead. Neither of you gave two fucks about Dolores. No, you went to the police because John Cullen raped your woman. Then you say that if Róisín gives evidence, she will be looking over her shoulder the rest of her life. The only place Róisín should be looking for John is six foot under clay. If you were any kind of man, you would have run him over on the road. Who'd blame you? No, Willy, seeing as you are gutless, you took the easy way out. You went to the cops to get John off your back. I might have got put away forever too, but you would sacrifice your own mother to get yourself off the hook. Róisín made *her* statement to get *me* to make one. You were both desperate by that time. That was not part of the deal Willy, was it, for Róisín to make a statement? You were just going to grass, then walk away. When the police told you I had not made a statement, you panicked. John would walk free, he would know you had tipped off the police. Your death warrant was signed. So, as Róisín told me, you gave her permission to make a statement to induce me to make one. You had to come out from under the rock you crawled under. After your coming-out ceremony you gave me all kinds of assurances. "We are your friends, Lyn. We will stick by you, Lyn." Oh God, you make me sick. But, you don't surprise me. So Lyn is on her own again, eh? Well, that's OK, Willy. I am well used to that. I'll face it on my own. But get one thing straight. I am going to make sure that everyone knows you for what you are, a slithering, gutless snake in the grass. You won't get off that lightly. You will never be able to show your face without people nudgin' each other and whispering. So I am declaring war on you, Willy. Don't be shocked when people come to you repeating things I've said. I am going to unmask you. I'm telling people all I know about you.'

'Lyn,' he whined, 'You don't have to be like that. I'm just worried about Róisín.'

Lyn said through clenched teeth, 'You don't give a damn about Róisín. The only person you care about is yourself. You should know John by now. You are too late. He knows you grassed him. You and Róisín are on the top of his hit list, after me. So either way your woman will be looking over her shoulder. It's a Catch 22 situation.'

Willy was unabashed. Now that he had told Lyn his intentions, he felt better. He brushed her threats aside. She knew he was thinking: 'Don't mind Lyn. She says things in temper, but she's not vindictive. She won't open her mouth to anybody.'

The talk got round to Kevin, Willy's mate. Kevin was still staying away from his flat with his wife and kids. Everyone liked Kevin. John liked him. Lyn asked Willy why Kevin was so scared. Surely he knew John had no argument with him.

Willy replied, 'Did you not know, Lyn? Kevin was going with Teresa for a while when John was doing his three years?'

'John did not care about Teresa,' Lyn pointed out, 'she also went with Belfast. John didn't bother him. Didn't Teresa have a baby for him while John was locked up, and John never even thought of revenge. Willy shrugged his shoulders in an 'I don't know gesture'. 'Anyway,' Lyn said, suddenly beyond patience, 'get out of my flat and never come near me again.'

The days, weeks, months sped by. Time, as Lyn had known it, ceased to exist. She would wake at 6.00 a.m., watch breakfast TV, go down to her police escort at 9.00 a.m. and stay out all day, driving all over the countryside. She did not notice her surroundings. She just had to get out of the flat. She would get out of the car at 10.00 p.m. some nights, stiff from sitting in the car and barely able to walk the two flights of stairs to her flat. She was trying to push the harsh reality of the forthcoming court case from her mind.

Thursday 5 May came anyway, and Lyn was taken to the District Court to give depositions for the murder trial. Before she left, Lyn took two Valium. She was still desperately nervous and when she got to the court she turned to her escort and said, 'Mary, I have to go to the loo. Will you walk over with me?' As they were crossing the courtyard she said, 'Oh God, Mary, there's John.' He was walking towards her, handcuffed to a prison officer. His head was thrown back, his shoulders erect. He smiled. Lyn was frozen, immobile, her eyes fixed on his mouth. She felt Mary grab her arm.

'Come on, Lyn. Don't look at him.' She pulled Lyn towards the toilets.

When she got inside Lyn said, 'Mary, keep a look out the door. Tell me when he's gone.'

When they got back to the court, Lyn met one of the Murder Squad detectives and told him shakily that she had seen John. He got quite annoyed at the fact that the prison officers had brought him over so soon, before the doors of the courtroom were open. The detective took Lyn to a room and left her there, under escort. Lyn took more Valium and then she was brought to court, a slim, lovely woman whose perfect beauty spot was the Borstal tattoo. She wore a black velvet jacket over a white blouse and straight grey skirt, stiletto heels. Curly dark lashes lay on her cheeks because she kept her eyes down when she entered the court and when she raised her hand to her face, it was fine boned, exquisitely delicate with pink fingertips. Those close to her got a whiff of 'Femme' perfume, and everyone tried to get a better look at her. At the press table someone whispered, 'Surely that's not her? She looks a bit like Joan Collins, doesn't she?'

Lyn stayed at the back of the court so that she would have no one behind her. When she turned to the public gallery, about six pairs of female eyes caught hers. Two pairs of eyes peered out of Dolores' face. Lyn faltered. It was like seeing a ghost. She knew that they were Dolores' sisters. Her legs shook as she sat down. She had been living in such dread of facing John Cullen in court that she had forgotten about the Lynches.

John turned around in his seat, pausing at each face in the gallery, the scar in his lip a grimace at each. Lyn squeezed her eyes closed. 'Oh Mary,' she said, and moved closer to the policewoman.

Mary patted her arm reassuringly. 'I know, Lyn. I saw him. Keep your head down. Don't let him laugh at you. He's only trying to frighten you.' Lyn was shaking. She opened her handbag and took another Valium.

The woman sitting directly in front of Lyn turned to face her. She said, 'Are you Lyn?' Lyn nodded her head, ashamed. 'I'm Kathleen, Dolores' sister. You must be terrified. Are you?' Lyn nodded her head again. Kathleen was smiling gently. 'Lyn, do you mind if I say something?' she said. Lyn shook her head in misery and braced herself for the onslaught. 'I would just like to thank you for what you are doing,' she said. 'We all would. We think you are very brave.' She was looking at Lyn kindly, no recriminations. Lyn had difficulty in answering.

'Oh my God, Kathleen. You don't have to thank me. I was there.' Lyn said.

Kathleen nodded her head gently. 'I know, Lyn. I still thank you,' she said softly.

Lyn had been utterly terror-stricken and Kathleen's few simple words gave her courage. Now, she could face her ordeal. She could stifle her fear of John; for Dolores, for the Lynch women sitting in the court who all looked so much like Dolores, for the Dolores who had just gently thanked her. Her fear was gone. Lyn raised her head to look steadily back at John Cullen. He was twisting in his seat, still lingering on each face, sneering at them. Róisín came into the court with her escort and sat down beside her policewoman. John had tuned in on Róisín, smirking at her, and at the same time rubbing his chin. Róisín slid rapidly along the seat out of his line of vision and ended up sitting almost on the policewoman's lap.

Two large detectives stood in front of John with their hands clasped behind their backs to obscure his view. Cullen was sliding left and right to see around them. Kathleen Lynch turned to Lyn and said, 'You see what he's doing, Lyn?' Lyn nodded. 'He does that every time the family is here. I have another sister and the last time he was up, he kept grinning into her face. She was ill after it. She was too sick to come to court today. Her nerves couldn't stand it. Lyn, I saw him grinning at you. Do what I do, grin right back into his face. I do that and he drops his eyes.' Lyn looked at Kathleen. So that was where Dolores got her courage. It ran in the family.

Lyn had not finished her depositions by 4.00 p.m. The case was put back until 31 May. Her ordeal was over for the day. Kathleen Lynch said goodbye and thanked Lyn. Her morale soared. She had been excellent in the box. She just wanted to get home and sleep.

Lyn was concerned about Joey. Obviously, he resented his mother's twenty-four hour police escort, and life became increasingly difficult for him. Although he would not admit it in a million years, Joey was frightened. He had been shattered the night he saw Dennis Black stab Lyn when she went over the balcony on a rope. His father had instilled in him that he must fight in defence of his family. And there he was, unable to defend his mother. Lyn had reminded him that he was only thirteen years old then and Black was a 'hard man' who had stabbed his own brother to death, but Joey's helplessness preyed on his mind. Now, here was his mother in worse trouble, this time with a £5,000 contract out on her for 'grassing'. To Joey, reared in the environment of criminals, there was nothing worse than a 'grass'.

Joey had difficulty sleeping and asked Lyn for Valium. At 3.00 a.m., Joey would arrive in Lyn's room, unable to sleep. Lyn gave him the money to go and live in England. He was sixteen years old. She was aware that she had failed him once more. Her heart ached as she watched him strip his bedroom walls of his Liverpool supporters' posters and fold them carefully. For a few short months, Joey had had a home again, been settled in his own little space, and now he was uprooted again. Lyn could not bear to watch his nerves going, nor could she be sure he was safe staying in Ireland. Someone might get him for John Cullen.

Lyn was alone. She went in to see Inspector Mick Connolly every two or three days, bringing him her fears and uncertainties, and always came away feeling reassured. He was Lyn's discovery of what fathers should be.

The High Court closed for the summer recess without setting a date for the murder trial. Lyn was in limbo. She spent most of her waking life touring the countryside with her escorts. She got on well with them, became very friendly with the policewoman, exchanged confidences and gossiped. Lyn says that she would have gone crazy without their companionship. When she was not out with the police, she worried about the forthcoming murder trial and brooded about the past. She could not bear to think of the Lynches.

Lyn went through hell those few months, torturing herself with recriminations. When she looked back over her life, she knew that the night she stood in the garden, watching her lover set fire to her friend's house and made no attempt to stop him, disaster was inevitable. Something terrible was bound to happen, eventually. She was still far from understanding why she had lived her life the way she had, or that it was possible to change.

26

For weeks Lyn's 'banners'* talked of nothing but the forthcoming wedding of their colleague Clare. Clare had invited the
'banners' from her graduation class and they were all obsessed
with what to wear. Lyn listened and marvelled that they had so
little to worry about. And the chat went on. Then one night, as
she was getting out of the escort car, Clare asked, 'Lyn, can I
have a word with you?' They moved away from the car and she
said, 'Lyn, John and I would like you to come to the wedding.'
She saw the shock on Lyn's face and said briskly, 'Yes or no?'
Lyn was too moved to answer. Clare repeated, 'Yes or no?' Lyn
still could not speak.

'Lyn, you're part of the family. You have to come,' asked
Clare.

'Thanks, Clare,' was all Lyn could manage before she ran
upstairs. She had never been to a wedding. She had a neighbour
once who was always showing her wedding album and asking
Lyn to show her wedding photos. Lyn had to keep making
excuses. Now, she knew a lot of married people in Dublin, but
they happened to be married to people other than the partners
with whom they lived. She could not go to sleep with thinking
about being asked to Clare's wedding.

Lyn was shattered by such acceptance. She began to live for

---

* Policewomen

253

the wedding and scoured Dublin and its surrounding thirty mile radius looking for an outfit. She bought a lovely cream dress but one of the policewomen advised her against wearing it, explaining that the bride had chosen cream. In the end she wore something borrowed from ban garda Marie.

Lyn was sick with nerves on the morning of the wedding. A non-believer, she sat at the back of the church with her escort. She was dazzled by the ceremony. She was nibbling her little finger, watching the two candles being lit, symbol of unity, when the garda took her hand off her cheek and started to shake it. 'What are you doing?' she asked him.

'Peace be with you, Lyn', he said, and as he shook the hand of the ban garda on her other side, he explained, 'It's part of the ceremony.' Everybody was shaking hands with people on either side of them, Lyn included. Tears came to Lyn's eyes and just then Clare and John walked back down the aisle. Clare was nodding to everyone as she passed, and when she saw Lyn her face broke into a delighted smile. 'Lyn,' she said.

That made Lyn weepier, but they were soon outside on their way to the reception. It was held in an hotel, once a castle, overlooking the sea. Lyn sat with the eight 'banners' singing songs about Templemore Garda Training School. She did not know the words, but hummed along with them. When she went out to the women's room, a woman remarked, 'I must say you women have lovely voices.'

'Thank you,' Lyn said, and went back to the party and danced. She was happy. When Clare and John were going away she kissed them both and burst into tears. People shook hands with her and she was overcome with feeling. She blew her nose.

'What's wrong, Lyn?' asked one of the policemen.

'You don't know how it feels to sit with people and be able to relax enough to get drunk and not have to worry about some lunatic picking up a glass and smashing it into someone's face.'

'All you need,' he observed, 'is a little tender loving care.'

'It wasn't an offer,' she says now. 'That was the amazing thing!'

After the reception Lyn went with a few of her escorts to Sach's nightclub where they danced until 3.00 a.m. Then it was back to a 'banner's' flat for coffee. Lyn arrived home around

5.30 a.m. and lay staring at the ceiling thinking that it had been the second happiest day of her life. The other happy day was when her first son, Chris, was born. She was not on the game then and thought things were going to be alright between Craig Nelson and herself.

The trial of John Cullen for the murder of Dolores Lynch began on 26 October. Lyn went to court dosed with Valium for the first morning of the trial. John's wife, his brother and his sister were there. Dolores' three sisters and some neighbours were in court. Róisín and Willy hung around outside the courtroom. Lyn did not look left or right as she entered, Inspector Mick Connolly motioned her to sit up in the front amongst the police witnesses; her escorts sat on either side of her. John Cullen was smiling. 'Have you got your gun handy?' Lyn quipped nervously to her escort.

'Relax', he replied.

The morning passed slowly with the opening address from the prosecuting counsel. Lyn stared straight ahead. During the midday recess, John had attacked a prison officer, hitting him in the face when the handcuffs were being taken off. The officer had to go to hospital. Now, when the jury returned, the prosecuting counsel asked that John Cullen be kept in handcuffs. Defending counsel argued that it would prejudice the jury against John Cullen. The judge asked the prison officer in charge if he thought it would be necessary for John Cullen to be handcuffed. The officer mumbled that he thought the prisoner had calmed down. 'My eye,' thought Lyn. 'He's makin' sure he won't be next.'

Lyn had thought that Mrs Lynch and her sister Hannah died in their sleep. The firemen told how they could not open the door of Mrs Lynch's bedroom because her body was behind it and that they had found her sister on the floor near a window.

'ELIZABETH MADDEN to the stand.'

Lyn walked with legs shaking, past John Cullen and into the witness box. Prosecuting counsel questioned her gently. She answered, but two or three times the judge asked her to speak up, as neither he nor the jury could hear her. Lyn's voice shook every time she spoke and somehow she got through until the recess. She swallowed more Valium. She knew the blood sport would start when the defending counsel cross-examined her. Lyn was an old hand in court and she would not have been in such a state if she had been allowed to answer in her own way. She was telling the truth and could pit herself against any barrister, but Lyn had been instructed by the police to answer 'yes' or 'no' only. They knew that she could get 'lippy' and feared she might get carried away.

'ELIZABETH MADDEN to the stand.'

Lyn was in the witness box, but at the same time, a familiar scene played in her head. It was a scene that, even now, sometimes replays itself when she least expects it: she is standing on a street corner and a car stops. The driver opens the window . . .

'Are you looking for business, luv?' Lyn asks. Eyes peer out and inspect her body.

'How much?' he asks, eyes continuing to assess her.

'Twenty pounds in the car, luv.'

'Give you fifteen.'

'The price is twenty.'

'I know, but it's cold. You'll be standing here all night. You'll take fifteen.'

'The sale starts 1 January, luv. Come back then,' and she slams the door. She would always rather freeze than drop her prices. Ten minutes later, he's back again.

'Come on, luv, I'll give you sixteen?' In court the scene in her head did not get as far as the bit where he comes back at 4.00 a.m., just as Lyn is hailing a taxi.

'OK,' he says then, 'I'll give you the twenty.'

'Stuff it.' Lyn says.

What brought the scene into Lyn's head was that, in the witness box, she was being assessed. Like a rape victim. Could she be believed? Every eye in court was glued to her, mainly because she was a prostitute.

Lyn was frustrated by the questioning. She wanted to tell the jury about Cullen, the kind of man he was. But the questioning was all about *her*, the kind of woman *she* was. To Lyn, it did not seem to matter that she was trying to give evidence against a dangerous man, the killer of three women who even now had taken out a £5,000 contract on her own head. Lyn was a prostitute, had been for twenty years. That was that. Nothing else was important.

The defence counsel told Lyn she could stand down, and Róisín was called to the stand. Róisín answered, 'I can't remember.' to all questions put to her. Counsel looked at the judge and shrugged his shoulders; he asked that Róisín be treated as a hostile witness. The judge agreed, and Róisín was allowed to stand down, which meant that her statement was read out. Lyn knew every word of it and she never took her eyes off the jury as it was being read. The last few words were: 'I would also like to state that while he was in my flat he had sex with me against my will.' That shook them. Lyn saw a ripple run through the benches of the jury. If only they knew what else Cullen had done to Róisín.

The trial lasted four days, with the jury retiring at 4.10 p.m. to consider their verdict. Lyn waited in the main hall, the Cullens waiting to her right, the Lynches to the left of her.

Lyn's hopes faded when the jury were still out at 6.00 p.m. She knew that if they did not return quickly there was a greater chance of their bringing in a 'not guilty' verdict. But who could blame them? It was Hobson's choice. The defence summing up rested on 'hell hath no fury like a woman scorned', emphasising to the jury that John had tried to leave her. And, there was the constant reminder that Lyn was, by her own admission, a prostitute of some twenty years' standing.

As she waited for the verdict, Lyn failed to get her mind away from John Cullen. There was a fifty-fifty chance he would be convicted. If so, it would be many days before he knew freedom again. She could not suppress the pity she felt for him. No one understood better than Lyn that Cullen had to be incarcerated for the common good, but she knew so much more about him, too.

He was one of nine children. His father died when John was eight years old. John played truant from school and first got in trouble for robbing sweets about a year after his father died. His mother sent him to stay with relatives in England, to avoid going to court, but he kept running away because he missed his mother. So she fetched him back. He refused to go to school and she had to let the police take him. He was sent to Upton Reformatory for six years.

During the first in-depth conversation Lyn ever had with John, he spoke at great length about the experiences in Upton, the beatings from the Christian Brothers, the hard work, for a child, cutting sugar beet. He said that anybody who transgressed was made to stand naked under a cold shower while a Brother beat him with a wet towel which was knotted at one end.

'A boy arrived with a suitcase of posh clothes, d'you know what I mean, like, and he had an American accent,' John told Lyn. 'He was an orphan and he didn't have anybody else belonging to him either. The Brothers took the kid's posh clothes away and he was beaten almost every day.' John was not looking for sympathy, recalls Lyn, merely recounting data that was as fresh in his mind as if it had happened yesterday. That had been the first of many such conversations; hardly a week had passed with Cullen without some mention of Upton.

Two of John's friends came to Lyn's flat one night and the three of them spoke for four hours non-stop about their experiences in Upton Reformatory. Lyn did not interrupt them, just handed around tea and sandwiches in silence. One of the guys was very violent, the other one a persistent robber. Hearing them talk, Lyn wondered would this have been the case had they not been at Upton. The robber recalled being sexually interfered with by one of the Christian Brothers. The men laughed as they reminisced. 'Do you remember Brother So-and-so'. As Lyn listened she was forcibly struck by the way they all remembered every minute detail, such as where Brother So-and-so had a spot on his face or the size of Brother So-and-so's hands. Upton Reformatory had a lot to answer for. John Cullen seethed with the urge for revenge every day he was there.

When John had bashed Scotch Sheila and her girlfriend, Lyn was terrified. She said, 'John, I'm scared. They'll pay someone to give it to you. Are you not scared?'

'No, Lyn,' he replied in that calm way of his. 'I told you before I have never been scared of anything in this world since I left Upton, d'you know what I mean like? I remember one Brother bashing me all over the place because I had not cut enough sugar beet. I was scared of my life. He was a massive big man, with enormous hands. I cried, but when I was in me bed in the dorm that night, I swore on me Ma's life that I would never cry again and I never did. I was scared shitless of that Brother, I was only a boy. I'm a man now and I'm frightened of nothin' and nobody.' Lyn had never known him to show a glimmer of fear. As Lyn waited for the verdict, she thought that even now, after two and a half years with John, she did not know when he was really smiling. She had known him for a full year before he pulled up his upper lip one day and showed her a scar that left his lip permanently upturned. He had been in a fight years ago, had a bottle smashed in his face which split his upper lip, and he never bothered having it stitched, with the result that the lip was permanently upturned. Even after she knew, Lyn was never relaxed about that 'smile'. If he was irate about something she could never take her eyes off his mouth. Was he smiling that smile, or . . . ?

John and his brother were both epileptics. She thought about the time she had seen John have an epileptic seizure and how impressed he was that it had not upset her. Lyn had been used to it; she palled around with a girl in her teens who had seizures. John's mother ruled the family with a rod of iron. When Lyn and Joey stayed with her in a caravan for a week, Joey had sworn at Lyn and Mrs Cullen was furious with him. She told Lyn that if any of her sons talked·to her like that, she would put them in hospital. When Lyn broached the subject of his mother's severity, 'Ah sure, it was nothin',' said John. 'Me Ma had it hard tryin' to bring us all up.' John adored his mother, as did all her children. Each one visits her every single day.

Lyn reflected on whether she could have prevented John from killing Dolores and her family. On the night it happened, she had been unable to think about anything but her own fear. And the trouble with Dolores was before Lyn's time with John. Her destiny had been decided seven years previously. Lyn believed that had John and she not had an affair, Dolores would have met her death sooner. When Dolores had gone down to the Canal to show the women her picture of herself with Pope John Paul, Lyn and John had been so happy and things were going so well that it never occurred to Lyn to mention John to Dolores. John had been so wrapped up in his affair with Lyn that he put Dolores' death on the long finger.

It was about that time that Dolores went to a priest known to all the prostitutes on the Canal and asked him what should she do to protect herself and her family against John Cullen. Should she leave the country? The priest said no, she should not let a man like John Cullen drive her out of her own country. Lyn found comfort in the fact that her affair with Cullen had probably given Dolores a few extra years of life. She had been fond of Dolores in life, but in death, the courage of the younger woman shone through the nightmare.

Now, perhaps John would never know freedom again. Lyn knew that every waking minute of his day would be filled with thoughts of revenge. Dolores had paid for his last incarceration. Róisín and herself would be his revenge targets for the future. John Cullen vowed, when he left Upton, that never again would he 'take messin' from man, woman, or child. Always get your enemies back'. He had impressed this on Joey who could not forgive Lyn for making the statement.

Lyn had been thinking and when she looked at her watch, it was 10.30 p.m. Jury still out. What if the jury foreman said, 'not guilty'?

Lyn could not stand waiting any longer so she called one of the Murder Squad detectives and asked if she could leave the court. The escort took her to the Burlington Hotel, where she waited until the verdict came. The judge had ordered a retrial. The jury could not agree. Lyn sank back into the chair. Why? Why? Why? 'I can't, can't face it all again. I can't,' she said. There was a rumour that one of the jurors was got at, which did not surprise Lyn.

Mick Connolly and Lyn's escort became everything to her between the murder trials. She often felt like overdosing with Valium and going to sleep forever. If it had not been for the police, she would have done that after the first trial. One night after she had given depositions, Lyn left the court feeling depressed and utterly drained. She barely spoke to the escort on the way home, remarkable for one who talks a great deal. She went into the flat at 6.30 p.m., barricaded the door, counted out her sleeping tablets to find only ten, swallowed them and passed out within minutes. She woke to a terrible racket. The door was being kicked off the hinges. It was 10.30 p.m. and Lyn staggered to the door. 'Who the bloody hell is it?' she screamed, her speech slurred.

'The milkman,' came the reply. She recognised the voice of Brendan, one of her escorts.

'For fuck's sake,' she yelled as she unlocked bolts, 'do you have to kick the bloody door off the hinges?' Lyn stood facing him, furious.

'Sorry, Lyn,' Brendan said. 'I was frightened you had done something stupid. The last shift said you were very down in yourself when you went into the flat. I've been knocking for ages. I got worried when you didn't answer.'

Lyn apologised for yelling at him. He laughed and said, 'I'm not worried about you Lyn. It's all the paperwork. Imagine if you killed yourself when I was on duty, I would be writing for-ever. Get dressed and we'll go for a drive. It will clear your brain.' He went down to the car to wait, and Lyn pushed her-self to get ready and went for a drive. Denise was on duty, too. They drove out to Malahide and watched the sea. Between the two of them, they managed to get Lyn to talk it out. She did not tell them that she had made plans to end her futile existence by swallowing liquid cleaning agents. Her courage was renewed when they dropped her home.

27

Lyn always thought there should be prizes given for survival. Yet for the third time in her life she thought that she was beaten when her prize should have been John Cullen's conviction. The jury's failure to reach an agreement could only mean they did not believe her. She felt washed up. John Cullen would get off scot-free and at best Lyn would have to live in a world where people accept 'not guilty' verdicts, no matter how ludicrous. Everyone who knew John Cullen would be terrorised. At worst, Lyn knew, she would be living on borrowed time.

She found herself wishing 'they' would get her soon, not make her wait, always conscious she was for the slaughter. She had thought that she was beaten when she prised her baby daughter's hands from her legs and ran from Craig Nelson. Yet she survived. She thought she was done for when she landed in hospital after Dennis Black stabbed her. She was physically wrecked, her home was gone, her belongings stolen, she was flat broke and her son was out in the street, yet she survived. Perhaps she would survive once again. Now, however, she stayed indoors, just wanting to be alone. Mercifully, Lyn was subpoenaed for the second murder trial for 7 November, three weeks away.

A feminist, with experience of Valium, was sitting at the press table during the first trial and recognised that Lyn was sedated to her own detriment. The woman told Lyn, 'You were like a garda giving evidence: "Yes", "No", "Correct". It was hard for the jury to know what to make of you. How do you feel?' Lyn replied that she had taken Valium because she was warned not to be lippy in the court. The woman advised, 'Don't take any tablets next time, just be yourself.' Lyn knew she was right. She went into court as she was, no Valium, terrified. And not being drugged, it seemed as if she was hearing the awful agony of Dolores' dying for the first time.

The firefighters had difficulty getting Dolores out of the window of her burning home because the burnt skin was slipping off her arms. As she lay on the roof she kept repeating, 'Help Mammy, save my mother.' Eighty per cent of Dolores' body was burnt and yet she lived all those hours. In court, the doctor gave evidence of the weight of her lungs and heart because of decompression, the necessity of slicing her flesh to release the fluid. Lyn moaned and looked at John Cullen. He was getting a kick out of hearing these details.

And then Lyn was called. The jury shifted in their seats as she walked to the witness box. Prosecuting counsel steered her gently through her evidence, but Lyn was aware that it was about to get rough.

Lyn was a different witness this time. Without the Valium she was definite and lucid. Her description of prostitutes' lives and the violence they experienced at the hands of their pimps was riveting. This time, Lyn was Lyn. She couldn't be shaken. Even experienced court reporters smiled as she answered.

At last the questions ended. Lyn became aware of the electric atmosphere in the courtroom. No one stirred. She could hear her own breathing. Her cheeks were flushed and she could feel all eyes glued upon her. She walked shakily from the stand, and as she passed John Cullen he muttered something about 'rat'.

Jurors and members of the public fidgeted as they made themselves comfortable again. Reporters scurried from the court to ring their papers or to write their copy. They had the air of people who felt things were reaching a conclusion. Watching them, Lyn felt better. They would phone in all the juicy stuff about pimps and prostitutes and then all they would have to do was add an 'intro' paragraph, giving the lesser information that a man had been convicted of murder and sentenced to life imprisonment.

As she left the court, Lyn's exit was blocked by John's brother. He pretended not to see her as he stuck his elbow into her. Lyn pretended not to notice, digging her stiletto heel into his foot. She had an armed escort and she was high because she had said everything she wanted to say. It was up to the jury now.

'Well done, Lyn.' 'You were great.' 'Brilliant.' People congratulated her. She had not only survived the ordeal without Valium, but been at her best. All she had wanted was to get the truth across, not just about the murder, but about the pimping business. She had, to use her own word, been a bit 'lippy', but the truth of her words resounded. The word flew around the Four Courts, the building in which the trial was held beside Dublin's River Liffey, and legal people crowded into the courtroom to witness the battle.

Lyn's triumph was short-lived: Rex Mackey asked that the case against John Cullen be dropped. His arrest under Section 30 of the Offences Against the State act was illegal. Mr Mackey's suggestion was overruled, but he came back with an encore that sent the jury home for four days while the legalities were fought. Rex Mackey argued that in accordance with the rules governing Section 30, any verbal statements made by John Cullen were inadmissible because he had been interrogated without rest for 19 hours non-stop.

The judge eventually decided that only statements made by John Cullen within five hours of his arrest were permissible. This spared everybody the tedium of an army of police giving their fragments of evidence one after the other. It was all the one anyway; John Cullen had not said much under interrogation. Now, as far as the jury was concerned, it was entirely up to Lyn. Could this jury agree to believe her? After four days going about their normal business, Lyn wondered could they even remember what she had said.

The judge's summing up was long and drawn out. He ended with, 'It is clear from her own evidence that Ms Madden was there, but you, the jury, must decide whether Cullen was with her. You will consider the way she gave her evidence and how she impressed you, or didn't impress you,' he added. Lyn went straight to the house of the woman who had warned her off the Valium, lay down in the darkness, closed her eyes. She must have dozed off. She woke at 11.00 p.m. to the phone ringing. 'It's for you,' her new friend said, and handed her the receiver.

'Hello? Hello, Mick. What happened?' She asked the inspector. She sat down quickly, in case. 'What?' Lyn asked. 'Can you say that again?' jumping to her feet. 'Guilty on both counts! Oh Mick, is it true?' Lyn stared at the empty wine glass. She had drained it without even noticing that it had been put in her hand.

'Mick, how did John react?'

'Not a bother on him. He was quite impassive.'

'When will he be sentenced?' Lyn asked.

'Tomorrow,' Inspector Connolly replied. Lyn slept deeply that night. She did not go to court to see John Cullen sentenced to life imprisonment for the murder of Dolores Lynch, with fifteen years for arson.

28

I visited Dublin on a summer's day in 1987 and passed over Baggot Street bridge. I was amazed at how lovely the Canal looks in daytime. People strolled along the banks, and I doubt if any of them could have imagined what it is like at night.

I was watching the television news that night and saw British soldiers on patrol in Northern Irish streets. They were wary and tense, looked right, left and behind them, their guns cocked, shoulders rigid in expectation of a sniper's bullet. That is how the Canal was for me. I could feel my shoulders lift almost to my ears as I stepped out of the car at night. My jaws would clench and I would take a deep breath as I took up my position on the path. Then I'd look to my left, then my right, across the road: 'Is that someone hiding in the garden over there? Who's that in the parked car? Are there two or three men in it?' Then I'd turn and peer into the bushes along the banks of the Canal. 'Looks OK. No, did that bush move? What's that noise? Coulda swore I saw someone lurking behind that tree, or was it an optical illusion?'

The dark plays strange tricks with trees and bushes. Sometimes a couple of us used to venture along the canal bank, to investigate what we thought was a man's elbow sticking out from behind a tree, only to find a misshapen branch, and we'd giggle in relief. You never knew who was lurking in the shadows waiting to hurt you in some way. The game acts as a magnet for life's weirdoes.

Getting into a car was even more scary. Your heart raced as you assessed the client. And as you got in the car, you checked that it had a door handle on the inside and a window catch, in case you had to get out in a hurry. The silent ones were the worst. 'Why doesn't he speak?' So you small talked, and I mean small talk. And if your client was the silent type your palms were sweating with fear and you heard yourself asking inane things in an effort to get him to say something so you could hear the tone of his voice. Was there any kindness in it? If he made any sudden moves you jumped out of your skin even though he was only reaching for his wallet. I could go on, but you've got the picture.

It does not end when the night's work is over. You go home and if you haven't a pimp to deal with, you get into bed and you're still in what psychiatrists call 'a state of extreme arousal'. I can only describe it as being like 'hearing stars'. I've seen stars, many a time, when I got a punch on the jaw. Hearing stars is different. It takes a lot of sleeping tablets to take you down from being so high.

I hate to think about the men, now. They came from all walks of life. Back then, I just thought I needed them as much as they needed me. I always thought that a good comparison could be made with wildlife. I watched lots of wildlife programmes on TV and learned how animals survive off other species, like the birds who ride on the backs of beasts and feed off their parasites and so on, down to the small fishes that clean the gills of larger fish. So clients and prostitutes needed each other, I figured. It was that sort of relationship, except that people are not wildlife. I needed those men more than they needed me. They could have masturbated.

I don't know how they saw me, except that when we met under other circumstances they pretended they did not know me. It's funny the little things that stick in the mind. I remember, years ago, one guy asking with interest what my routine was when I got home after a night's work and I replied, 'The four bees: bath, bed, book, a cup of cocoa, then bliss.' He looked taken aback, and something else I could not identify immediately. I thought about him when I got into bed and then I laughed out loud. Disappointment, that was what it was. He was probably disappointed to learn that I didn't go to an orgy after the Canal.

I also remember the one who was so drunk he fell asleep on top of me, urinated into the condom and drowned me. God!

On my thirty-fifth birthday I went to work in a dark cloud of depression because I always made it a rule never to work on my birthday. I had not got a single birthday card, no present. The girls didn't know it was my birthday so I hadn't even heard 'Happy Birthday!' I felt ever so sorry for myself. I was unloved. A car pulled up beside me and the guy (an ex-regular) told me to get in. He said, 'Many happy returns of the day, Lyn,' and handed me a birthday card. I cried. I asked how on earth he knew and he said the last time we'd done business together two years ago, we'd talked of star signs and I'd told him I was an Aquarian. He had asked the date and I told him and he'd written it down in his diary when he'd got home. He had come across the diary a few weeks ago and thought it would be nice to surprise me with a card.

I also remember the guy who pulled a screwdriver from his inside pocket and held it under my chin and forced me to kiss him while he climaxed. Afterwards he said with a chuckle, 'Sorry darlin', makes it more exciting, y'know?'

I'll never forget the young man who, three years after our last business together, still came down the Canal on the first Tuesday of every single month to bring me all the paperback books he'd read since the previous one. Róisín said he was down every Tuesday for six months after I retired.

And there was the man I picked up one night, a clean, well-spoken guy in his mid twenties who paid me, soft talked me, then got out of the car to take a leak (supposedly) and opened the boot to let another guy out. The 'nice' one pulled a knife to my throat and threatened to end my life if I didn't do everything they asked. He had sex with me, robbed all my money while his mate leaned over the seat and held the knife steadily against my throat.

Maybe I ought to end on the guy who gave me £200 to spend the night in a posh hotel, and I was so nervous of being locked in a room with him I found myself babbling, 'Nice Mercedes you've got, they're fuel-injected aren't they?' I said. To this day I don't know what that means, but I remembered Craig Nelson telling me. The guy looked amazed. 'Jesus Christ! D'you know I could talk to the most well-educated woman I know and she wouldn't know what fuel injection was. You're remarkable.' And we started to talk and after two hours he yawned, laughed and said, 'Well, you've talked that much you talked yourself out of a job,' and he told me to go home and keep the £200.

I remember them all, the good and the bad. Fortunately, there were more 'good' guys than bad. Don't forget we're talking about clients; I wasn't looking for a partner for life.

What happened to Craig Nelson? Friends breathed a sigh of relief when I got him off to Israel that time before I met Dennis Black. Before that, he used to make relentless threatening phone calls to two of my Prisoners' Rights Organisation friends. They breathed a sigh of relief and replaced their telephone receivers when he left. About a month later, Frank, my PRO friend, received a live .303 bullet from Israel accompanied by a note which read 'This one's got your name on it.' Then the phone calls began again. Apparently, every time Craig found himself alone with someone's phone he dialled Dublin. Two months after he left, I received a postcard from Bethlehem with the simple message: 'Things are bad. Can't speak the language. Coming back. Craig.'

I met Craig in Liverpool just after the murder trial and we went for a drink and talked about those times. The immigration was a fiasco, starting with the taxi driver who drove them from Tel Aviv Airport to Jerusalem, overcharging £20. Upon arrival in Jerusalem, Craig decided to try out the local bars. He left the children in the market place saying he'd be back in half an hour, forgot the time, and ended the day sitting in the gutter with an Arab, drinking the local brew.

They got places on a kibbutz, but Craig could not take the work. He was put to catching chickens. 'Have you ever tried catching chickens?' he asked me. He discovered chickens did not like being caught. They squawked and clawed; his hands were scratched to bits. Chris, at fourteen, had worked in the bakery where it was 120 degrees. Joey and Fiona were well looked after there, happy.

Craig said it was the saddest thing to watch old Jews who had been in the concentration camps 'stealing' food which was available in abundance. People pretended not to notice them 'stealing'. According to Craig, there are no store detectives in Israel because there are no shoplifters. I asked him why and he said, 'Who are the Jews going to steal from, each other?'

In all our dreaming, Craig hadn't figured on working on learning the language, so he decided to call it a day. He appealed to the Israeli immigration authorities to repatriate him, but they refused: 'We're not asking you to leave.' He tried the British Embassy, but got nowhere with them either. The British ambassador was getting tired of listening to Craig's raving and asked him to leave. Craig looked at Chris, nodded towards the portrait of the Queen of England which hung on the wall of the office and said, 'Smash that, Chris.'

Chris broke the glass and hurled the picture to the floor. The ambassador became visibly scared, but still refused what Craig asked. 'Right,' said Craig, 'now the desk, Chris.' Chris picked up a chair and smashed it over the desk. Three security guards rushed into the room and Chris and his father were arrested and sent to Abukabee Prison for a week. Visiting time was totally chaotic and relatives and friends of the Arab prisoners stood outside the wire surrounding the prison, shouting messages in, so no one got a wink of sleep. Fiona and Joey had already flown out of the country to Craig's mother in England.

In court, Craig and Chris were fined £20. They moved into a top hotel and stayed for a month without paying. They were asked to leave, but they refused and the staff kept slipping food to them, in spite of the management. Eventually, the British ambassador intervened and Craig and Chris were repatriated.

Today my sons are quite bitter about the fact that their father had made no attempt to fit in and learn Hebrew. They loved Israel.

A year before I left Ireland, Professor Ivor Browne, the psychiatrist, suggested that I 'could do with some therapy'. I did not think there was anything 'wrong' with me, but when he suggested that I would never know unless I had the 'bottle' (a word he learned from me) to find out, I thought, 'What have I to lose?'

I found out there was plenty wrong with me. I had also thought that therapy would be a cakewalk. The reality was different. I went through hell. I had lived with violence all my life, but nothing had prepared me for what I went through in therapy. After each session I was convinced that I would not be able to cope with the suffering until the following week and when the next session was 'now', I'd tell myself I could not go through with it, while knowing I had to. In the early days of treatment, I *felt*, rather than *knew*, that if I didn't see my therapy through I would find no salvation. It was in discovering my own buried history that I was able to look towards a different future.

Each time I went to Ivor Browne I thought I would not be able to endure any more pain, and when I devised tricks of avoidance, he reasoned, explained, cajoled and warned me that I could no longer go back to being my old self. I had to go forward. I owed it to myself. He showed endless patience and if I had to describe Ivor Browne with one word, I would say 'compassionate'. I suppose it was partly to please him, for all his kindness, that I persevered.

At the end of treatment I emerged more whole than I ever thought possible, but raw. I could no longer cut off my emotions, and perhaps more important, I could no longer dismiss the suffering of others. I am now aware of the reasons why I could not escape from the violent, brutalised life I was living. I learned why through therapy.

I was forty years old before I could admit to myself that my father had sexually abused me. I was four years old when he first began to 'play' with me. Being four meant pain, and for twenty years I suffered pains in my jaws, brought on by a deep-seated subconscious effort to stop my father from forcing his penis into my mouth. By the time I had reached five, Daddy had a new game to play. 'I'm only playing, Lynda,' he said. The game forced my face into the mattress and he called me by my mother's name when he was hurting me in the bed.

In therapy, I lived a lot of other trauma I had suppressed. I learned that, above all, I was convinced that I was not good enough for anybody to love. So, long ago, I had decided, 'sod it, if I'm not good enough, I'll be as bad as I can'. For years I felt as if I was on a helter-skelter going down, down, down, always towards some new disaster, but unable to stop. And I relived the night of the fire, but this time, from the inside of the Lynches' house. I became Dolores and I screamed as the flames devoured my skin. Until then, I'd just felt shock and guilt at my involvement. Reliving that night, in that way, made my emotional pain harder. But it also helped me find the courage to finally be able to look at myself in the mirror and say, 'Right. It cannot be undone, so you have got to go forward and try to be a better person. Try to think of others. They have their suffering, too'. Therapy gave me an understanding of the Craig Nelsons and John Cullens of this world, but it also enabled me to see that I do not have to put up with such people. I am no longer a doormat.

The other thing I brought with me after therapy was a deep fear of men. Logical, you might say. Not so. Before therapy I was distrustful of men and scared of them in close situations, like in a house etc., yet they loomed high on my horizon. After therapy, and until the spring of 1987, every day was a nightmare I had to get through to survive contact with men. I felt danger from them in the street, shops, offices, everywhere. If I was walking to the shops and there was a man on the path, I'd have to hold down a scream until I passed him. When the gas or electricity man called I'd stand and shake until he'd gone. I could not talk to them.

I babysat for a friend one night and her brother called round to wait for them to come home, and I ran from the house in fright. Once outside I thought that he could abuse one of the children, yet I could only stand outside trembling, unable to force myself to go back. Luckily my friends happened along soon afterwards.

I watched a BBC *Man Alive* programme about Birmingham's young prostitutes and I just cried and cried. One young girl was bright and chatty and reminded me of myself at that age. She knew it wasn't a life fit for a dog and yet she was so defiant. It was like watching a caricature of myself as a youngster. Why is she there? What happened to her as a child to convince her that she was worthless? With Social Welfare, it is not just the money that sends a girl into the streets. In other parts of the world, you starve if you can't work. Not in the West.

I wanted to reach out and touch that girl and say, 'It doesn't have to be this way. You can have a better life. Let me help you. I was on the game, too, and I know. It's not too late. Never.' But

272

I'm still healing and I feel I've a little way to go before I dare offer help.

I did numerous interviews in the past where I justified prostitution, believing everything I said at the time. Through therapy and the love of friends, I've learned that there can be no justification for that life. It is no way for people to relate to one another, and every single woman is far too precious to be wasted on 'the game'.

I would never have gone back on the game after Dolores died, but without therapy I would have drifted back among criminals, no matter where I lived. The therapy opened up a can of worms for me, but was also instrumental in helping me to get in touch with feelings for others. Many people think of therapy as selfish. Perhaps it is, but at the end of the soul-searching I've reached a stage where I realise that other people matter. All my life I was totally wrapped up in myself, and although I loved my kids, I never really saw beyond their physical and material needs. In fact I only 'saw' people as they affected me.

I'm not living happily ever after. How can I, after my experience? At least I feel equal to my struggle, most of the time. Sometimes I think, 'If only the fire hadn't happened, if only I could live in Dublin'.

I live in a place now I never would have chosen before. It was written up in the national papers recently because it is such a deprived area where everyone is unemployed and the odds are stacked against us. I'm unemployed too. The people round here are still angry and insulted, say the media picked on a few who live in extreme poverty and abject misery. Not so. The misery affects us all.

I stood at my window this morning and felt despair because the first thing I saw when I opened the curtains was a black cross-bred Alsatian dog squatting in the front garden. I banged on the window in fury at him. Vandals ripped out the fencing so we cannot keep out the dogs which maraud in packs. I've never seen so many dogs anywhere, most of them stray. I put on rubber gloves once a day and feel sick while I clean up after the dogs. And the rubbish amazes me. The Council doesn't bother cleaning up. There is a junior school at the end of the road and the kids dump everything in the gardens, on the roads; crisp packets, sweet wrappers by the ton, soft drink tins. You'd never see an apple core or even a wrapper from peanuts. And most of the kids are so puny and whitefaced with dark smudges under their eyes. I've never seen so many obese women in one area, not even in Ballymun. For the first nine months I lived here I would watch those roly-poly women and their whitefaced kids and shake my head and say, 'Why?' Now, I *feel* why.

When I lived in a little flat in London I never paid any bills because I knew I was leaving there, and like Dublin, no one would be bothered to catch up on me. How wrong I was! I was chased for the bills. I even have a TV licence which I paid for out of a Christmas gift someone sent from Dublin and I buy £2 worth of stamps each week for the next one. Bills amount to £22 a week before I even think of food, and there's the cigarettes. I pretend to myself I'm cutting down and buy only ten at a time. With another eight days until I get my Bank Giro, I have £4.75. The woman next door borrowed some bread for her kid's tea, so now I'll have to buy bread at least, and ten fags. I'm looking forward to publishing this book, but for now if I can't even have a fag, what's to look forward to? Sure, I know there's worse off, but . . .

I'm taking leatherwork classes, and I can't go today because I can't afford the 75p. There's free butter and cheese offered to pensioners and unemployed, but I can't swallow my pride and queue for it. Maybe if I had kids, but I'd sooner eat dry bread. The kids on either side don't seem to get enough to eat; they are always ravenous and their mothers look old before their time. I'm not whining, just trying to tell you about poverty in the Western world.

I just looked out the window and saw an extremely elderly woman trudging across the road to the old people's bungalows, wearing a pair of ragged running shoes. She isn't wearing them because she's got bunions; it's pissin' out of the heavens, and her clothes are just as ragged. The runners looked so incongruous with her bent, old frame and it made me feel afraid. When I got this place, the Council officer informed me that, when I reached fifty years of age, I would be entitled to one of the bungalows providing I had been a good tenant. I'm wondering what that means around here? Everybody keeps a dog to protect

themselves, and because of pigeons which make drying clothes difficult, to put it mildly. The man two doors away had to go to hospital and he has left his dog locked up in his bedroom; imagine the state of it.

Most of the people around here have substitute meters. I always thought older people were too straight to bypass meters, but all age groups do it. I guess they can't afford to be honest. Everyone spends £1.20 a week on the Littlewoods Pools, and the man comes to every door. A win would be a way out of here.

I couldn't get over the beauty of Dublin when I went back to visit. And I saw Powerscourt Gardens and a field of yellow gorse on the way there. Today, I can see beauty. I always knew that trees were bare in winter. I knew this because you'd have nowhere to hide from the cops then. But that was all I noticed of nature. I did not realise how trees became bare, just that all of a sudden, they were bare. In 1986, three and a half years after the fire, I suddenly noticed that everything grows. Grass, hedges, tulips, daffodils and primroses appear in the spring. And magnolia trees. Of course I'd been in parks, but I didn't see what was around me.

Now, I watch all the gardening programmes on TV and read gardening books and it's a great treat to stroll around a garden centre. I know the names of different flowers as well as the difference between trees. I mean, in the past, I bought pot plants like anyone would, but only as ornaments; I never realised that they were alive. Definitely, the therapy did this for me. The highlight of this year, so far, was waiting for the daffodils I planted to push their way up. Next time I'll know to plant them in a clump, instead of a straight row, but that's the first time I ever planted anything.

I feel sorry for that old woman in the runners, can't get her out of my head as I write. Was I looking at my future? Next step is to learn a skill. June Levine suggested a creative writing course. Then she thought I should get a knitting machine with the advance from this book. I like to knit and to try to buy a ball of wool every fortnight. It might work. I could sell things on a stall at the market. I have choices. So long as John Cullen does not find me when he gets out of prison.